PLANNING THE METROPOLIS

PLANNING THE METROPOLIS

The Multiple Advocacy Approach

Donald N. Rothblatt

PRAEGER

PRAEGER SPECIAL STUDIES • PRAEGER SCIENTIFIC

575611

Library of Congress Cataloging in Publication Data

Rothblatt, Donald N.
　　Planning the metropolis.

　　Bibliography: p.
　　Includes index.
　　1. Metropolitan areas—United States—Planning.
　2. Regional planning—United States.　　I. Title
　HT334.U5R67　　　307.7'6　　　81–20965
　ISBN 0–03–057364–5　　　　　AACR2

Published in 1982 by Praeger Publishers
CBS Educational and Professional Publishing
a Division of CBS Inc.
521 Fifth Avenue, New York, New York 10175 U.S.A.

© 1982 by Praeger Publishers

23456789　　　145　　　987654321

Printed in the United States of America

For Ann, Joel, and Steven

ACKNOWLEDGMENTS

This book would not have been completed without the help of numerous individuals, public institutions, and representatives of private business. In gratitude, I would like to thank Victor Jones, Arthur Maass, Arie Shacher, and Stanley Scott for their thoughtful comments about the conceptualization and design of the multiple advocacy model. I am also grateful to Sheila Baumgarten, William Bennett, Kathleen Ebright, Sylvia Ehrenthal, Sally Harvey, Charlene Hasmann, Susan Hootkins, Elizabeth Kilham, Susan McBain, Fred Musser, Vivian Olmos, Stephen Olsen, Michael Ottenstein, Deborah Schreiber, Marlene Stevenson, Celeste Wixom, Aida Wohl, Cynthia Wordell, William Zavlaris, and William Ziebron for their assistance with organizing the case studies of the San Jose metropolitan area. In addition, I would like to thank the many urban planning graduate students at San Jose State University who helped me conduct the fieldwork and research on the metropolitan case studies, and the many representatives of public and private organizations who were willing to be interviewed and share a part of their metropolitan world with us.

Special thanks are due to my colleagues in the Department of Urban and Regional Planning at San Jose State University, especially Earl Bossard, Daniel Garr, Vincent Milone, and Bert Muhly; and to the dean of the School of Social Sciences, Gerald Wheeler, for their support and encouragement while completing this study.

For financial support I am grateful to the California State University and Colleges, which provided funds for research assistants; and the National Science Foundation, which provided assistance with a faculty research grant.

I would like to express my appreciation to Marti Carsel, Marilyn Ledoux, Phannee Nitayasoothi, and Ann Rothblatt for their invaluable editorial assistance. Special thanks also go to Carolyn Danielsen and M. Christine King for their diligent typing and retyping of the original manuscript. All errors are, of course, my own responsibility.

CONTENTS

LIST OF TABLES

LIST OF FIGURES

INTRODUCTION

In light of the accelerating transformation of our postindustrial society with its intricate network of large-scale spatial dependencies, the need for regional planning is becoming increasingly apparent. While a case has been made to decentralize some of our more socially sensitive urban services such as education, it is clear that metropolis-wide management is needed increasingly in order to deal with the growing number of large-scale problems that transcend the boundaries and resources of local governments, such as the provision of adequate low-cost housing and public transportation facilities.

Yet, because of the decentralization of political power and authority of American government, most regional planning institutions in the United States have been ineffective. With the exception of efficiency-oriented, narrowly defined, single-purpose institutions, such as a water supply authority, American regional planning agencies have seldom had the ability to implement their plans and resolve a major metropolitan problem.

This book provides a framework for dealing effectively with regional planning problems that confront most large urban areas in the United States. First, the study presents an overview of metropolitan problems in the United States—from our limited concern about linking suburban enclaves to the dominant central city at the turn of the century to our struggle to cope with the diverse and often overwhelming problems of existing polycentric metropolitan areas. Since governmental machinery needed to deal with these problems is not likely to develop in the foreseeable future, the second chapter of the book presents an alternative approach to resolving regional planning problems—the multiple advocacy approach. This approach attempts to articulate the points of view of the major individuals, groups, and organizations (actors) involved with a metropolis-wide problem and to foster a diplomatic rather than an authoritative resolution of a problem to the satisfaction of the actors involved.

The next four chapters of the book demonstrate how the multiple advocacy approach has been used in four case studies of metropolitan conflicts in the San Jose area that typify regional planning problems in much of urban America: the expansion of air transportation facilities; the supply of sufficient open space and recreational facilities; the supply of low- and moderate-cost housing; and the creation of adequate public surface transportation facilities. Each study identifies the actors involved, articulates their views, and discusses the possibility of a real world resolution of the problem examined.

Findings and conclusions of the case studies are presented in the seventh chapter. We examine the findings of these studies to see the extent to which the multiple advocacy approach helps to perform the tasks required in conflict resolution and consensus formation. Our conclusions address the major question underlying our study: what is the relative utility of the multiple advocacy approach in helping to resolve metropolis-wide planning problems?

The book closes with a discussion of the implications of our case studies and literature review for metropolitan America. In this last chapter, we focus on the public policy implications of the multiple advocacy approach for increasing citizen participation in, and control over, metropolitan issues that affect the majority of our national population.

PLANNING THE METROPOLIS

1

METROPOLITAN PLANNING IN THE UNITED STATES

Although urban civilization has been emerging for millennia, urbanization as a worldwide phenomenon was just beginning to be noticed two centuries ago. For example, it is estimated that in 1800 only 1.7 percent of the world's population lived in cities of 100,000 or over, and not one city in the Western world had even 1 million people.[1]

During the past 100 years, the cities themselves have become engulfed as centers of expanding clusters of communities—metropolitan areas. By 1900, 11 such areas with more than 1 million inhabitants had come into existence, including Berlin, Calcutta, Chicago, Moscow, New York, Philadelphia, St. Petersburg, Tokyo, and Vienna.[2] On virtually every continent this growth of metropolitan areas has continued unabated through the twentieth century. As Lewis Mumford pointed out:

> By the middle of the twentieth century there were a host of new metropolitan areas, with bulging and sprawling suburban rings that brought many more [people] within the general metropolitan picture.[3]

Other observers claim that an even higher level of urban complexity has evolved in the form of constellations of metropolitan areas creating vast megalopolitan regions such as those urban agglomerations in Western Europe and on the East Coast of North America.[4] Yet, whether singularly as central places, or as part of vast megalopolitan structures, metropolitan areas have become the predominant form of large-scale urban development throughout the world, and are likely to be so in the foreseeable future.

AMERICAN METROPOLITAN DEVELOPMENT

In the United States the metropolitan pattern began in the last quarter of the nineteenth century with the establishment of suburbs at the edges of the then emerging cities. This phenomenon was made possible by transportation innovations, such as the establishment of commuter trains and streetcar lines, which opened many new sites for development beyond the city limits, and by the emerging middle class of industrial America, with its desire to escape the negative aspects of city life and find its own healthful and pastoral miniature republic in the hinterland.[5] Thus, by the turn of the century, substantial suburban development around major American cities such as Boston, Chicago, Philadelphia, and New York had occurred, setting the stage for the modern American metropolis.[6] At the same time, numerous smaller metropolises began to emerge, so that by 1900 almost one-third of the national population lived in 52 metropolitan areas.[7]

The outward movement of the central city population to the suburbs was reinforced further with the advent of automobile usage during the 1920s and 1930s, which opened up still larger areas for suburban development for middle- and upper-middle-income families.[8] This pattern continued, so that by 1940, America had become primarily metropolitan, with 51.1 percent (67 million) of its national population living in 147 metropolitan areas.[9]

Yet, it wasn't until after World War II that the United States experienced the large-scale expansion of our metropolitan areas as we know them today through massive suburbanization. The pent-up demand for housing during the war years; the baby boom; government programs that encouraged suburban home ownership, such as mortgage insurance and massive highway projects; the desire of the middle class to escape the central city poor and minorities; and the mutually reinforcing factors of rising incomes, industrial decentralization, and the almost universal use of the automobile accelerated the outward push of metropolitan development on an unprecedented scale.[10] As shown in Table 1.1, by 1960, 113 million people, nearly two-thirds of our national population, lived in 212 metropolitan areas; and by 1970 a majority of the residents of the 243 metropolitan areas were suburbanites.

The proportion of our national population living in the current 284 metropolitan areas may be stabilizing.[11] Nevertheless, the trend for suburban growth seems likely to continue during the 1980s.[12] As Table 1.2 indicates, after the turn of the century, the growth of suburban rings lagged behind that of the central cities until 1920. At that point the pattern changed to an increasing suburban growth dominance during the 1920–50 period, building up to the spectacular suburban population

Table 1.1 Population in Metropolitan Areas in the United States: 1900–80

Year	Number of SMSA's	Total Metropolitan Population[a]	
		Number (millions)	Percent National Population
1900	52	24.1	31.7
1910	71	34.5	37.5
1920	94	46.1	43.7
1930	115	61.0	49.8
1940	125	67.1	51.1
1950	162	85.6	56.8
1960	212	112.9	63.0
1970	243	139.5	68.6
1980	284	164.2	72.8

[a]Standard Metropolitan Statistical Areas (SMSAs) as defined at the dates indicated.

Sources: 1900–50 data from Donald J. Bogue, *Population Growth in Standard Metropolitan Areas 1900–1950* (Washington, D.C.: Housing and Home Finance Agency, 1953) p. 47: 1960–70 data from U.S. Department of Commerce, Bureau of the Census, *Census of Population* (1960, 1970); 1980 data from U.S. Department of Commerce, Bureau of the Census, *Preliminary 1980 Census* (March 1981).

booms after 1950, when the growth rate outside of the central city exceeded that within by a factor of almost five.

With the establishment of a suburbanization pattern as the predominant mode of American middle-class life, our metropolitan areas spawned a plethora of independent outlying communities, and school and other special districts. As shown in Table 1.3, there were 25,869 local governmental units in the 272 Standard Metropolitan Statistical Areas (SMSAs) in 1977, an average of 95 local governments per region. Thus, since the turn of the century, our urban areas have shifted from a primarily central city form to a polycentric development pattern reflecting the diverse public constituencies in our expanding metropolitan regions.[13]

PROBLEMS OF METROPOLITAN AREAS

Because of the dispersed pattern of political power generated by the large number of local political units in our metropolitan areas, broad regional management has been difficult to establish. Indeed, the development of American metropolitan areas has been thought of as the unconscious product of an "ecology of games" of the various private and

Table 1.2 Central City and Suburban Population Changes in Metropolitan Areas in the United States: 1900–80

	Percent Change in Metropolitan Population[a]		
Time Period	*Central Cities*	*Suburban Rings Outside Central Cities*	*Total*
1900–10	35.3	27.6	32.6
1910–20	26.7	22.4	25.2
1920–30	23.3	34.2	27.0
1930–40	5.1	13.8	8.3
1940–50	13.9	34.7	21.8
1950–60	10.7	48.6	26.4
1960–70	6.4	26.8	16.6
1970–80	−0.6	17.4	9.4

[a]Standard Metropolitan Statistical Areas (SMSAs) as defined at the dates indicated.

Sources: 1900–50 data from Donald J. Bogue, *Population Growth in Standard Metropolitan Areas 1900–1950* (Washington, D.C.: Housing and Home Finance Agency, 1953) p. 49; 1960–70 data from U.S. Department of Commerce, Bureau of the Census, *Census of Population* (1960, 1970); 1980 data from U.S. Department of Commerce, Bureau of the Census, *Preliminary 1980 Census* (March 1981).

public entities pursuing their individual interests, rather than the result of systematic policy of a regional planning institution.[14] As Robert C. Wood put it, in his study of the New York Metropolitan region, " . . . responsibility to maintain law and order, educate the young, dig the sewers, and plan the future environment remains gloriously or ridiculously fragmented."[15] In short, it seems that development of our metropolitan areas has been collectively unconscious in the absence of regional policy.

While the call for metropolitan guidance has long been made in the United States, it appears that the existing polycentric political organization of metropolitan areas can efficiently respond to many of the diverse consumer demands in urban areas, particularly those demands for services that require face-to-face activity, are labor-intensive, and have economies of scale that are exhausted at a relatively small size.[16] Indeed, a strong case has been made to decentralize, rather than consolidate, some of the more socially sensitive of these services (such as police patrol and education) in order to facilitate community control of neighborhoods and suburbs in large metropolitan areas.[17]

Still, the decentralized political structure has been unable to cope effectively with large-scale problems that transcend the boundaries and

Table 1.3 Governmental Units in Metropolitan Areas in the United States: 1977

Types of Units in Metropolitan Areas	Number	Total Independent Units	
		Number	Per Metropolitan Area[a]
General government		11,069	40
Counties	594		
Municipalities	6,444		
Townships (including New England towns)	4,031		
Special districts		9,580	34
With property taxing power	5,327		
Without property taxing power	4,253		
School units		5,220	21
Independent school districts	5,220		
Dependent School systems[b]	601		
Total units of local government (excluding dependent school systems)		25,869	93

[a]Standard Metropolitan Statistical Areas (SMSAs). There were 272 SMSAs in 1977.

[b]A dependent school system operates as a subunit of local general government, and doesn't have independent taxing power.

Source: U.S. Department of Commerce, Bureau of the Census, *1977 Census of Governments*, Vol. 5, *Local Governments in Metropolitan Areas* (1977). Table 1.

resources of local and even state governments, and that seem to justify regional and perhaps national intervention. Some of the most important problems in this category appear to be the following:

1. Interregional migration. Migration of unskilled population from poor rural regions to large metropolitan areas has generated the social and economic isolation of large ghettos of minorities and poor in urban centers, and at the same time has drained the rural areas of the labor force needed for economic and social viability. Migration has recently been moderated, if not reversed, from such rural areas as Appalachia.[18] However, metropolitan regions still have large concentrations of urban poor from earlier migration patterns.[19]
2. Intraregional migration. The movement of jobs and the middle class to the suburbs has reinforced the social and economic isolation of the central city poor and minorities. While some gentrification has occurred recently in the central city, earlier movement to the suburbs has left the central city with a

declining fiscal capacity resulting from the increased demand for its public services and the decline of its tax revenues.[20]

3. Inefficient public services. The dispersed political system has resulted in the provision of fragmented community services, such as mass transportation, which often are inefficiently supplied at below scale economies.[21]

4. Social and economic inequalities. Inequalities exist for minorities and the poor in terms of job opportunities, housing, education, health facilities, and transportation. Many of the inequalities are related to discrimination, limited skills, social and physical distance, and the uneven quality of public services in urban and rural areas.[22]

5. Environmental deterioration. A by-product of the uncontrolled growth of large urban areas is a regionwide deterioration of the environment in terms of pollution and the misuse of land and natural resources, and the decline in the quality of life with respect to the amount and accessibility of open space, character of housing, land use relationships, transportation options, and urban aesthetics.[23]

Thus, it appears that metropolitan or regional management is needed for a variety of purposes, such as limiting the diseconomies between governmental units generated by the provision of fragmented and inadequate public services and policies for multijurisdictional problems. Even the most skeptical critics of planning agree that regional management is needed, on the ground of economic efficiency alone, for such regional problems as provision of adequate public transportation facilities, low-cost housing, open space, pollution control, and water supply.[24] Beyond efficiency, regional planning and governance also seem desirable in order to foster equity in the distribution of resources for public services in communities throughout a metropolitan area, such as bridging the financial and quality gaps between school districts serving the central city poor and more affluent suburbs.[25] And, if established by an electoral process, regional government could lessen the social isolation of the central city poor and minorities through broad citizen participation and conflict resolution abilities at the regional level, and could enable many metropolitan problems to be dealt with more fairly and openly than is presently the case.[26]

ATTEMPTED GOVERNMENTAL APPROACHES FOR MANAGING THE METROPOLIS

In order to cope with the increasingly complex problems of our expanding metropolitan areas, various institutional approaches have been attempted. At first, the adaptation of existing governmental units was tried, such as expanding the influence of the central city itself through annexation of surrounding land, merging with adjacent suburbs, broadened and extraterritorial powers over outlying areas; then, transforming county government from a limited administrative branch of state government into a general purpose "urban county" offering a wide range of public services; and even central city-county unification.[27] These adaptation approaches, however, met with very limited success, since the influence of central cities and urbanized and unified counties was usually overwhelmed by the explosion of metropolitan development and the growth of numerous independent suburban municipalities well beyond their boundaries.[28]

Another approach involves the creation of new units of government to provide areawide specialized services such as school and special districts. While these districts may be able to deliver their specialized services efficiently, they also tend to add to the functional fragmentation of services and lack of coordination at the regional level.[29] School districts have often reinforced differences in educational opportunities between the central city and suburbs; and special districts, whose governing boards are usually appointed, are frequently autonomous and unresponsive to citizen concerns.[30] Even mulitpurpose authorities, such as those in Boston and Seattle, provide for only "hardware" services, like water supply and sewers, and suffer the same accountability disadvantages of the single purpose districts.[31]

Other efforts involve varying forms of federation that have been described as "two-tiered metropolitan governmental systems where the policy making of the area-wide tier is controlled by governments of the first tier."[32] Regional institutions such as the councils of governments (COGs), regional planning commissions (RPCs), and economic development districts (EDDs) were formed during the 1960s and 1970s in response to the various national incentives, with their numbers reaching about 200 in metropolitan areas in 1976.[33] While these regional councils and planning institutions often generate worthwhile metropolitan studies, and provide a useful review function for local grant applications for federal aid, their influence has been quite constrained because they are almost always advisory, their boards being controlled by local elected officials.[34] As the National Academy of Sciences concluded about one of the most promising of these institutions:

> Councils of governments have been put forward as one solution to the metropolitan governmental problem. Although COG's are easily organized, flexible, and adaptable governmental units, none of the large number created in the 1960's has solved a major metropolitan problem. There is no evidence to date that they are beginning to take on a metropolitan governance function.[35]

Apart from a few notable exceptions, such as the Metropolitan Council for the Twin Cities area in Minnesota (which has considerable influence over, and independence from, local city and county governments because its functions and membership come with state authority), most regional councils have been largely ineffectual.[36] To be sure, some promising models have been generated for effective metropolitan governance, such as the proposal of the Committee for Economic Development (CED) for a two-tier system of shared powers:

> To gain the advantages of both centralization and decentralization we recommend as an ultimate solution a governmental system of two levels. Some functions should be assigned in their entirety to the area-wide government, others to the local level, but most will be assigned to each level.[37]

But such a balance of federated interests between regional and local concerns has yet to emerge in our major metropolitan areas.[38] It may be possible to increase gradually the influence of our regional institutions as instruments of federal policy and as guardians of metropolitan resources. As things stand now, other approaches to managing metropolitan America appear to be needed.

NOTES

1. Lewis Mumford, *The City in History* (New York: Harcourt, Brace & World, 1961), p. 529.
2. Ibid.
3. Ibid.
4. Jean Gottmann, *Megalopolis* (New York: Twentieth Century Fund, 1961).
5. See David Ward, *Cities and Immigrants: A Geography of Change in Nineteenth Century America* (New York: Oxford University Press, 1971), ch. 4; Joel A. Tarr, "From City to Suburb: The 'Moral' Influence of Transportation Technology," in *American Urban History*, ed. Alexander B. Callow (New York: Oxford University Press, 1973), p. 202; and Robert C. Wood, *Suburbia: Its People and Their Politics* (Boston: Houghton Mifflin, 1958).
6. See, for example, Sam B. Warner, *Streetcar Suburbs: The Process of Growth in Boston, 1870–1900* (New York: Atheneum, 1969), ch. 1.
7. Donald J. Bogue, *Population Growth in Standard Metropolitan Areas 1900–1950* (Washington, D.C.: Housing and Home Finance Agency, 1953).
8. Scott Greer, *Governing the Metropolis* (New York: John Wiley and Sons, 1962), pp. 9–21.
9. John C. Bollens and Henry J. Schmandt, *The Metropolis: Its People, Politics, and Economic Life* (New York: Harper and Row, 1975), ch. 1; and Bogue, *Population Growth*.

10. John R. Meyer, John F. Kain, and Martin Wohl, *The Urban Transportation Problem* (Cambridge, Mass.: Harvard University Press, 1965), ch. 2.
11. Some observers argue that since 1970, we have entered a new phase of decreasing concentration of our national population in metropolitan areas. See James Heilbrun, *Urban Economics and Public Policy* (New York: St. Martin's Press, 1981), ch. 3. Others suggest, however, that most of the recent nonmetropolitan growth is occurring on the edges of existing metropolitan areas. If so, this pattern could be viewed as primarily an extension of metropolitan development. See William Alonso, "Metropolis Without Growth" *The Public Interest* 53 (Summer 1978): 68–86.
12. Ibid.; and "Profile of America: What '80 Census Will Show," *U.S. News and World Report,* April 7, 1980, pp. 64–67.
13. Greer, *Governing the Metropolis,* ch. 3.
14. Norton E. Long, "The Local Community as an Ecology of Games," in *Urban Politics: Past, Present, and Future,* ed. Harlan Hahn and Charles Levine (New York: Longman, 1980), pp. 107–18.
15. Robert C. Wood, *1400 Governments* (Cambridge, Mass.: Harvard University Press, 1961), p. 1.
16. Robert L. Bish and Hugh O. Nourse, *Urban Economics and Policy Analysis* (New York: McGraw-Hill, 1975), ch. 5.
17. See John Hamer, "Neighborhood Control," in *Neighborhood Preservation, Hearings Before the Committee on Banking, Housing, and Urban Affairs,* U.S. Sen., 94th Cong., 2nd Sess. (June 1976), pp. 139–57; F. Stevens Redburn, "On 'Human Services Integration,'" *Public Administration Review* 37 (May/June 1977): 264–69; and Bruce W. Shepard, "Metropolitan Political Decentralization," *Urban Affairs Quarterly* 10 (March 1975): 297–313.
18. William H. Miernyk, "An Evaluation: Tools of Regional Development Policy," *Growth and Change* 11 (April 1980): 2–6.
19. Heilbrun, *Urban Economics and Public Policy,* ch. 10.
20. Ibid., ch. 14.
21. Donald N. Rothblatt, "National Development Policy," *Public Administration Review* 34 (July/August 1974): 369–76.
22. Melvin B. Mogulof, *Governing Metropolitan Areas* (Washington, D.C.: Urban Institute, 1971).
23. Donald N. Rothblatt, "Issues Underlying a National Urban and Regional Development Policy," in *National Policy for Urban and Regional Development,* ed. Donald N. Rothblatt (Lexington, Mass.: D. C. Heath, 1974), pp. 325–37.
24. Edward C. Banfield, "The Uses and Limitations of Metropolitan Planning in Massachusetts," in *Taming Megalopolis,* ed. H. Wentworth Eldredge (New York: Praeger, 1967), pp. 710–19.
25. Mogulof, *Governing Metropolitan Areas,* ch. 2.
26. Robert C. Embry, "Embry Proposed Regional Solutions to Urban Problems," *Practicing Planner* 7 (September 1977): 4–6; and Adepoju G. Onibokum and Martha Curry, "An Ideology of Citizen Participation: The Metropolitan Seattle Transit Case Study," *Public Administration Review* 36 (May/June): 269–77.
27. Bollens and Schmandt, *The Metropolis,* ch. 11.
28. James F. Horan and G. Thomas Taylor, Jr., *Experiments in Metropolitan Government* (New York: Praeger, 1977), pp. xii–xvii.
29. Howard W. Hallman, *Small and Large Together: Governing the Metropolis* (Beverly Hills, Calif.: Sage Publications, 1977), ch. 4.
30. Ibid.
31. Charles R. Warren, "Developing Alternative Models for Servicing Metropolitan

America," in *Organizing Public Services in Metropolitan America,* ed. Thomas P. Murphy and Charles R. Warren (Lexington, Mass: Lexington Books, 1974), pp. 3–14.

32. Melvin Mogulof, *Five Metropolitan Governments* (Washington, D.C.: Urban Institute, 1972), p. 13.

33. Hallman, *Small and Large Together,* ch. 6.

34. Melvin R. Levin, *Community and Regional Planning* (New York: Praeger, 1977), ch. 11.

35. National Academy of Sciences, *Toward an Understanding of Metropolitan America* (San Francisco: Cornfield Press, 1975), p. 120.

36. See Horan and Taylor, *Experiments in Metropolitan Government,* ch. 9; and Hallman, *Small and Large Together,* ch. 6.

37. Committee for Economic Development, *Reshaping Government in Metropolitan Areas* (New York: Committee for Economic Development, 1970), p. 19.

38. Hallman, *Small and Large Together,* ch. 6.

2

THE MULTIPLE ADVOCACY APPROACH

Despite the importance of regional problems in our nation, they are often left unresolved because of the lack of governmental machinery to deal with metropolitan issues.[1] Recent studies indicate that, while some promising metropolitan institutions have developed in the nation during the past decade, such governmental machinery has not been very effective and is not likely to be so in the near future.[2]

This chapter will present an alternative method for dealing with metropolitan problems that confront most large urban areas in the United States: the multiple advocacy approach, a regional planning method that attempts to present the various points of view of the major participants involved with a metropolitan problem.

THE METHOD

In the spring of 1974, the Urban and Regional Planning Department of San Jose State University began to develop an alternative to metropolitan government for handling metropolitan problems. Given the polycentric political structure of metropolitan areas, the approach attempted to deal with regional problems by facilitating a "diplomatic" rather than authoritative resolution of those problems to the satisfaction of the various interests concerned with each issue. Accordingly, the method was designed to include the following characteristics:[3]

1. Openness. Enable the various points of view of the major individuals, groups, and organizations (actors) involved with a metropolitan planning problem to be expressed to public decision makers.
2. Broad representation. Provide the professional skills and resources needed to

11

ensure that all actors involved would be represented accurately, competently, and vigorously.

3. Fairness. Establish a system of inquiry that would treat all of the actors equally, especially in terms of resources (including time) made available to each actor for research, planning, and presentation.

4. Hostility reduction. Provide a decision environment that would help to de-escalate the hostility and alienation that could develop between conflicting actors, so as to enable each actor to consider more objectively the views of others.

5. Provide information. Present each view, together with supporting documentation and analysis, in a manner that would help clarify the issues involved and provide useful information for all parties concerned.

6. Encourage broad citizen participation. Develop a mechanism that would expose the metropolitan community to the range of views concerned with regional problems, and provide a means of registering preferences for the resolution of these problems.

7. Responsiveness. Create a setting that would induce decision makers to really listen to, consider, and be responsive to the concerns and proposals of the actors directly involved, and to the metropolitan public.

The method attempts to draw upon the concept of a pluralistic planning process originally introduced by Paul Davidoff[4]—a process by which alternative plans representing the views of all parties involved with an issue can be examined by decision makers. Although Davidoff argued for advocacy planning mostly on behalf of the disadvantaged, in order to remove inequities in the planning process, our method attempts to provide advocate planning services to all major actors associated with a particular planning problem—the affluent as well as the poor; private organizations as well as public institutions; and regional interests as well as local groups. It was believed that this method, called the multiple advocacy approach, might provide, as Stephen Skjei[5] suggests, the parity, fairness, and information needed to examine and reconcile systematically the diverse views associated with a large-scale or metropolis-wide planning problem.

The first step was an attempt to identify the major actors involved in each metropolitan planning problem. Following preliminary research on the existing situation,[6] the identification of most actors associated with each problem was relatively straightforward. However, other actors who stand to gain or lose substantially from a possible change in the existing situation (such as the implementation of a particular plan) were not always highly visible. These low visibility actors, sometimes called "potential groups,"[7] were identified in the form of neighborhoods that could suffer housing relocation or be environmentally damaged if plans for locating public facilities, such as highways or airports, were implemented.

Another difficulty encountered in the actor identification process was the inability (due to financial and time contraints) to represent every interest that could conceivably be affected by a particular metropolitan planning problem. In order to simplify the identification process, major actors were defined as groups who have or could have important stakes in the resolution of particular problem, and organizations whose involvement seems essential for problem resolution. For example, as many as 14 actors, including public, private, environmental, and minority group interests, were chosen to represent the spectrum of views concerned with the issue of surface transportation in the San Jose metropolitan area.

After identifying the actors, their representatives were given the opportunity to present their views of the problem individually to the research staff (planning students and faculty at San Jose State University). While some of the actors were not always anxious to participate in the process, particularly the dominant groups whose views appeared to prevail, they were induced to do so. Since it was known that the process would represent the views of all the major actors to public decision makers and the metropolitan community in a highly visible manner, each actor believed self-interest required it to participate in order to ensure that its position would be presented accurately. In order to give a contextual sense of the environment of each actor's operating world, and to maximize the ease of presentation, the research staff met with each group in its own environment.[8]

Next, the research staff formed teams for the purpose of developing advocate plans for each actor. It became apparent, however, that a considerable overlap (if not congruence) existed among some of the client groups. Consequently, it was determined that a few teams could accurately represent the spectrum of views expressed by the original number of actors indentified earlier. Each team was given equal resources, accessibility to information, and time for the preparation of its advocate plan.

The next step involved the teams' presenting their advocate plans at a session with all the actors present. Thus a range of alternative solutions to each problem was made available to the actors and public decision makers involved. Finally, the problem was reexamined, and an attempt was made to generate a plan that reflected the range of views held by the interests involved more closely than was previously recommended.

SUMMARY

While holding the promise of great participatory rewards, our approach to formulating regional development policy for our urban areas can be both time-consuming and difficult.[9] For example, it was not easy for each advocate team to crystallize and articulate its client's view of a San Jose metropolitan problem or to plan for a solution. Often a client group held a range of views reflecting membership diversity,[10] and in some instances an advocate team represented more than one group. Despite these difficulties, through careful interviewing of group representatives and examining available written materials (such as position papers, reports, documents, newpaper articles), each team was able to develop a position reasonably representative of its client's view (as judged by the clients themselves, who were present during team presentations). As a result, the teams in the multiple advocacy process often generated basically different perceptions of the problem and related solutions.

In order to examine the potential of our participatory approach to regional planning, the next four chapters will demonstrate how the multiple advocacy approach has been used in case studies of metropolis-wide issues in the San Jose area that typify regional planning problems in much of urban America: the expansion of air transportation facilities; the supply of sufficient open space and recreational facilities; the provision of low- and moderate-cost housing; and the creation of adequate surface transportation facilities. Each study will identify the actors involved, articulate their views, and discuss the possibility of a real world resolution of the problem examined.

The San Jose metropolitan area (Santa Clara County), which represents the largest and fastest growing urban focus in the San Fransisco Bay Region, brings these metropolitan problems into sharp relief. Located in the southern portion of the Bay Region, the San Jose SMSA, with its 15 cities, numerous special districts, and nearly 1,000 square miles of unicorporated land,[11] posesses all the political, social, economic, and physical complexities of most American metropolitan areas (see Figures 2.1 and 2.2) Since the end of World War II, most of the electronics industry in the Bay region has settled in Santa Clara County, near the centers of technological innovations of Stanford University and the National Aeronautics and Space Administration (NASA). As Table 2.1 indicates, during the 1950–80 period the metropolitan population grew from 290,500 to 1,295,000 (446 percent), placing it among the 30 largest of the 284 SMSAs in 1980.[12] Consequently, the rapidly expanding San Jose metropolitan population has greatly increased its demand for region-wide services and facilities, clearly delineating the nature of its metropolitan problems. The San Jose SMSA, therefore, provides us with a very useful setting for examining the metropolis-wide issues presented in the following four chapters.

FIGURE 2.1. The San Francisco Bay Region*. *Source:* 1970 USGS—
San Francisco Bay Region Map.

*"Localities" include cities and unincorporated places of 2500 or more popu-
lation in 1970 Census. Unincorporated localities are indicated (u).

15

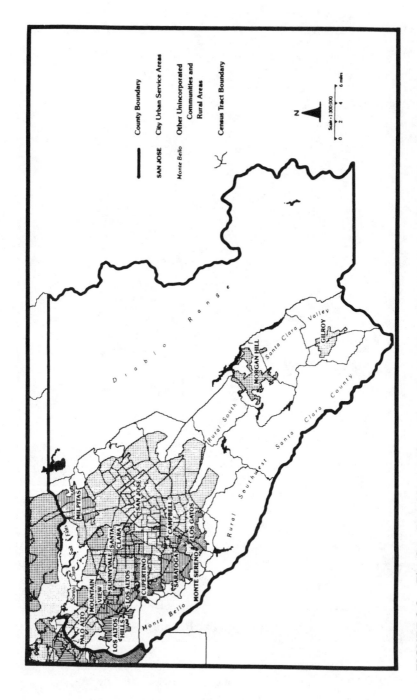

FIGURE 2.2. **The San Jose Metropolitan Area (Santa Clara County).** *Source: Association of Bay Area Governments, Projections 79* (Berkely, Calif.: ABAG, 1979), p. IV–29.

Table 2.1 Population of Cities and Unincorporated Areas in Santa Clara County: 1920–80

	1920	1930	1940	1950	1960	1970	1980
Alviso	500	400	700	700	1,174	a	a
Campbell	—	—	—	—	11,863	23,797	27,067
Cupertino	—	—	—	—	3,664	17,895	34,420
Gilroy	2,900	3,500	3,600	4,900	7,348	12,684	21,641
Los Altos	—	—	—	—	19,696	25,062	25,769
Los Altos Hills	—	—	—	—	3,412	6,871	7,421
Los Gatos	2,300	3,200	3,600	4,900	9,036	22,613	26,593
Milpitas	—	—	—	—	6,572	26,561	37,820
Monte Sereno	—	—	—	—	1,506	2,847	3,434
Morgan Hill	600	900	1,000	1,600	3,151	5,579	17,060
Mountain View	1,000	3,300	3,900	6,600	30,889	54,132	58,655
Palo Alto	5,900	13,700	16,800	25,500	52,287	56,040	55,225
San Jose	39,700	57,700	68,500	95,300	204,196	459,913	628,283
Santa Clara	5,200	6,300	6,700	11,700	58,880	86,118	87,746
Saratoga	—	—	—	—	14,861	26,810	29,261
Sunnyvale	1,700	3,100	4,400	9,800	52,898	95,976	106,618
Total incorporated	59,800	92,100	109,200	161,000	481,433	922,898	1,167,013
Total unincorporated	40,900	53,000	65,000	129,500	160,882	142,415	128,058
County total	100,700	145,100	174,900	290,500	642,315	1,065,313	1,295,071

[a]Annexed into the city of San Jose.

Note: Dash indicates city not yet incorporated.

Sources: Santa Clara County Planning Department, *Housing Characteristics, Cities, Santa Clara County, 1970* (San Jose, Calif.: Santa Clara County Planning Department, 1971); and Santa Clara County Planning Department, *Advanced Final Count of 1980* (San Jose, Calif.: Santa Clara County Planning Department, April 1981).

NOTES

1. Melvin B. Mogulof, "A Modest Proposal for the Governance of America's Metropolitan Areas," *Journal of the American Institute of Planners* 41 (July 1975): 250–57.
2. Melvin R. Levin, *Community and Regional Planning* (New York: Praeger, 1977), ch. 11.
3. These characteristics are based on concepts of conflict resolution presented by Stephen LaTour et al., "Some Determinants of Preference for Modes of Conflict Resolution," *Journal of Conflict Resolution* 20 (June 1976): 319–56; Bernhardt Lieberman, "Coalitions and Conflict Resolutions," *American Behavioral Scientist* 19 (March/April 1975): 557–81; and Donald N. Rothblatt, "Multiple Advocacy: An Approach to Metropolitan Planning," *Journal of the American Institute of Planners* 44 (April 1978): 193–99.
4. Paul Davidoff, "Advocacy and Pluralism in Planning," *Journal of the American Institute of Planners* 31 (November 1965): 331–38.
5. Stephen S. Skjei, "Urban System Advocacy," *Journal of the American Institute of Planners* 38 (January 1972): 11–24.
6. Interviewing knowledgeable public officials, professionals, and citizens, and examining position papers, reports, documents, and newspaper articles about the planning problem.
7. In group theory a "potential group" can be defined as a collection of individuals with common attitudes who will interact to form a group if other groups threaten their interests. See Enid Curtis Bok Schoettle, "The State of the Art of Policy Studies," in *National Policy for Urban and Regional Development*, ed. Donald N. Rothblatt (Lexington, Mass: D. C. Heath, 1974), pp. 3–33.
8. See the discussion of the important influence the social and political environment has on actors in the planning process in Richard S. Bolan and Ronald L. Nuttal, *Urban Planning and Politics* (Lexington, Mass.: D. C. Heath, 1975). For an examination of the positive effect environmental continuity (familiarity) has in group interaction and decision making, see Harold D. Lasswell. *A Pre-View of Policy Sciences* (New York: American Elsevier, 1971).
9. For a discussion about the possible tradeoff between the amount of consensus and social interaction costs needed for collective decision making, see Robert Mayer, Robert Moroney, and Robert Morris, eds., *Centrally Planned Change* (Urbana: University of Illinois Press, 1974), ch. 9; and Robert L. Bish, *The Public Economy of Metropolitan Areas* (Chicago: Markham, 1971), ch. 3.
10. It has even been argued that substantial divergence of attitudes often develops between a group's spokesperson and the group membership. See Donald F. Mazziotti, "The Underlying Assumptions of Advocacy Planning," *Journal of the American Institute of Planners* 40 (January 1974): 38.
11. Santa Clara County Planning Department, *Information*, June 1980.
12. U.S. Department of Commerce, Bureau of the Census, *Preliminary 1980 Census* (March 1981).

3

THE EXPANSION OF
AIR TRANSPORTATION
FACILITIES

As has been the case in many urban regions of our nation, an enormous post-World War II expansion in air transportation use has occurred in the San Jose metropolitan area. An indication of this growth is the change in annual passenger use of the San Jose Municipal airport, which rose from 80,000 passengers to 1,590,000 during the 1960–70 period.[1] Then, between 1970 and 1978, it more than doubled, increasing to 3,400,000 passengers.[2]

With few exceptions, such as the outlying airports of Dallas-Ft. Worth and Chicago, the expansion of air travel has created increasingly serious noise and air pollution problems for substantial portions of our urban regions. Indeed, the environmental pressure of our expanding air transportation system may have as much influence on the urban morphology as do our surface transportation networks. The San Jose metropolitan area is no exception. Its conveniently located airport, which is only three miles from the central business district, has seriously constrained downtown redevelopment because of building height regulations, and has rendered nearby residential neighborhoods unlivable. A consequent large scale acquisition of adjacent residential properties is presently under way. A 1980 report indicated:

> To date, the City has acquired 322 parcels (77 in fiscal year 1979–80) and relocated about 300 families. Relocation costs per household have averaged $6,100. Approximately 300 parcels are yet to be acquired, involving about 420 households.[3]

Finding an appropriate alternative outlying airport site is difficult at best, because of the limited public funds available for such a facility and the opposition of surrounding communities that might be environmentally harmed by the new airport. This is the basic question of air transportation in the San Jose metropolitan area: how to balance the demand for increased air transportation facilities against the environmental requirements of the region. This chapter will examine how such a balance might be made.

ACTORS' VIEWS

As a result of the identification process described in the previous chapter, the following actors were found to reasonably represent the different views involved in the San Jose air transportation case:

1. Central City Airport Authority (Airport Department, city of San Jose)
2. Community groups representing neighborhoods suffering from high levels of air and noise pollution due to increasing use of the existing airport site (Save Our Valley Action Committee, North Side Residents Association, United New Conservationists)
3. Business interests (San Jose Chamber of Commerce)
4. A representative inlying community environmentally damaged by the expanding use of the existing airport (city of Santa Clara)
5. A representative outlying community in the metropolitan area threatened by the location of a proposed new airport site (city of Milpitas)
6. Metropolitan planning organizations for the San Jose area (Santa Clara County Airport Land Use Commission and Santa Clara County Planning Department)
7. Bay Area regional planning agencies (Association of Bay Area Governments, Metropolitan Transportation Commission)
8. Federal government (Federal Aviation Administration).

Because of the overlapping views of some of the actors, it was determined that five teams could accurately reflect the spectrum of views expressed by the actors identified above.

Central City and Business Interests
(City of San Jose, San Jose Chamber of Commerce)

Problem: San Jose Municipal Airport is one of three major airports in the San Fransisco Bay region (see Figure 3.1). The San Jose airport and its surrounding streets and highways occupy about 1,000 acres. The greater portion of this area (895 acres) is in the City of San Jose; the remaining portion is in the city of Santa Clara. Although the predominant features

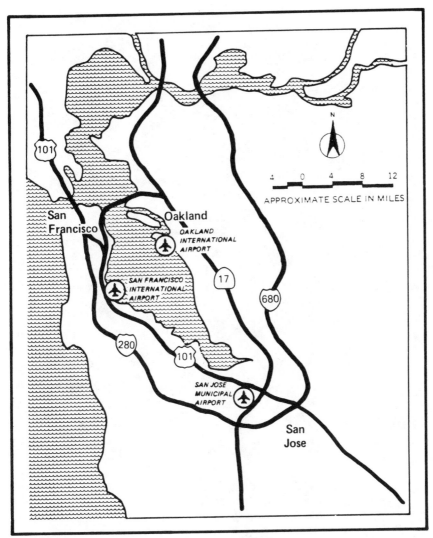

FIGURE 3.1. San Jose Municipal Airport Location. *Source:* San Jose Planning Department (1980).

of the site are the airfield, the passenger terminal facilities for air carrier operations, and the general aviation facilities, much of the property is open agricultural land surrounded by major freeways and city streets (see Figure 3.2).

These existing airport facilities, which accommodated about 4.0 million annual passengers (MAP) in 1980,[4] do not have the capacity to

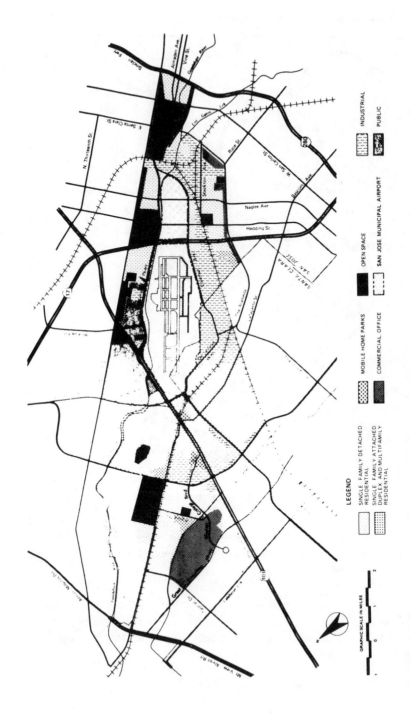

FIGURE 3.2. **San Jose Municipal airport and Surrounding Land Use: 1980.** *Source:* San Jose Planning Department (1980).

safely handle expected 1987 and 1997 air transportation demands of the San Jose metropolitan area of approximately 5.3 and 8.3 MAP, respectively (See Tables 3.1 and 3.2).[5] Even today, members of the business community complain about the inadequacies of the passenger

Table 3.1 Air Transportation Demand for the San Jose Municipal Airport: 1975–97

Activity	1975	1978	1987	1997
Annual passengers (in thousands)				
Interstate and intrastate				
carriers	2,248	3,346	5,310	8,278
Commuter carriers	14	56	28	44
Total	2,262	3,402	5,338	8,322
Annual cargo and mail (by passenger airlines, in tons)	8,882	15,936	17,340	28,480
Annual aircraft operations				
Interstate and intrastate carriers				
Scheduled service	54,054	n.a.	57,316	82,432
Unscheduled service	457	n.a.	485	697
Subtotal	54,511	56,692[a]	57,801	83,129
Other commercial carriers	1,309	n.a.	1,301	1,871
Commuter carriers	6,324	10,370	5,400	6,300
General aviation				
Itinerant	154,929	186,339	229,400	309,200
Local	211,961	203,817	292,000	362,900
Subtotal	366,890	390,156	521,400	672,100
Military	751	1,100	800	800
Total operations	429,785	458,318	586,702	764,200
General aviation aircraft parking	548	548	686	804

Table 3.2 Physical Facilities Requirements for the San Jose Municipal Airport: 1978–97

Facility	1978	1987	1997	Reserve[a]
Passenger terminal complex				
Aircraft parking positions				
Intrastate and interstate				
airlines	14	17[b]	24[b]	—
Commuter airlines	1	1	1	—
Total	15	18	25	31[b]
Passenger boarding lounges	11	14	25[b]	31[b]
Terminal building				
(square feet)	147,000	255,000	400,000	500,000
Automobile parking spaces				
Public	2,934	4,700	7,300	12,000
Employee	513	1,000	1,600	2,000
Rental car	1,200	2,500	3,940	—
Total	4,647	8,200	12,840	—
Curbside for noncommercial				
vehicles (linear feet)	890	1,200	1,750	—
Airline air freight building				
area				
(square feet)	19,200	38,000	62,000	100,000
All-cargo aircraft area				
(acres)	—	25	25	—
General aviation area				
(acres)	53	64	73	—

[a]The "reserve" requirements are established to assure the longevity of the airport site and to accommodate the effects of unanticipated traffic growth in the development of the Airport Master Plan.

[b]These estimates reflect 1977 airline estimates. Previous forecasts were based on assumptions that airlines would, over time, significantly increase their peak-hour gate utilization.

Source: San Jose, Environmental Assessment and Environmental Impact Report on the Airport Master Plan and airport Vicinity Area Actions (April 1980).

and air cargo terminals and the limitations of general aviation facilities to handle the variety and volume of desired air transportation activity.[6] If left unchanged, this situation will artificially limit the economic and social development of the San Jose area.[7]

Also, as Figure 3.2 indicates, the existing site location (three miles from downtown San Jose) and design (all major runways point to the city's center) are creating difficult environmental problems for the surrounding urban areas.[8] Aircraft noise, generated principally from commercial air carrier operations, has been a significant problem at San Jose Municipal Airport for many years.[9] The airport's proximity to urban development—particularly residential areas to the north and south—results in a major incompatibility between aircraft operations and these adjacent land uses.[10] In addition, air pollution due to airport operations is traceable both to aircraft emissions during landing and takeoff operations and to automobile emissions related to travel to and from the airport by travelers, employees, and others.[11]

Finally, opportunities for physically expanding the airport site are severely constrained by the Guadalupe River and Guadalupe Parkway to the east, Highway 17 to the south, Coleman Avenue and related industrial development to the west, and De La Cruz Boulevard, U.S. Highway 101, and industrial development to the north.[12] (See Figures 3.2 and 3.3.)

Solution: When the burgeoning air transportation volume and concomitant environmental problems began to emerge during the late 1960s and early 1970s, the Airport Authority and business interests argued for developing a new airport in a sparsely settled portion of the San Jose metropolitan area (such as the North San Jose area), with a capacity and design that would accommodate the long-term growth of air transportation demand in the metropolitan region while minimizing noise and air pollution to the surrounding population.[13] In 1975, however, San Jose decided to modify its long term plans to develop a new airport site because of the associated economic and environmental costs.[14]

The city consequently drew up a program to guide the future planning of the existing site in May 1976 retaining Peat, Marwick, Mitchell and Company, which prepared *An Economic and Planning Management Program for San Jose Municipal Airport.*[15] The program was adopted as the *Airport Master Plan and Airport Vicinity Area Actions* by the San Jose City Council on July 15, 1980.[16]

The airfield improvements shown in Figure 3.4, as well as the overall land use and design of specific facilities (such as passenger terminal building, automobile parking, and airport access), are important features of the city's Airport Master Plan. All of these components are summarized in the following sections.[17]

Airfield

Improvement recommendations include extensions of Runway 11/29 to 3,800 feet and widening to 100 feet, Runway 12R/30L to 10,250 feet and Runway 12L/30R to 7,425 feet. Development of general aviation facilities on the west side of the airfield requires an upgrading of Runway 11/29. Extension of this runway to 3,800 feet and widening to 100 feet will permit it to accommodate nearly all types of general aviation

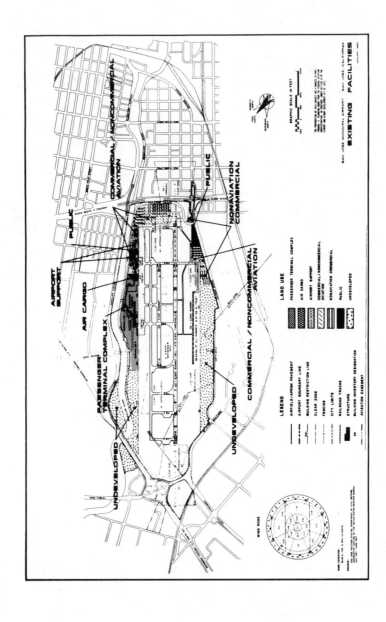

FIGURE 3.3. San Jose Municipal Airport Facilities: 1980. *Source: San Jose, Environmental . . . Impact Report on the Airport Master Plan and Airport Vicinity Area Actions* (April 1980).

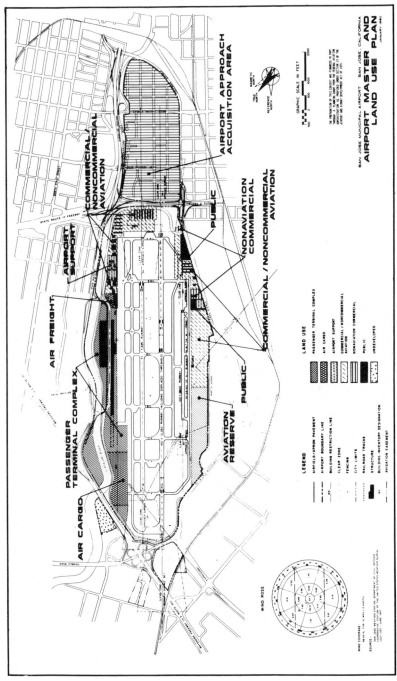

FIGURE 3.4. San Jose Municipal Airport: Planned Development. *Source: San Jose, Environmental Assessment and Environmental Impact Report on the Airport Master Plan and Airport Vicinity Area Actions (April 1980).*

propeller aircraft expected to use San Jose Municipal Airport in the future. Basically, during moderate to heavy traffic conditions, Runway 11/29 will be primary runway for itinerant general aviation operations flying to and from southern areas such as Los Angeles. Business jet aircraft will continue to use other runways at the airport.

In addition to runway modifications, a significantly improved taxiway system will be designed to improve aircraft ground traffic circulation to and from the west-side general aviation area.

The existing 8,900-foot Runway 12R/30L is adequate to serve nearly all commercial aircraft traffic forecast for the future. Under high summer temperature conditions, certain aircraft in the current fleet may be required to take off with less than maximum takeoff weight levels. Extension of Runway 12R/30L 1,350 feet to the north would permit large commerial aircraft to fly to distant cities, but such operations are not anticipated in the demand forecasts. However, the extension could bring about a small reduction in air carrier noise impacts.

The third airfield improvement is the extension of Runway 12L/30R to 7,425 feet. This runway would continue to be designated as a nonprecision runway. Design studies will still have to be conducted to evaluate possible cost savings that could be achieved by considering minimal construction for pavement strength (due to infrequent use by heavy aircraft), as opposed to full air carrier strength.

Prudent airfield management policies indicate that wherever possible, a major airline airport should have secondary air carrier runway capability. The FAA considers this flexibility to be a high priority in managing aircraft movements for airport traffic safety and efficiency.[18]

Runway 12L/30R, as extended, would serve as the primary runway for itinerant general aviation arrivals from the northeast and for airline and large business aircraft when Runway 12R/30L is closed for maintenance or emergencies. It will provide an additional degree of flexibility in airfield operations. Two runways would be available for simultaneous air carrier operations under visual flight rule (VFR) conditions when there are momentary peaks in traffic, thus reducing delays.

With two runways of air carrier length, runway maintenance can be carried out with minimal impact on air carrier operations. Pavement tests have indicated that Runway 12R/30L must be reconditioned in the near future. If Runway 12L/30R is extended as planned, such reconditioning can be accomplished more readily.

Other recommended airfield improvements include the addition of helipads at the northwestern corner of the general aviation area on the west side, and near the passenger terminal building; the construction of a bypass taxiway between taxiways 1 and 2 south of Taxiway B; and the construction of holding aprons at both the north and south ends of Runway 12R/30L.

During the Economic and Planning Management Program, air traffic and airspace considerations were analyzed. It was determined by the FAA that the type and number of aircraft expected to use the airport can be accommodated with the programs recommended in the proposed Airport Master Plan.[19]

Overall Land Use

General Aviation. The recommended plan for general aviation calls for the development of expanded facilities, including new fixed base operations on the west side of the airfield and south of the aviation reserve area. As a result of new development on the west side of the airport, space will be available for improved aircraft service and maintenance facilities to accommodate the needs of a wide range of commercial and personal aircraft. In addition, shops providing specialized aviation services can be located on the west side of the airport.

Growth in air carrier passenger and cargo activity, with an attendant growth in the need for airport services, may require expansion of areas for related facilities on the east side of the airport. Such development may require conversion of existing properties for these purposes in the future.

When general aviation development takes place on the west side of the airport, some of the existing fixed base operators may desire to move to the west side and become a part of the new development.

Public Land Uses. Public land uses in the airport include the San Jose State University Aeronautics Department, the General Aviation District Office (GADO), and the control tower. There are no plans for expanding the San Jose State University site. The tower can be relocated to the west-side aviation reserve to improve the safe and efficient operation of the airport. At the FAA's option, the GADO could be consolidated on the west side with the relocated control tower.

Nonaviation Commerical. No additional nonaviation-related commerical facilities would be permitted in the airport.

Air Cargo. The existing airlines' air freight building would be expanded to twice its current size, meeting short-term requirements. Beyond that point, additional air freight could be located north of the terminal building or south of the existing air freight building, with final resolution depending on economic and operational circumstances.

In the northeast corner of the airport, an all-cargo center is located on a site of approximately 25 acres. Cargo processing buildings can be developed to provide for consolidation and transfer from trucks to aircraft. To provide access to this cargo center, a separate road would be developed, entering the airport from De La Cruz Boulevard, south of Central Expressway.

Aviation Reserve. About 40 acres in the northwest corner of the airport are designated as aviation reserve. This area will be set aside for future development that cannot be foreseen at the present time. Among the facilities that might be located there, in addition to general aviation, are those for airport support (fueling, commissary, and airport maintenance), the FAA, and crash/fire/rescue operations.

Sound long-range planning dictates a need for flexibility where economics, environmental considerations, and technological improvements are key factors in the planning and implementation process. The establishment of an aviation reserve provides the ability to react to future needs.

Passenger Terminal Building

On the Master Plan the passenger terminal building is shown on the existing site, with expansion both north and south as dictated by future demand. Additional terminal facilities would be provided by removing the existing baggage claim and rental car wing and placing these facilities at designated locations along an extended linear terminal. A roadway would be constructed along the face of the linear terminal, thus providing improved access to and from the building.

Automobile Parking

Automobile parking would be located at various places on the east side of the airport. It is estimated that 67 acres are now available to accommodate passenger, visitor, employee, and rental car parking. This acreage is not sufficient to provide for all automobile parking at grade and, as part of the Passenger Terminal Complex shown in Figure 3.4, a parking structure will be required to satisfy all long-term requirements.

Airport Access

Airport access proposals include three major programs. The first is interim intersection improvements at Brokaw Road and Guadalupe Parkway, Brokaw Road and Airport Boulevard, and Airport Boulevard and Coleman Avenue. These improvements are deemed necessary to help alleviate expected congestion caused by the rise in access traffic attributed to the increase in air passenger growth. The intersections would be modified by the addition of stacking and turning lanes and by the installation of signal systems that improve traffic flow.

The second access program calls for the upgrading of Guadalupe Parkway to a freeway with the development of interchanges at Guadalupe Freeway and Brokaw Road and Guadalupe Freeway and Highway 17. This improvement is currently in the freeway plan of the California Department of Transportation.

The third access program is for future development of general aviation facilities on the west side of the airport, which requires consideration of airport access problems along Coleman Avenue, Martin Avenue, and De La Cruz Boulevard. The frontage of the west-side general aviation development along Martin Avenue is such that, depending on detailed planning, a separate internal access roadway, parallel to Martin Avenue, might be constructed to improve traffic movements and to control land development and parking. Such a decision depends on the future detailed design of the general aviation facilities.

Other Considerations

The Master Plan also included consideration of aircraft obstruction. The first major issue concerns FAA regulations on clear zones.

At the south end of the airport, a sizable proportion of general aviation T-shelters are, and have been for many years, within the clear zone for Runway 12R/30L. The general aviation terminal building lies within the clear zone for Runway 12L/30R. There are other buildings in the clear zones (shown in Figure 3.3) at both ends of the airport.

It is FAA policy that all existing structures in clear zones be removed.[20] However, FAA permits exceptions to this policy for indeterminate periods of time at many airports. The San Jose Airport management is optimistic that such as exception can be secured for this area.[21] Without FAA approval these areas should be cleared. These functions could be provided at an alternative location.

The second aircraft obstruction issue concerns the potential for aircraft accidents in the community surrounding the airport. For the most part, FAA obstruction considerations have been developed primarily for the purpose of promoting aircraft safety rather than reducing the hazards to people on the ground. Aircraft obstruction regulations are usually enforced through a jurisdiction's adoption of *Federal Aviation Regulation Part 77—Objects Affecting Navigable Airspace.*[22] These regulations require that notice of construction or a possible obstruction to navigable airspace be given to the FAA. However, the FAA does not have the power to demand compliance. The responsibility ultimately lies with the jurisdiction where the proposed project is to be built.[23]

Part 77 delineates imaginary surfaces around an airport.[24] Structures are subject to height limitations based on their distance from the runways. Additional criteria may include the prohibition of uses or devices that may be hazardous to aircraft by causing glare, radio interference, smoke, and the like. Above-ground bulk storage of hazardous materials, such as petroleum products, may also be prohibited.

In order to enforce Part 77, the affected jurisdictions usually incorporate the regulations into their zoning ordinances. To date, such regulations have not been adopted for San Jose Municipal Airport by the cities of San Jose and Santa Clara.[25]

Another consideration is the possible hazard that aircraft pose to the land uses and inhabitants on the ground, particularly in the immediate vicinity of an airport.

In 1977 an airport planning consultant[26] performed a brief investigation to determine the extent to which aircraft actually pose a hazard to the public. It was found that a large percentage of aircraft accidents at air carrier airports occur on approach or takeoff, primarily near the extended runway centerline. However, documentation of the danger from civilian aircraft was too sparse to substantiate the imposition of restrictive land use regulations in these areas.

As part of the investigation, the "Air Installation Compatible Use Zone" (AICUZ)[27] study for Andrews Air Force Base was reviewed. Although the results of that study do provide some indication of the areas most prone to aircraft hazards, it was not possible to translate them directly to a civilian airport for the following reasons:

—As of 1977, no analysis similar in depth to the Air Force's aircraft accident study had been conducted by the FAA or civilian airports.
—The operations in the AICUZ study could not be compared with civilian aircraft operations because military flights include a large number of training flights; also, the average age of the military pilots is lower and they have far less experience than air carrier pilots.
—The types of aircraft used for military purposes are not the same as civilian aircraft.

The Santa Clara County Airport Land Use Commission (ALUC) has designated safety areas to the north and south of Runways 12R/30L and 12L/30R.[28] Much of the safety area to the south of Highway 17 is currently within the Coleman Loop (Airport Approach Acquisition Area in Figure 3.4), and future land use in this area is expected to be compatible with all obstruction and noise criteria.

Much of the area to the north is already developed or owned by the airport. In the Vicinity Area Actions it is proposed that new development in the area be required to meet all safety criteria as specified in FAR Part 77.

In the Santa Clara County study, the ALUC adopted a population density standard of 10 persons per acre for the defined hazard areas.[29] This standard could be translated into 3 dwelling units or 10 employees per gross acre. The ALUC has defined the safety zones to be within the FAA-designated approach areas (2,200 feet by 5,000 feet for air carrier runways, and 1,250 feet by 2,500 feet for general aviation runways).

Vicinity Area Alternatives

Seven concept alternatives for noise compatibility in the San Jose Municipal Airport Vicinity Area represent action programs that can be enacted by the cities of San Jose and Santa Clara to help mitigate the noise impacts caused by airport and aircraft operations.[30] The primary objective is to achieve the maximum amount of land use compatibility with the minimum amount of neighborhood disruption and cost.

All but two of the seven alternatives were eliminated early in the planning process because they did not meet the primary objective. The alternative that became the recommendation for the Vicinity Area Actions contains the following major programs.[31] (See Figure 3.5.)

—Acquisition includes the relocation of residents and sale or lease of the property for a nonresidential, noise-compatible use.
—The noise remedy program consists of remedial sound attenuation in existing structures, paid for with airport revenues and funds in exchange for a navigation easement granted by the property owner to the city of San Jose. The program is contingent on the results of a pilot noise insulation study demonstrating the viability of a full-scale program.
—New Development may be permitted in areas between CNEL 65 and CNEL 76 aircraft noise exposure, provided that structures for noise-sensitive land uses, such as residential, are constructed with adequate soundproofing to assure that the interior noise level does not exceed CNEL 45.[32] Also, all new or redeveloped property would be subject to the dedication of a navigation easement to the city of San Jose as a condition of approval.

In addition to the noise programs, it was recommended that the local zoning ordinances be amended to conform with height regulations in FAR Part 77, and that special regulations be applied to prevent other ob-

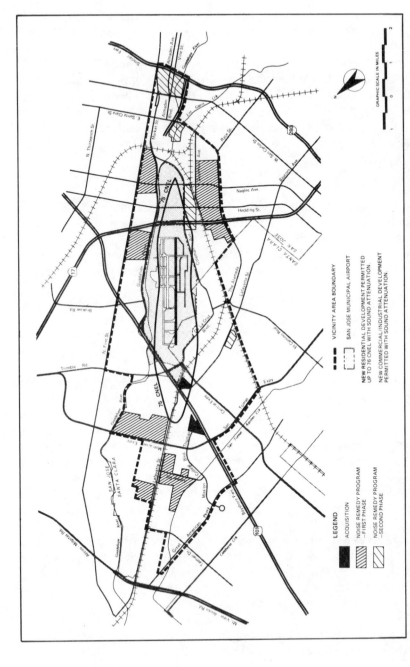

FIGURE 3.5. San Jose Municipal Airport: Planned Actions for Noise Compatibility. *Source: San Jose, Environmental Assessment and Environmental Impact Report on the Airport Master Plan and Airport Vicinity Area Actions* (April 1980).

structions or navigational hazards, such as reflection of sunlight on glass and flashing lights.[33]

Thus, the city of San Jose and local business interests believe that the measures proposed in San Jose's *Airport Master Plan and Airport Vicinity Area Actions* will enable the existing airport site to meet the expected demand for air transportation and the environmental needs of the metropolitan community.

Community Groups and Cities
Representing Areas Adjacent to the Airport
(Save Our Valley Action Committee, North Side Residents
Association, United New Conservationists, City of Santa Clara)

These actors primarily represent residents on inlying neighborhoods adjacent to the airport that suffer from high levels of air and noise pollution due to the increasing activities of the airport. They are concerned with maintaining a livable level of environmental quality and conservation of environmental resources, and believe that any expansion of the existing airport would be contrary to such concerns.[34]

Opposition to airport expansion is based on three major problems directly affecting the quality of life in the Santa Clara Valley. The first problem, noise pollution, is probably the most serious difficulty associated with the airport.[35] As one observer living near the San Jose Airport stated:

> The airport, as it presently exists, is a terrible noise nuisance to some 4,000 North Santa Clara residents and probably twice as many San Jose residents.[36]

Those most affected live either directly beneath or adjacent to a flight path, and have experienced problems ranging from minor subjective effects such as annoyance and disturbance to behavioral problems such as interference with speech communication, sleep, and learning activities, and even physical effects such as permanent hearing damage and the cumulative physical results of prolonged sleep loss.[37] While the airport has met the noise standard established by the State Division of Aeronautics, the measurement used (CNEL) is not sufficient to properly assess the noise impact on the community, since it is an average value and does not isolate the individual aircraft event noise level.[38]

The second problem is air pollution.[39] The state of California has established ambient air quality standards that should not be exceeded for reasons of health and comfort of the public. The Bay Area Pollution Control District (BAPCD) has rated the air pollution potential of the airport location between stage IV (heavy) and stage V (severe).[40] The Air

Quality Reports have been available from the BAPCD since September 1975.[41]

The final area of concern is safety.[42] Although difficult to predict, accidents during takeoff or landing would involve several hundred residences.[43] Not only must potential accidents be considered, but for many people low-flying jets cause emotional or physical fear reactions.

In summary, these three areas of concern—noise, air pollution, and safety—seriously affect the health of individuals in the community; the property value of homes near flight paths; neighborhood viability (the impacted areas, once populated primarily by homeowners, now contain many renters); and the social and individual quality of life in the Santa Clara Valley, by encouraging further growth of the San Jose metropolitan area.

Solution: Economic and population growth is the main focus of pro-expansion business interests. These interests have promoted and encouraged a development policy justified on the basis of a broadened tax base, but it has resulted in higher taxes and fewer and poorer services for residents.[44] The need for economic growth in the Santa Clara Valley and its relation to business and recreational travel needs is recognized, as is San Jose's position as the population center of the South Bay area. But, in the absence of city policies setting a limit to growth or even committing the city to rationally planned growth, there is little reason to believe that future growth perpetuated by airport expansion will be any less harmful to the quality of life in San Jose than in the past.[45] Therefore, in accordance with the desire to preserve the living environment, rather than merely to transfer the airport's detrimental environmental effects to another populated area, and at the same time to meet the transportation needs caused by economic and population growth, the following alternative is proposed to expand air service within the Santa Clara Valley.

Both Save Our Valley Action Committee (SOVAC) and the North Side Residents' Association (NSRA) argued for the closing of the San Jose Airport.[46] SOVAC recommended the development of a high-speed ground transportation (HSGT) system linking San Francisco, Sacramento, Oakland, San Jose, Los Angeles, and San Diego, providing for the largest portion of Bay Area air travel demand.[47] It is predicted that 35 percent of all destinations will be to Southern California by 1985.[48]

The HSGT has several assets, and avoids the disadvantages of airport expansion as outlined. It is technologically feasible and ecologically sound in relation to air and noise pollution. It will not displace entire neighborhoods, and could eventually satisfy Santa Clara County's business and pleasure travel needs, as well as the Bay Area's commuter and cargo-carrying requirements to Southern California. HSGT would not demand that Oakland Airport (OAK) and San Francisco International

(SFO) accept more passengers in place of an expansion of Santa Clara County air service, because OAK and SFO would be relieved of much of their own commuter service by HSGT. In addition, using the 1985 demand projection of 72 MAP made by the Regional Airport System Study Committee (since reduced to between 37 and 43 MAP), it can be illustrated that the present combined capacities of OAK and SFO would have been sufficient to carry total regional demand until 1980.[49] An additional runway at OAK would extend this date until the proposed ground transit system could be constructed.[50] It is contended that expansion of transportation services prior to this is unnecessary. In fact, if construction was begun immediately, San Jose Municipal Airport could be dissolved in 1985 without burdening SFO and OAK by using an interim improved high-speed rail (IHSR) system until completion of the HSGT.[51] Cost of the IHSR would approximate the outlay for air service expansion until 1985.

The cost of HSGT could be borne by income from IHSR, government subsidies, an auto toll system, or some combination of these. Employment provided for low- or semiskilled labor by airport expansion would most likely be transitory, since it would consist primarily of construction and maintenance-type jobs. In contrast, the IHSR and HSGT would provide employment for unskilled labor in all phases—construction, maintenance, and operation. The suggested alternative, therefore, encompasses a more permanent redistribution of income for the numerous low-income households in the San Jose metropolitan area.

The HSGT will serve a broader travel market with respect to cost and accessibility than would expanded air service. Expansion of the airport necessarily involves the purchase of more residences within a specified area under flight paths. The time sequence of acquisition may affect the eminent domain process. That is, as it becomes publicly known that certain residences are within the acquisition area, the market price may decline. The city has, in effect, reduced the market value of the residences and purchased them at below fair market value by condemning the area, and then taking a long period of time to purchase the residences. This problem is further complicated if new housing must be constructed to accommodate relocated families. Relocation may also increase out-migration to peripheral areas, possibly giving rise to additional urban sprawl. The suggested alternative avoids relocation and its attendant problems. Using the railroad's existing right-of-way, the HSGT will not disturb established, viable neighborhoods.

Finally, the plan provides enough benefits for different factions to make it politically feasible. The federal government and the California Department of Transportation are both seriously interested in a West Coast HSGT plan.

The HSGT plan recommended by SOVAC would not only avoid the negative effects of increased air service but, by servicing the central city, it might also encourage new social and economic development in the downtown area. It would eliminate access problems associated with airports on the urban fringe, reduce dependence on the automobile (especially if an adequate interface with BART is developed), and help curb urban sprawl.

However, NSRA realizes that the likelihood of shutting down the airport is low, so the concept of reliever airports and enforcement of stringent operating rules is suggested as a means by which to reduce present and future impacts, since noise is considered to be the primary impact in North Santa Clara.[52]

NSRA, for example, suggests that Oakland International Airport has the capability to increase its air carrier traffic, and such an increase could reduce air traffic and associated impacts presently affecting North Santa Clara.[53] NSRA believes that Oakland would not suffer adverse impacts if its airport could accommodate a larger share of the air carrier traffic. NSRA further suggests that San Jose should explore the possibility of developing a new airport, perhaps in the southern portion of the city.[54] NSRA stresses, though, that efforts to increase the use of existing airports or to develop new airport sites should proceed wisely, in order to prevent the transfer impacts from one city or community to another.

With regard to the specific elements of the proposed San Jose Airport Master Plan, the City Council of Santa Clara recommended the following:[55]

a. The northerly extension of Runway 12R/30L should be re-evaluated, on the basis of the potential adverse noise impact on Santa Clara and admitted marginal benefits to San Jose. Noise over Santa Clara will increase if takeoffs to the north use the extra length. Planes taxiing to the north will bring noise closer to the residential areas beyond.

b. The report should discuss the effects of the enlarged clear zone at the north end of Runway 12R/30L on existing industrial properties in Santa Clara. The problem is not necessarily solved by asking the FAA for waivers or variances.

c. The plan should include a more detailed discussion of the impacts of the voluntary night flight curfew upon noise mitigation, and of the potential for expanding the curfew. The Airport Master Plan and the Vicinity Area Actions do not contain commitments by the airport to maintain and consider expansion of the night flight curfew. Expansion of air freight facilities will put much greater pressures on the airport for night flights. The curfew should cover the "freighters" specifically.

d. The "pilot studies" to determine the effectiveness of construction elements in reducing interior residential noise should include situations where SENL criteria are used, as well as CNEL standards.[56] This will establish a cost differential needed to comply with the higher standards. The City Council of Santa Clara felt that the CNEL standards appeared to be more feasible for both new and existing dwelling units. Residents in the noise-impacted area indicated that even where air conditioning, double-paned windows, and insulation have been installed, single event noise is still uncomfortably loud and outdoor living is extremely unpleasant.

    e. The report should include an expanded discussion of transit service as a mitigating measure for traffic congestion. Santa Clara County's current light rail feasibility study (Guadalupe Corridor study) provides an excellent opportunity for such planning. The projected traffic congestion at airport access points and the high cost of improving these points could provide support for the Guadalupe Corridor transit project. The airport might even contribute funds to such a project in lieu of making some street and parking improvements.

    f. The report should include a statement that adding noise insulation to certain nonconforming residences in the city of Santa Clara's industrial zone may conflict with its objective of eliminating these uses. For example, Santa Clara's Zoning Ordinance limits nonstructural improvements to nonconforming buildings to 15 percent of their value within one year. More extensive improvements require a use permit. The plan should also present the alternatives to complying with state noise standards if the installation of insulation is not feasible.

    g. Mitigation should include an explicit policy of minimizing the total number of flights using the airport. This could be accomplished by the following:

        1. Shifting general aviation growth to reliever airports. The plan should be designed to accommodate only the expansion of current fixed base and private users, not the total general aviation demand

        2. Not becoming a major air freight center

        3. Preventing air "hops" between Bay Area airports

        4. Promoting the use of Moffett Field for large commerical flights.

    h. Noise mitigation should require that any new airlines requesting San Jose flights use only wide body and/or quieter airplanes. It has been reported that some airports actually ban noisy planes, allowing only the quieter planes to operate to and from their facilities.

    i. Mitigation of social impacts on the approximately 850 persons living in mobile homes could be accomplished by immediately setting a plan and time schedule for acquisition and relocation. The occupants should know how value will be established and what the relocation benefits are. Payments to owners to prevent filling of vacancies as they may occur is another method to begin the acquisition process.

Given the environmental and social diseconomies of airport expansion, San Jose must begin to accept its responsibility to the region, as well as the state and the nation, with respect to providing pollution-free, energy-conserving transportation alternatives.

An Outlying Community Threatened by the Location of a New Airport Site (City of Milpitas)

Problem: Located in the northeastern portion of Santa Clara County, Milpitas is bordered by Highway 17 to the west, Trimble Road to the south, and the Fremont-Alameda County boundary to the north. Since 1968 six sites for a major jetport have been proposed to the west of Highway 17 in the vicinity of Milpitas. The most likely site is on the present Agnews State Hospital property (east annex). This plan would accommodate 10 MAP in accordance with the regional allocation of air passengers proposed by the Association of Bay Area Governments (ABAG).[57]

Although relocation of the San Jose Airport is presently not being pursued, Milpitas officials believe that this issue could be revived in the future, and that the most likely relocation site would be in North San Jose, adjacent to Milpitas and the nearby communities of Fremont and Newark.[58]

Two of the numerous aspects of the relocation issue are still apparently of crucial concern to Milpitas:[59]

a. The proximity of the relocation site to Milpitas will cause an increase in noise levels throughout the city, particularly in the residential district at the city's southwestern corner adjacent to Highway 17. The two-segment airplane approach pattern, quieter jet engines, and other technological advances will reduce the adverse impacts of airport noise, compared with current levels. However, any noise increase whatsoever would be considered a strong negative impact. The orientation of the runways and location of the maintenance shop area would be of prime concern to Milpitas.

b. Milpitas anticipates a significant increase in automobile traffic due to the relocated airport. This is considered to be primarily a problem of design that can be solved. Milpitas will pay close attention to the specific proposal in order to ensure that the solution is appropriate for Milpitas.

Air pollution and physical safety are concerns of secondary importance to Milpitas.[60] The air pollution situation in the entire South Bay area, including Milpitas, is such that it is believed that the relocation of the airport would cause a minimal increase in pollutants for Milpitas. Physical safety is not considered significant because all proposals indicate the placement of runways parallel to Milpitas, thus not creating landing approach zones over the community. Several additional issues that have no direct impact, such as geologic hazards of the site, the Alviso relocation, and the proximity to the wildlife refuge, would most likely be brought up by Milpitas.[61] City officials admit that the community stands to benefit substantially from the relocation of the airport.[62] However, they also admit that the citizens will discount any potential economic benefits because of cynicism toward government predictions regarding economic improvements, and an uncertainty about whether the individual citizen would actually reap the benefits if economic activity did increase.[63]

The San Jose Municipal Airport Master Plan, as adopted in July 1980, does not represent a problem for the city of Milpitas. However, if it is amended in the future, so that the existing airport site is transformed into a "super-airport," Milpitas officials would be concerned about additional noise pollution resulting from increased aircraft traffic over their city.

Solution: The most likely airport relocation site would accommodate the allocated 10 MAP. Proponents believe that expansion at the present airport location would be undesirable because of environmental and size constraints. According to airport sources, the most likely site, adjacent to Milpitas, would be the best for relocation because it has fewer constraints than other areas.[64] The proponents concede that there will be environmental impacts, but that they will be less severe than at any of the other suggested relocation sites. Noise pollution from aircraft, which is of great concern to Milpitas, will shift, but the ultimate impact would be on a smaller population.

Much recent work has been done to examine some of the implications of expanding the capacity of the existing airport site.[65] Nevertheless, little is known about the full environmental impact of developing a new airport site at the 10 MAP level.[66] The *Regional Airport Systems Study* presented general environmental impacts according to their regional allocations.[67] Numerous subsequent studies compiled by the county of Santa Clara, the city of San Jose, the Planning Policy Commission, private consultants, and others have presented and discussed the proposed site alternatives and some of their general environmental impacts.[68] These impacts include noise, air pollution, geologic hazards, and destruction of natural biotic associations. This information has added greatly to the general knowledge of possible environmental effects of airport expansion and/or relocation. Little of it, however, is specific enough for the consideration of expanding airport services at either site to the 10 MAP level.[69]

The city of San Jose should be aware of all the factors involving the sites it might consider before deciding on any one location in which to expand or relocate the airport. The city should also determine development policies for geologically unstable areas before they even consider a large development such as the airport proposal. Citizens in all affected areas should be made aware of the regional impact that an enlarged airport may place upon them.

Furthermore, neither the proponents nor any of the studies have investigated the most important questions dealing with airport expansion, such as whether the citizens of this area want to accommodate the 10 MAP; whether they want to live in and accept the level and combination of the projected environmental impacts; and whether air traveler needs and demands should take precedent over needs in the San Jose metropolitan area. It is Milpitas' contention that any expansion of air service to the magnitude proposed for the San Jose Municipal Airport would severely degrade the quality of life in Santa Clara County, far outweighing any subsequent benefit.

While it is common practice for neighboring municipalities to assume a cautious position when dealing with an issue being sponsored by another city, it is Milpitas' opinion that an issue with as many facets and as regionally oriented as the airport proposal is demands input from all affected areas. This input should occur from the initial consideration through project completion.Therefore, prior to any decision, specific environmental information should be gathered concerning both the present airport site and the proposed site. This information should be used to project and assess living conditions in the South Bay area as a result of airport expansion and/or relocation. The reported information should be presented as a cost-benefit analysis allowing comparisons between present living conditions and the benefits accrued under airport expansion. In other words, this report should not be an expanded environmental impact report (EIR) that enumerates impacts and mitigating measures, such as that made in 1980 for the expansion of the existing site,[70] because EIRs tend to come too late in the planning process, when many of the crucial decisions have already been made. Such a cost-benefit analysis should commence immediately, while flexibility is still possible.

The FAA provides impacted citizens with an opportunity to request a public hearing to present and discuss these types of issues. "The FAA . . . requires the sponsor to afford the opportunity for a hearing, and conduct the hearing if one is requested, before submitting a request for aid for a project" under the Airport Development Aid Program (ADAP).[71] This program requires that transcripts of public hearings be submitted to the FAA when requested.

The content of the final report should include the recommended subjects proposed by the FAA in the guidelines for public hearings. These include the following:

a. Safe and efficient air transportation
b. Economic activity
c. Public health and safety
d. Property values
e. The human and natural environment
    1. Displacement of persons and replacement housing
    2. Noise, air, and water pollution
    3. Neighborhood character and location
    4. Aesthetics, parks, and recreation areas
    5. Natural and historic landmarks
    6. Conservation (erosion, sedimentation, wildlife, and general ecology of the area).[72]

Social, economic, and environmental effects should be defined as the direct and indirect benefits or losses to the community as a result of the proposed development.

The consultant performing the cost-benefit analysis should be chosen by a regional body, preferably the Santa Clara County Airport Land Use Commission (ALUC). It is hoped that this will eliminate consultant bias in favor of the clients. Funding for the analysis could be obtained from the FAA, since monies for a hearing are an allowable project cost.

In summary, Milpitas is opposed to both the relocation and the expansion of airport facilities in the Santa Clara Valley.[73] Richard Delong, the former city manager of Milpitas, explained this position several years ago when he stated:

> The moral of the story, as we in Milipitas see it, is not to make the same mistakes over again. We believe also that this is just what is about to happen in the case of the airport. The same shortsighted thinking that located the present airport is about be be repeated all over again, only this time the consequences are many times over.[74]

The proposed cost-benefit study should publicly expose the facts supporting Milpitas' present position regarding the airport controversy.

Despite the ability to review the EIR for expanding the existing airport site, there are no decisive governmental mechanisms available to local jurisdictions whereby they could substantially influence a project in a neighboring jurisdiction that would produce spillovers adversely affecting their community. This applies even to regionally oriented projects such as the airport expansion or relocation proposal. Affected communities can only appeal their concerns to the lead agency or to a higher jurisdictional body. With regard to the airport, both the present site and the most likely relocation site are completely within the municipal boundaries of San Jose. Furthermore, the proposed site is situated so that it is not within the area regulated by the San Fransisco Bay Conservation Development Commission (BCDC), one of the few Bay Area regional agencies that has regulatory power. This means that San Jose is the sole lead agency for the airport project, needing approval from only the ALUC and the FAA. A denial from the ALUC can be overturned by the San Jose City Council with a 4/5 majority vote. The Association of Bay Area Governments (ABAG) has an opportunity to review the EIR through A-95 review.[75] However, as experience has shown, this may prove to be a mere procedure rather than an avenue for appeal.

As one of the outlying communities, Milpitas has a choice of two approaches to convey its concerns about the airport proposal. It can appeal to San Jose, the lead agency in this case, or it can turn to concerned regional bodies for assistance. Despite its concerns about the limitations of regional planning institutions, Milpitas has taken on a regional-level argument, believing it to be the most effective route for two reasons.[76] First, the relocation or expansion of the San Jose Municipal Airport is a multijurisdictional issue that will produce important regional impacts. It is sound planning to grapple with a metropolitan problem on the regional planning level. Second, because of their perspective and function, regional agencies are the potential allies of outlying communities affected by the San Jose Municipal Airport. Since these regional agencies represent many communities, they may have a greater ability than an individual city to influence San Jose's airport plans. Milpitas will therefore attempt to influence decisions about the San Jose Airport through the regional planning institutions.

The Metropolitan View (Santa Clara County Land Use Committee, and Planning Department)

Problem: While acknowledging the metropolis-wide importance of expanding air transportation facilities at the existing airport, the Santa Clara County ALUC and Santa Clara County Planning Department find that San Jose's *Airport Master Plan and Airport Vicinity Area Actions* are inconsistent with the ALUC plan for the San Jose Airport,[77] and would be harmful to this area with respect to noise pollution and safety.[78] In particular, the Santa Clara County-wide actors find that the San Jose Airport plans conflict with metropolitan county-wide policy in the following ways:[79]

a. New residential uses will be permitted in areas having CNELs up to and including 76 decibels (dB), whereas current ALUC policy places an upper limit at 70 CNEL.

b. The soundproofing standard for new residential structures has been set by the Vicinity Area Plan as 45 CNEL, whereas current ALUC policy recommends attenuation to between 40 and 60 dB SENL.

c. New commercial and industrial uses will be permitted in any noise exposure area, whereas current ALUC policy places upper limits at 76 and 70 CNEL, respectively.

d. The soundproofing standard for new commercial and industrial uses has been set by the Vicinity Area Plan as 55 CNEL, whereas current ALUC policy recommends attenuation to between 55 and 75 SENL, depending upon the specific use.

e. Safety areas, as defined and described in the ALUC plan, are omitted from both the Airport Master Plan and the Vicinity Area Plan.

Thus, the county is concerned that the proposed San Jose Airport Plan would allow the airport activity to generate noise pollution and safety risks beyond those acceptable under county-wide policy. Under these circumstances the County expects that

> ... during overflights of jet aircraft, conversation will be interrupted, radio/television listening will be disturbed and awakening probable. Some work situations may also experience interruption, especially in offices, hotels, and institutional uses.[80]

Solution: In general, the county recommends the amelioration of airport noise and safety hazards through the compliance of the San Jose Airport Plan with the ALUC plan. Specific recommendations and contrasts with San Jose proposals follow.

Effects of Jet Noise

ALUC and Vicinity Area Plan Boundaries. The ALUC referral boundary for the San Jose Municipal Airport is currently defined by the 65 dB CNEL contour of October 1968, and will expand or contract on a yearly basis, depending upon its annual fluctuation. Recent evidence suggests that during 1979 it remained nearly stationary because of a slight decrease in total jet aircraft operations (passenger traffic increased by 6 percent, to 3.6 MAP, during the same year).[81] Over the long term, however, the 65 dB contour is expected to have a slight outward creep as the passenger load approaches 8.3 MAP by 1997.[82]

San Jose used the consultant's projected 1997 contour of 65 CNEL as a general limit for the Vicinity Area Plan, and modified it to produce a plan boundary conforming to existing and planned living areas that will be retained or redeveloped for residential use of varying densities.[83] This modification appears conservative, and will not materially affect ALUC referrals or actions through the target year. ALUC may desire to consider using an expanded boundary as its current referral area to ensure that new or converted uses, which may later become noise-impacted, are constructed to ALUC noise attenuation standards.

Residential Noise Attenuation. The thesis upon which the 1973 ALUC plan was founded held that within the referral boundary, no new residential uses (whether single family detached, townhouse, duplex, or any of various multiple densities) should be permitted. Recent ALUC Hearing Board decisions have tended to liberalize this policy, however, and certain changes will probably be recommended in the forthcoming Policy Plan update. But in all cases of residential approvals (65–70 CNEL), the ALUC standard of SENL for the noisiest aircraft operating from San Jose Municipal Airport (1973 through 1985)[84] was consistently used as the design criterion in recommending noise quieting to interior levels of 60 dB (day), 55 dB (night), and 40 dB (sleeping rooms).

In contrast, the Vicinity Area Action plan, whose principal thrust is to ameliorate existing noise-impacted dwellings in the 65–76 CNEL range[85] by means of an acoustical treatment program, proposes the state standard of 45 CNEL[86] for all interior residential spaces, using the argument that ALUC single event criteria are virtually impossible to meet and can be attained only at considerable additional expense for new structures, ALUC's principal concern.

A critical assumption in the Vicinity Area Actions Plan is that during the normal sleeping hours, 11 p.m. to 7 a.m., only a negligible portion of the total operations in a 24-hour period occurs. While it is true that San Jose Municipal Airport discourages jet operations between midnight and 6 a.m., no prohibition exists, and occasional cargo or general aviation jet aircraft will doubtless violate this policy.[87]

Both ALUC staff and the Santa Clara County noise control engineer are concerned at the proposed relaxation of soundproofing standards for new residential construction.[88] It is suggested that this portion of the Vicinity Area Plan is inconsistent with adopted ALUC policy, and would prove harmful to future residents in areas adjacent to the airport, notwithstanding grants of navigation easement to the city of San Jose.

Commercial and Industrial Uses Noise Attenuation. The ALUC Policy Plan recommends permitting new commercial uses in locations of up to 65 CNEL without special consideration as to soundproofing. Between 65 and 77 CNEL soundproofing is recommended to produce an interior level of 40 to 75 dB, depending upon specific use. Above 77 CNEL, the plan suggests avoidance of land use unless it is related to airport service.

Similar recommendations have been established for new industrial uses, with correspondingly higher CNEL limits and interior noise levels allowed (up to 75 dB for machine shops).

The Vicinity Area Plan would allow any new commercial or industrial use without regard to exterior CNEL, and with interior quieting required only to 55 CNEL (about 75 SENL). Implementation of this proposal clearly would be inconsistent with the current ALUC Policy Plan, and no changes to it are presently contemplated.

ALUC Safety Areas

North Safety Area. This 2,200 by 5,000-foot rectangle, lying entirely within the City of Santa Clara, was based on the northerly end of Runway 12R/30L, which has remained constant since the 1973 adoption of the ALUC plan. It is also the landing threshold for jet aircraft approaching from the northwest (about 15 percent of all operations).[89] There will probably be no need to extend the North Safety Areas beyond its present limits, but the matter will be considered in the ALUC Policy Plan update.

South Safety Area. The South Safety Area was based on the existing displaced threshold for Runway 30L (about 1,500 feet north of its southerly terminus).[90]

As adopted by ALUC and currently configured, it measures 2,200 by about 3,700 feet, less the area under airport ownership.[91] The addition of 1,300 feet on the south to increase the safety area to a standard 5,000-foot length seems academic, since the Airport Master Plan proposed shifting will displace the threshold 1,400 feet further north when the runway is lengthened in the 1980–87 period.[92]

New Uses Within ALUC Safety Areas. Since 1973, ALUC policy has recommended the following controls over new uses in both safety areas:

a. Nonresidential
b. "10/25 population density" (the presence of no more than 10 persons on an annual average, and no more than 25 persons at any one time on each net acre)[93]
c. Maximum of 100 gallons of flammable fluids stored per net acre.

In the South Safety Area, which is entirely within the "Coleman Loop" or "South Acquisition Area," noise-impacted residential units and neighborhood commercial facilities have been purchased and removed. The entire "Coleman Loop" is designated "Airport Approach Zone" in the San Jose *General Plan,* but has not yet been rezoned to reflect the restrictiveness that the Vicinity Area Actions Plan implies. The stated goal of this acquisition program is to provide a clear and safe approach area south of the airport and beyond mandated (FAA) clear zones, and to establish a land use pattern that is compatible with the noise of airport operations.[94]

The future uses of properties in the South Safety Area are proposed as follows:[95]

a. Those acquired by the city of San Jose will conform to FAA guidelines and grant restrictions (for example, will be retained in open space).

b. Those not under city ownership will continue to be regulated in accordance with the Airport Approach Zone policies of the San Jose *General Plan* (for example, a low-intensity light industrial development for an industrial park may be expected, which would conform to ALUC policy if the proposed 10/25 population density is not exceeded).

No mention is made of the North Safety Area in Santa Clara, and presumably ALUC policy would continue to govern new uses within its perimeter.

In summary, Santa Clara County recommends that San Jose be notified that certain portions of the Vicinity Area Actions Plan are inconsistent with ALUC's land use plan for areas surrounding Santa Clara County airports, including noise attenuation requirements for new residential, commercial, and industrial uses.

Bay Area and Federal Planning Institutions (Association of Bay Area Governments, Metropolitan Transportation Commission, Federal Aviation Administration)

Problem: The need for a regional overview of airport planning has long been apparent. The use of Bay Area airspace is already "managed" by a quasi-regional agency, FAA's Terminal Radar Approach Control Facility, since aircraft operations at one airport interact with operations at other Bay Area airports.[96] Several other factors are also relevant:[97]

—Airports in the Bay Area serve a broad regional demand for

passenger and cargo service extending well beyond the immediate jurisdiction of airport operators.

—Noise from aircraft landings and takeoffs and from aircraft "overflights" affects a large number of Bay Area communities. Certain communities have borne the major effects of the growing regional demand for air transportation simply because they are located near the airports.

—Emissions from aircraft and automobiles affect regional as well as local air quality.

—Ground transportation improvements often involve coordination among several political jurisdictions. The programming of funds for highway and transit improvements takes place at the regional level.

—Conservation of energy has emerged as a major goal in transportation planning. How new airline service is developed in the region will have a significant impact on the consumption of transportation energy both on the ground and in the air.

—Airport expansion has historically resulted in some filling of the bay. Protection and enhancement of the bay as one of the region's most significant environmental resources is an important concern.

The San Francisco Bay area is the fifth most attractive airport "hub" in the United States behind Chicago, New York, Atlanta, and Los Angeles. San Francisco Airport, the region's major facility, handles 78 percent of the passenger traffic and almost all of the air cargo.[98] International service as well as a significant portion of domestic service is located there. Private investment in passenger service facilities, aircraft service facilities, and air cargo facilities is substantial.

Oakland Airport's share of Bay Area passenger traffic averages between 9 percent and 10 percent.[99] Oakland's activity rose sharply in the late 1960s when intrastate carriers inaugurated new service in California markets. Between 1965 and 1969 there was also rapid growth in service to Europe and Hawaii by supplemental air carriers headquartered at Oakland. This service declined in the early 1970s as scheduled carriers introduced competing low group fares. Development of new interstate service has fluctuated with the economy and airline profitability.

San Jose Airport's share of Bay Area passenger traffic is about 12 percent, and has been gradually increasing on the strength of economic and population growth in the South Bay and of new airline service.[100] Like Oakland, San Jose's development received a major impetus in the late 1960s with the inauguration of new intrastate service. The airport has been somewhat more successful than Oakland in attracting and retaining new interstate service.

There will be continuing growth in the demand for airline services in the Bay Area, although changing economic and energy price and supply conditions will result in peaks and valleys in the growth curve. The major impact of energy-related factors on air travel and cargo growth will be lower growth rates compared with those experienced in the past. For example, passenger forecasts indicate a 4.2–5.8 percent annual growth rate during the 1977–87 period and a 3.1–4.2 percent annual growth rate in 1977–97. (See Table 3.3.)

Regional forecasts show that San Jose Airport would be the most convenient airport for 22.2 percent of the Bay Area air passengers in 1987, and for 23.1 percent in 1997.[101] The Regional Airport Plan indicates that the San Jose Airport should handle at least 16 percent of the Bay Area's air passengers in 1987, and 18 percent in 1997 (compared with 12.5 percent in 1979).[102] Essentially, this means that the San Jose Airport should accommodate a progressively larger share of passengers generated within its own trade area (approximately 6–7 MAP in 1987, and 10–13 MAP in 1997).

The regional benefits associated with having the San Jose Airport serve a greater share of its air trade area include reduced noise impacts in communities around other Bay Area airports, reduced surface travel (with attendant improvements in energy consumption and air quality), and reduce delays for aircraft using other Bay Area airports. For example, the difference between serving 5.3 MAP in 1987 (San Jose Airport Master Plan) and 7.0 MAP (Regional Airport Plan) is a reduction of approximately 4,250 persons impacted by noise of 65 CNEL or greater in the vicinity area. In contrast, shifting almost 2 million passengers to San Francisco Airport results in an equivalent and slightly larger increase in the number of persons exposed to adverse noise levels in San Mateo County.[103]

Thus, a major concern of regional and federal planning institutions is that local demand that cannot be served at San Jose Airport will add to airport environmental and traffic problems at other airports in the Bay Area.[104] Yet, from a regional perspective, it is not desirable to develop a new airport site in the San Jose area because of regionwide policies to limit urban sprawl and the potential negative environmental (noise, air, and water pollution) and ecological (destruction of wildlife areas and encroachment on the bay) effects of such development.[105]

Solution: Because many issues concerning airport development are regional in nature, the Association of Bay Area Governments (ABAG) and the Metropolitan Transportation Commission (MTC) have prepared a plan to guide future aviation growth in the nine-county San Fransisco Bay area.[106] This plan is designed to provide guidance for the development of

Table 3.3 Air Transportation Demand in the Bay Area: 1977–97
(annual activity)

Year	Forecast Range	Bay Area Passengers	Air Cargo (tons)	Aircraft Operations	Passengers/Operation	Commuter Operations
1977		24,465,000	490,000	358,000	73.5	62,000
1987	Low	37,000,000	790,000	406,000	92.0	43,000
	High	43,000,000	838,000	485,000	98.3	85,000
1997	Low	45,000,000	1,284,000	429,000	109.0	68,000
	High	56,000,000	1,784,000	532,000	119.0	110,000

Source: Association of Bay Area Governments and the Metropolitan Transportation Commission, *Summary of the Regional Airport Plan* (July 1980).

both air carrier airports an general aviation airports serving smaller aircraft.

The main objective of the plan is encouragement of a better distribution of commercial air traffic among the Bay Area's three major airports. Getting airlines to use Oakland and San Jose airports, rather than concentrating their activities at San Francisco, can result in less noise, less air pollution, fewer delays due to congested airspace, and greater convenience to the Bay Area air passenger.[107]

As shown in Table 3.4, the plan recommends traffic allocations for the three major airports—San Francisco, Oakland, and San Jose—with each having its unique role in the regional system.[108]

—San Francisco Airport will continue in its role as the major supplier of airline service for the region. Most air cargo and international flights will remain there, as will the region's connecting passenger traffic. The rate of passenger growth will, however, gradually decrease as new airline service is provided at other Bay Area airports. The policy limit of 31 MAP is retained because of the need to control and abate airport noise, because of deficiencies in airport landslide capacity, and because of the need to better utilize airport and airspace capacity in the Bay Area.

—Oakland Airport would serve 7–8 MAP in the midrange (1985–89) and 10–13 MAP in the long range (1994–2000). Air service at Oakland will be expanded and improved in order to accommodate a larger share of future Bay Area traffic. Most new airline service will be domestic; however, some international service will also be developed. In addition to serving the East Bay, Oakland Airport will relieve San Francisco Airport by providing convenient ground transportation for passengers with destinations in downtown San Francisco. New airline service, as well as improved ground transportation, will enhance the attractiveness of Oakland for resident and visiting air travelers and for the airline industry. Other direct benefits from using Oakland will be reduced airspace delays and limited noise restrictions resulting from the availability of overwater approaches and departures. Air cargo will also increase as a result of expanded domestic service. Oakland's traffic can be accommodated on a single runway.

—San Jose Airport would serve 6–7 MAP in the midrange (1985–89) and 8–13 MAP in the long range (1994–2000).

Continuing development in the South Bay will place pressures on San Jose Airport to provide expanded airline facilities. Accordingly, the capacity of the air transportation facilities there should be enlarged to an environmentally safe volume.[109] New service to major domestic markets will be selectively increased; however, the supply of new service will be controlled by airport noise abatement policies. Traffic growth may have to

Table 3.4 Recommended Regional Air Traffic Allocations: 1977–97

1977 Conditions

Airport	Passengers[a]		Aircraft Movements		PPO[b]	Air Cargo Tons	
	Millions	% Region	Thousands	% Region		Thousands	% Region
San Francisco	18.9	77.3%	256.3	71.6%	81.2	470.0	95.9%
Oakland	2.5	10.2	43.7	12.2	57.7	7.9	1.6
San Jose	3.1	12.5	58.0	16.2	53.7	12.2	2.5
Total	24.5	100.0%	358.0	100.0%	73.5	490.1	100.0%

1987 (Low Forecast)

Airport	Passengers[a]		Aircraft Movements		PPO[b]	Air Cargo Tons	
	Millions	% Region	Thousands	% Region		Thousands	% Region
San Francisco	24.0	64.9%	248.3	58.7%	104.1	717	90.8%
Oakland	7.0	18.9	89.4	21.1	80.3	40	5.0
San Jose	6.0	16.2	85.6	20.2	71.0	33	4.2
Total	37.0	100.0%	423.3	100.0%	92.0	790	100.0%

Table 3.4 (continued)

1987 (High Forest)

Airport	Passengers[a]		Aircraft Movements			Air Cargo Tons	
	Millions	% Region	Thousands	% Region	PPO[b]	Thousands	% Region
San Francisco	27.0	62.8%	271.2	56.0%	107.2	756	90.2%
Oakland	8.0	18.6	104.0	21.4	80.3	43	5.1
San Jose	7.0	16.3	97.8	20.2	72.6	36	4.3
North Bay	1.0	2.3	11.7	2.4	85.6	3	.4
Total	43.0	100.0%	484.7	100.0%	93.6	838	100.0%

1997 (Low Forecast)

Airport	Passengers[a]		Aircraft Movements			Air Cargo Tons	
	Millions	% Region	Thousands	% Region	PPO[b]	Thousands	% Region
San Francisco	27.0	60.0%	257.4	58.8%	113.3	1,137	88.5%
Oakland	10.0	22.2	98.6	22.5	106.1	87	6.8
San Jose	8.0	17.8	81.8	18.7	99.6	60	4.7
Total	45.0	100.0%	437.8	100.0%	109.0	1,284	100.0%

Table 3.4 *(continued)*

1997 (High Forecast)

Airport	Passengers[a]		Aircraft Movements			Air Cargo Tons	
	Millions	% Region	Thousands	% Region	PPO[b]	Thousands	% Region
San Francisco	31.0	55.4%	281.9	52.9%	118.9	1,524	85.3%
Oakland	13.0	23.2	126.5	23.8	107.4	150	8.4
San Jose	10.0	17.8	102.2	19.2	99.6	105	5.9
North Bay	2.0	3.6	21.9	4.1	91.3	5	.4
Total	56.0	100.0%	532.5	100.0%	111.1	1,784	100.0%

[a]On and off passengers. Includes "connecting" passengers but excludes "through" passengers.
[b]Passengers per operation (excludes charter, nonrevenue, and air cargo flights; also excludes "through" passengers).
Source: Association of Bay Area Governments and the Metropolitan Transportation Commission, *Regional Airport Plan: Draft Environmental Impact Report* (June 1980).

be constrained in the short range by the limited availability of aircraft incorporating new noise reduction technology. However, the potential for handling up to 10 MAP exists in the long range with advanced aircraft in service. Development of local transit services needs to be stressed because of congestion of surrounding freeways and the limited amount of airport land for new parking and circulation.

—A North Bay airport would serve up to 1 MAP in the mid range (1985–89) and up to 2 MAP in the long range (1994–2000).

Regional traffic allocations to the North Bay contemplate the introduction of limited intrastate service at one or more existing airports— Hamilton AFB, Sonoma County, Napa County, or Travis AFB (joint use). In addition to the convenience for the local air traveler, the placement of new airline service in the North Bay would provide an incremental measure of noise relief for communities around other Bay Area airports and some reduction in airspace delays. The volume of passengers attracted depends on the specific airport location. The decision to recommend such service is primarily a local one based on the air service benefits and community impacts. However, the long-range regional impacts on other airports in the Bay Area and on communities in the North Bay are sufficient to warrant a cooperative study of aviation requirements in this area. Such a study would involve ABAG, MTC, BCDC, and local North Bay jurisdictions.

The Regional Airport Plan includes an extensive analysis of potential measures to mitigate the effect of increased aviation activity. Regional policy now calls for the development of improved airport ground transportation, noise abatement, and air quality improvement programs by the major airport operators when large scale expansion is anticipated.[110]

A fundamental regional approach to determining what future airport traffic levels should be, given the noise conditions around the airport, is to first determine the amount of noise that will be accepted. The Regional Airport Plan recommends that a noise "budget" be established for each Bay Area airport that reflects the role of the airport in the regional plan, as well as reasonable measures to abate and control future noise levels.[111] As shown in Table 3.5, this budget is represented by the number of acres or dwelling units within the projected 65 CNEL contour. The amount of traffic the airport could ultimately handle would be determined by the ability of the airlines to operate within the noise budget. The role of the airport would be to monitor noise levels and exercise controls on airport activity if the budget is exceeded.

The regional and federal planning institutions see the key to resolving future traffic levels as more a question of defining how the San Jose

Table 3.5 Regional Airport Noise Allocations: 1976–97

(projected dwelling units within 65 CNEL[a]contour)

Airport	1976	1981[b]	1986[b]	1987	1997
San Francisco	12,000	10,690	8,970	8,630	8,630
Oakland	80	1,730	3,390	3,720[c]	3,320
San Jose	1,630[d]	3,800	5,970	6,400	2,990
Regional total	13,710	16,220	18,370	18,330	14,940

[a]Community noise equivalent level (CNEL) is a method for estimating the cumulative aircraft noise that affects communities in airport environs. The higher the CNEL, the greater the noise impact.

[b]Interpolated on straight line basis for years when State Airport Noise Standards change to more stringent criterion.

[c]Assumes departure routes are modified to eliminate noise impacts in North Alameda.

[d]Based on 1975 noise contour.

Source: Association of Bay Area Governments and the Metropolitan Transportation Commission, Summary of the Regional Airport Plan (July 1980).

Airport wants to control its noise impacts over time. It is recommended that the airport adopt the concept of a noise budget and establish appropriate monitoring mechanisms. This budget should be reviewed and coordinated with the regional agencies. It would probably result in some increase in noise over current levels—as forecast in the San Jose Airport Master Plan—but would reflect the imposition of reasonable controls, such as restricting late night operations and requiring all airlines to use aircraft that meet federal aircraft noise certification standards.[112]

The San Jose Vicinity Area Actions Plan is a substantial program that will ultimately achieve compliance with the California Airport Noise Standards. While the Regional Airport Plan recognizes that there will be some filling in of existing residential areas, large new developments in the vicinity of Bay Area airports would be inconsistent with regional policies. The ABAG/MTC Regional Airport Planning Committee has, however, reviewed the proposed new developments in the Vicinity Area Actions Plan and believes that they are acceptable, providing that higher residential densities are achieved so as to take advantage of the better sound insulation properties of apartments and other multifamily-type construction.[113] The committee's recommendation is also based, in part, on the consideration of other regional policies calling for greater supply of housing in certain parts of Santa Clara County in order to provide more convenient access to jobs and transportation.

Regional policy recommends that airport development programs also give full consideration to surface transportation requirements, particularly the potential for expanding transit and ride-sharing programs.

The need for such a program at the San Jose Airport is evidenced by the relatively low level of airport transit use, local air quality conditions, the limited availability of funds for major roadway improvements, and increasing commercial development and traffic growth in the immediate vicinity.

The airport should take a leadership role in coordinating improvements in transit services and facilities, including expanded bus service, and in developing a formal program that provides the timing and commitment of funds for the future transportation improvements (such a program is required under existing regional policies in order to obtain favorable review of major expansion programs).[114] Also, the need for airport parking should reflect, in part, the overall transit and ride-sharing objectives for the airport.

As noted in the San Jose plan, some access improvements in the form of improved connections to adjacent freeways and connections to a future light rail system would be desirable. However, such improvements may not be forthcoming for some time. This possibility emphasizes the need for well-defined interim alternatives. The airport should continue to review the scope and location of proposed freeway interchange improvements so that these projects can proceed if new funds become available.

Aviation safety has become a primary concern at all airports in the country, and particularly at those serving both general aviation and air carrier activity. While the need to improve the supply of general aviation facilities and the quality of these facilities will continue to exist at San Jose Airport, the forecast volume of air carrier and general aviation traffic there and at surrounding airports calls for prudent traffic management policies. Regional and federal policy recommends the maintenance or lowering of existing numbers of general aviation operations at San Jose Airport in order to enhance air safety.[115] This, in turn, would be consistent with a change in the general aviation role of the airport—away from training to a more corporate/itinerant pattern of use. While the commitment of the airport to pursue development of reliever airports is important, a positive interim program—exclusive of reliever airports—should also be developed in line with the regional policies stated above.

Air quality analyses performed by ABAG and MTC at all three Bay Area airports show the major areas of concern to be the terminals (which experience large numbers of idling autos) and areas off the ends of the runways (which experience aircraft engine emissions and, often, auto emissions from nearby freeways).[116] At San Jose Airport, exceedances of the carbon monoxide standards were calculated for both locations under varying sets of conditions.[117] Terminal problems can be mitigated by minimizing the number of autos, increasing transit use, and maintaining relatively smooth traffic flow. Areas within the "Coleman Loop," south of the main runway, would experience high concentrations of carbon monoxide pollution due to aircraft operations and automobile traffic on Route 17. As the San Jose Airport Master Plan indicates, adverse air quality impacts in this area are being mitigated as a result of the land acquisition program and relocation of residents. At the same time, proposals for redevelopment of this area should recognize that there is a significant potential for high levels of air pollution.[118]

SUMMARY

Clearly, perceptions of problems in air transportation varied widely, from not enough air capacity thwarting the economic growth of the San Jose metropolitan area to the presence of too much air activity destroying the regional environment; the corresponding proposals ranged from developing a new site for a large jet port to no air facilities at all for the metropolitan area.

Yet, each of the actors involved came to understand the other points of view and was able to suggest a flexibility it might have in resolving this metropolitan conflict. With regard to developing an outlying airport site, for example, the Save Our Valley Action Committee indicated that if its high-speed ground transportation proposal were not feasible, the next best alternative would be a properly designed airport on a new outlying site, such as that suggested by residents of the city of Santa Clara. Representatives of the city of Milpitas also hinted at the possible acceptability of developing a new outlying airport site (even in the nearby North San Jose area) if they had a say in the airport site selection and design, and could share in the economic benefits of the facility. Some of the representatives of the regional and federal planning institutions even suggested that they might endorse a new airport for the San Jose metropolitan area if it could be demonstrated that the evnironmental and ecological impacts of the project would not be excessively harmful.

With similar flexibility, the city of San Jose and local business interests indicated that they had altered their plans (in the short run) to develop a new airport site because of the stakes involved for other actors in the region (such as environmental destruction of outlying communities) and because of the expected development cost of a new airport site as well as the availability of alternative ways of meeting their air transportation needs (such as San Francisco and Oakland airports' ability to absorb some of the expected increased demand for air travel in the San Jose area). Consequently, San Jose decided to stay with the existing airport site and accommodate a smaller increase in air transport than previously expected in ways that would minimize the environmental impact on surrounding areas (for instance, flight path alterations), and to compensate those residents who would unavoidably be affected (e.g., through such programs as home purchase and relocation payments). At the same time San Jose conducted thorough feasibility studies for the long-term development of the existing and outlying airport sites.

In addition, San Jose's planning process for expanding the capacity of the existing airport site was open to actor and public participation. During the more than three years it took to prepare the *Airport Master Plan and Airport Vicinity Area Actions,* 43 public meetings were held so that all the actors had many opportunities to express their views.[119] Again this interactive process enabled the actors to relate to one another's concerns and become flexible on their own positions. For example, some of the actors most opposed to the operation of the existing airport site, such as the City of Santa Clara and the Santa Clara County ALUC, were willing to accept San Jose's plans to expand airport facilities with the proviso that appropriate measures would be taken to ameliorate the negative impacts of airport activities on the surrounding community (such as timing of flights, soundproofing buildings). This local acceptance of San Jose's plans for the existing airport site related well with the regional views of ABAG and MTC to have San Jose carry its fair share of the Bay Area's demand for air transportation, balanced against a tolerable level of noise pollution.

In response to these requests, San Jose modified its plan for the existing airport site. Examples are these additions to its formal planning documents:

> . . . and the gradual phase-out of older aircraft to be replaced by newer, quieter aircraft. Currently, the Airport Department is negotiating with the air carriers to expand the existing, voluntary curfew from 6 hours (midnight to 6 a.m.) to 7 hours (11:30 p.m. to 6:30 a.m.).[120]
>
> The cities of San Jose and Santa Clara should continue their active support of federal laws and regulations requiring air carrier and other aircraft to comply with the strictest possible noise emission standards. The two cities should support federal legislation designed to broaden the allowed off-airport use of federal monies for improving the noise-insulation properties of public and private structures.[121]
>
> The Airport and Property Departments of the City of San Jose should consider the earliest possible meeting with the residents/ owners of properties targeted to be acquired in the Master Plan to fully explain how the value of property will be established for purposes of acquisition, what options and benefits are available to them under the City's relocation program, and to seek their views on the desirability of establishing a replacement mobile home park outside the noise impact areas. The City could also consider renting vacancies as they arise in the mobile home

parks and other rental housing to reduce its ultimate relocation responsibilities.[122]

Thus, through the mulitiple advocacy approach, the San Jose *Airport
Plan and Airport Vicinity Area Actions* was amended to reflect the range
of views of the major actors associated with the issue of air transportation.
As such, this most recent airport planning document should help to
resolve democratically the very difficult air transportation problem of the
San Jose metropolitan area for the rest of the century.

NOTES

1. Metropolitan Transportation Commission, *Airport Accessibility in the San Francisco
   Bay Area* (January 1974).
2. Peat, Marwick, Mitchell, and Co., *An Economic and Planning Management Program for
   the San Jose Municipal Airport: Aviation Activity Forecasts* (San Jose, Calif.: February
   1977).
3. San Jose, *Supplemental Report to Environmental Impact Report/Environmental
   Assessment for San Jose Airport Master Plan* (June 1980), p. 1.
4. Estimated annual passenger demand from Peat, Marwick, Mitchell, *An Economic and
   Planning Management Program for the San Jose Municipal Airport.*
5. Based on interview with James Mettler, manager, San Jose Municipal Airport, June
   1976; interview with Edward Marin, airport planning engineer, San Jose Municipal
   Airport, June 1980; San Jose, *Airport Master Plan and Airport Vicinity Area Actions*
   (July 1980); interviews with James F. Tucker, executive director, economic development and communication, San Jose Chamber of Commerce, June 1980 and March
   1981; and San Jose Chamber of Commerce. *Airport Master Plan Recommendations*
   (September 1979).
6. Interviews with Tucker.
7. San Jose Chamber of Commerce, *Airport Master Plan Recommendations.*
8. Interview with Marin.
9. Ibid.
10. San Jose, *Airport Master Plan.*
11. Ibid.
12. Ibid.
13. See Frank Sweeney, "Massive San Jose Jetport Local Decision," *San Jose Mercury,*
    October 20, 1979, p. 1; and Rothblatt, *Regional Advocacy Planning,* ch. 1.
14. This change of position is expressed in Ted Tedesco, city manager, City of San Jose,
    "Airport Relocation Issue," memorandum to mayor and City Council of San Jose
    (September 23, 1975); and interview with Mettler.
15. Peat, Marwick, Mitchell, and Co., *An Economic and Planning Management Program for
    San Jose Municipal Airport: Airport Master Plan* (San Jose, Calif.: January 1980).
16. San Jose, *Airport Master Plan.*
17. Ibid.

18. San Jose, *Environmental Assessment and Environmental Impact Report on the Airport Master Plan and Airport Vicinity Area Actions* (April 1980), p. 3-3

19. Ibid.

20. U.S. Department of Transportation, Federal Aviation Administration, *Airport Development Aid Program: Authority, Program Policy, Eligibility and Allowability Criteria* (August 1971, as amended), bk. I.

21. Peat, Marwick, Mitchell, and Co., the consultant for the Economic and Planning Management Program for San Jose Municipal Airport, recommends the removal by airports of all structures, aircraft parking, and automobile parking from clear zones, and the projection of the approach surface on the ground, from runway ends to the airport boundary. Airport management has reviewed this suggestion, and has decided to recommend retention of general aviation development that currently exists in these areas. Costs of removing structures from clear zones or of eliminating obstructions penetrating the FAR Part 77 surfaces are therefore not included in the plan. See note 20.

22. U.S. Department of Transportation, Federal Aviation Administration, *Federal Aviation Regulations, Part 77—Objects Affecting Navigable Airspace* (January 1975, as amended).

23. San Jose, *Environmental Assessment*, p. 3–6.

24. U.S. Department of Transportation, *Federal Aviation Regulations, Part 77*.

25. Interview with Marin.

26. Peat, Marwick, Mitchell, and Co.

27. Andrews Air Force Base, "An Installation Compatible Use Zone: A Report to the Citizens of Andrews Air Force Base Environs" (December 1974).

28. Santa Clara County Airport Land Use Commission, *Land Use Plan for Area Surrounding Santa Clara County Airports* (San Jose, Calif.: Santa Clara County Planning Department, (August 1973).

29. Ibid.

30. San Jose, *Environmental Assessment*, p. 3–26.

31. Ibid, p. 3–32.

32. CNEL (community noise equivalent level) is a method for estimating cumulative noise that affects communites in airport environs. The higher the CNEL, the greater the noise impact.

33. San Jose, *Environmental Assessment*, p. 3–33.

34. Based on interview with Maureen Hanson, spokesperson, Save Our Valley Action Committee, June 1980; interviews with Michael Winton, president, North Side Residents Association, June 1980 and February 1981; interview with Lilyan Branon, president, United New Conservationists, June 1980; interview with Olney Smith, director, Planning Department, city of Santa Clara, June 1980; and interview with Michael Downey, deputy city attorney, city of Santa Clara, February 1981.

35. Ibid.

36. R. Robinson, North Santa Clara City resident, letter to the San Jose Planning Commission concerning the EIR on plans to expand the San Jose Municipal Airport (June 20, 1980).

37. Interviews with Hansen, Winton, Branon, and Smith; and San Jose, *Supplemental Report to Environmental Impact Report*, pp. 8–9.

38. William A. Gissler, mayor, city of Santa Clara, letter to the San Jose Planning Commission concerning the EIR on plans to expand the San Jose Municipal Airport (June 11, 1980).

39. Interviews with Winton and Branon.

40. John Piper, "The Position of a Community Group Representing People Suffering the

Negative Environmental Effects of the Existing Airport Site," in *Regional Advocacy Planning: Expanding Air Transport Facilities for the San Jose Metropolitan Area,* ed. Donald N. Rothblatt (San Jose, Calif.: San Jose State University, 1976), pp. 18–21.
41. Ibid.
42. Interviews with Winton and Smith.
43. Piper, "The Position of a Community Group."
44. Interview with Hansen.
45. Piper, "The Position of a Community Group."
46. Interviews with Winton and Hansen.
47. Ibid.
48. Piper, "The Position of a Community Group."
49. Association of Bay Area Governments, *Regional Airport Systems Study: Final Report* (June 1972). See also Piper, "The Position of a Community Group."
50. Ibid.
51. Ibid.
52. Interviews with Winton.
53. Ibid.
54. Ibid.
55. Gissler, letter to San Jose Planning Commission.
56. Single event noise level (SENL) criteria with respect to the noisiest aircraft in use would provide greater sound protection than community noise equivalent level (CNEL) criteria which are based on a weighted average noise level during a 24-hour period.
57. Association of Bay Area Governments, *Regional Airport Systems Study.*
58. Based on interviews with James R. Connolly, deputy city manager, city of Milpitas, June 1980 and February 1981; interviews with city staff, city of Milpitas, March 1981.
59. Ibid.
60. Michael Dorn, "The Position of an Outlying Community Threatened by the Location of a New Airport Site: City of Milpitas," in *Regional Advocacy Planning: Expanding Air Transport Facilities for the San Jose Metropolitan Area,* ed. Donald N. Rothblatt (San Jose, Calif.: San Jose State University, 1976), pp. 22–28.
61. Ibid.
62. Interviews with Connolly and city staff, city of Milpitas.
63. Ibid.
64. James R. King, assistant city manager, city of San Jose, memorandum about airport expansion and alternative sites to Ted Tedesco, city manager, city of San Jose (May 29, 1973).
65. San Jose, *Environmental Assessment.*
66. Dorn, "The Position of an Outlying Community."
67. Association of Bay Area Governments, *Regional Airport Systems Study.*
68. Dorn, "The Position of an Outlying Community."
69. Interviews with Connolly and city staff, city of Milpitas.
70. San Jose, *Environmental Assessment.*
71. U.S. Department of Transportation, Federal Aviation Administration, *Airport Development Aid Program,* Advisory Circular no. 150/5100-7 (January 1971, as amended), para. 7.
72. Ibid, para. 8.
73. Interview with Connolly.
74. Interview with Richard Delong, former city manager, city of Milpitas, May 1974.
75. The A-95 review is a federal requirement that gives regional planning agencies such as ABAG the opportunity to review and comment on a local community's grant proposals to the federal government.

76. Dorn, "The Position of an Outlying Community."
77. San Jose, *Airport Master Plan,* Santa Clara County Airport Land Use Commission, *Land Use Plan for Area Surrounding Santa Clara Airports.*
78. These views are based on interview with John C. Hau, staff coordinator with the Santa Clara County Airport Land Use Commission and Santa Clara County Planning Department. June 1980; interviews with staff members, Santa Clara County Planning Department, February 1981; John C. Hau, staff coordinator, Santa Clara County ALUC, "Analysis of the Proposed Vicinity Area Plan for the San Jose Municipal Airport," memorandum to ALUC Hearing Board (September 10, 1980).
79. Ibid.: and Santa Clara County Airport Land Use Committee, "Resolution of the Santa Clara County Airport Land Use Commission Relating to the San Jose Airport Master Plan and Vicinity Area Plan" (September 10, 1980).
80. Hau, "Analysis of the Proposed Vicinity Area Plan," p. 5.
81. Metropolitan Transportation Commission, Regional Airport Planning Committee, *Airport Activity Statistics* (1979).
82. Peat, Marwick, Mitchell, *An Economic and Planning Management Program* (January 1980), p. 4.
83. San Jose, *General Plan, 1975* (1979, as amended).
84. Public Law 96–193 (February 18, 1980) granted exemptions to three-engine jet aircraft not meeting FAR Part 36 standards for noise emissions from 1983 to 1985 if binding contracts have been entered into for replacement aircraft by January 1, 1983.
85. The 76 CNEL, employed as an upper limit for residential uses, is not based on the California Airport Noise Standards, but on the San Jose General Plan limits "in conformance wth EPA hearing loss criteria."
86. The standard for remedial treatment of existing dwellings only.
87. In September 1980, the last evening passenger operation was an 11:10 p.m. departure, and the earliest a 6:26 a.m. arrival (both daily). No others were scheduled between 11:00 p.m. and 7:00 a.m. See Hau, "Analysis of the Proposed Vicinity Area Plan," p. 3
88. Ibid. interviews with Hau and Santa Clara County Planning staff.
89. The Airport Master Plan proposes lengthening this runway about 1,400 feet to the north but the landing threshold for Runway 12R would remain as at present, becoming a "displaced threshold."
90. Termination of glide slope and touchdown point for jet aircraft approaching from the southeast—about 85 percent of all operations.
91. See Santa Clara County Airport Land Use Commission, *Land Use Plan* (August 1973), "Safety Areas—San Jose Municipal Airport" (map).
92. Peat, Marwick, Mitchell, *An Economic and Planning Management Program* (January 1980).
93. Santa Clara County Airport Land Use Commission, *Minutes,* meeting of November 29, 1973, p. 7.
94. Hau, "Analysis of the Proposed Vicinity Area Plan," p. 4.
95. Ibid.
96. Association of Bay Area Governments and the Metropolitan Transportation Commission, *Summary of the Regional Airport Plan* (July 1980), p. 2.
97. These views are based on interview with Gordon D. Jacoby, senior planner, Association of Bay Area Governments, June 1980; interview with Chris Brittle, airport planning engineer, Metropolitan Transportation Commission, June 1980; interview with Donald Cartright, airport planning engineer, FAA, June 1980.
98. Association of Bay Area Governments and the Metropolitan Transportation Commission, *Summary,* p. 6.
99. Ibid.
100. Ibid.

101. Gordon Jacoby and Chris Brittle, Regional Airport Planning Committee, Association of Bay Area Governments, and the Metropolitan Transportation Commission, "San Jose Municipal Airport Master Plan and Vicinity Area Plan Draft Environmental Impact Report," letter to San Jose City Planning Department (June 4, 1980).
102. Association of Bay Area Governments and the Metropolitan Transportation Commission, *Regional Airport Plan: Draft Environmental Impact Report* (June 1980), p. II–3.
103. Jacoby and Brittle, "San Jose Municipal Airport," p. 1.
104. Interviews with Jacoby, Brittle, and Cartright.
105. Ibid.
106. Association of Bay Area Governments and the Metropolitan Transportation Commission, *Regional Airport Plan.*
107. Ibid, p. II-1.
108. Ibid, pp. III-15–16.
109. Interviews with Jacoby, Brittle, and Cartright.
110. Ibid.
111. Association of Bay Area Governments and the Metropolitan Transportation Commission, *Summary*, pp. 7–8.
112. See, for example, the federal noise standards outlined in U.S. Department of Transportation, Federal Aviation Administration, *Federal Aviation Regulations, Part 36—Noise Standards: Aircraft Type and Airworthiness Certification* (December 1969, as amended).
113. Jacoby and Brittle "San Jose Municipal Airport," p. 2.
114. Ibid.
115. Interviews with Jacoby, Brittle, and Cartright.
116. Jacoby and Brittle, "San Jose Municipal Airport," p. 3.
117. Ibid., p. 4.
118. Interviews with Jacoby, Brittle, and Cartright.
119. San Jose, *Airport Master Plan*, p. 8–1.
120. San Jose, *Supplemental Report to Environmental Impact Report*, p. 16.
121. Ibid.
122. Ibid, pp. 16–17.

4

OPEN SPACE AND
RECREATIONAL FACILITIES

Declining open space resources and inadequate recreational facilities are problems that confront most large urban areas across the nation. In a nation accustomed to a plentiful supply of open expanses, recognition of the issue of open space has occurred only in recent years. Open space has become a limited resource that must be actively preserved, especially in urban regions. As pointed out by the President's Commission on National Goals:

> The people in an urban area need open space for many different purposes: to conserve water and other natural resources; as a reserve for future needs, often unpredictable; to maintain special types of agriculture which must be near cities; to prevent building in undesirable locations in order to avoid flood hazard or a wasteful extension of services; to provide a rural environment for people who want to live that way; for pleasant views from urban areas, for a sense of urban identity; for buffers against noise and other nuisance; but above all, for recreation, which can be combined with many of the other uses.[1]

Yet problems arise, in that open space preservation efforts impinge upon urban growth. While the problems associated with urban sprawl and unconstrained growth have highlighted the importance of open space, opposition to curtailment of property rights and development makes open space preservation a controversial subject.

The issue of open space cannot be fully understood without also considering urban development. The complementarity of the two issues is now documented at different levels of government. The *1980 President's National Urban Policy Report*[2] links low-density dwelling patterns and farmland consumption, and cites both the amount of agricultural acreage given over to urban use and the increasing amount of urbanization occurring outside urban service boundaries. This report suggests that urban design is not likely to ever be the primary means for conserving the nation's natural resources.[3]

The state of California, through such documents as the *Urban Development Strategy for California*[4] and various planning-related legislation, expresses concern for containing urban sprawl, recognizing that "open-space land is a limited and valuable resource which must be conserved wherever possible."[5] One policy developed by the state is to develop vacant land within existing urban neighborhoods before expanding into rural areas.

The San Jose metropolitan area is also committed to the idea that urban development should take place within cities. The *Urban Development/Open Space Plan*, adopted in 1973 by the Santa Clara County Board of Supervisors, describes the rapid growth in the Santa Clara Valley that contributed to "scattered, uncontrolled urbanization."[6] This plan contained county policies specifically aimed at preserving open space resources and at establishing urban development policies to guide future growth. Yet, as shown in Tables 4.1 and 4.2, during the 1970s urban areas continued to expand while total agricultural bearing acreage declined by more than 50 percent in the San Jose metropolitan area.

In response to this trend, Santa Clara County reaffirms its commitment to preserve open space in two policies of its 1980 *General Plan*.[7] The first policy is that all new development should take place within the urban service areas of the cities.[8] The second is that all land outside the urban service areas not already committed to development should be maintained as some form of open space.[9]

This chapter will study how collective efforts to preserve open space and recreational facilities might be reconciled with the relentless pressure for urban expansion in the San Jose metropolitan area.

ACTORS' VIEWS

Our study of the issue of open space and recreational facilities in the San Jose metropolitan area uncovered the following actors:

1. Federal government (U.S. Department of the Interior)
2. State of California (Office of Planning and Research)
3. Bay Area regional planning agency (Association of Bay Area Governments)
4. Metropolitan planning organizations in the San Jose area (Santa Clara County

Table 4.1 Area of Cities in Santa Clara County: 1950–80

City	Area of Incorporated Land (square miles)[a]												
	1950	1960	1970	1971	1972	1973	1974	1975	1976	1977	1978	1979	1980
Alviso	9.9	13.7	c	c	c	c	c	c	c	c	c	c	c
Campbell	b	2.9	4.6	4.6	4.7	4.7	4.7	4.7	4.7	4.7	4.7	4.8	4.8
Cupertino	b	4.9	7.7	7.7	7.8	7.8	7.8	7.8	7.8	7.8	7.8	7.9	9.3f
Gilroy	1.5	2.2	4.9	5.0	5.4	5.5	5.4e	5.7	6.0	6.1	6.5	6.9	7.1
Los Altos	b	5.8	6.1	6.2	6.2	6.3	6.3	6.5	6.5	6.6	6.6	6.6	6.6
Los Altos Hills	b	9.5	9.5	9.5	9.5	9.5	9.5	9.5	9.5	9.5	9.5	9.5	9.5
Los Gatos	1.5	5.8	8.7	8.7	8.7	8.7	8.7	8.7	8.7	8.7	8.8	8.9	10.1
Milpitas	b	7.6	9.3	9.3	9.4	9.4	9.4	9.4	9.4	10.2	10.3	10.8	10.8
Monte Sereno	b	1.4	1.5	1.5	1.6	1.6	1.6	1.6	1.6	1.6	1.6	1.6	1.7
Morgan Hill[d]	2.2	3.6	8.0	8.7	8.8	9.2	9.5	9.6	9.7	9.7	9.9	9.9	9.9
Mountain View	1.1	7.4	11.0	11.0	11.0	11.0	11.0	11.1	11.5	11.7	11.7	11.9	12.0
Palo Alto	6.9	21.6	25.2	25.2	25.2	25.2	25.2	25.2	25.8	25.9	25.9	25.9	25.9

San Jose	17.2	53.0	136.4	138.3	143.0	145.6	146.8	147.4	149.2	150.5	152.2	154.7	156.6[f]
Santa Clara	4.9	11.3	16.6	17.4	17.6	17.8	18.5	18.5	18.6	18.6	18.7	18.9	19.1
Saratoga	b	11.7	11.7	11.7	11.7	11.7	11.7	11.7	11.7	11.7	11.7	11.7	11.7
Sunnyvale	6.1	17.3	22.2	23.1	22.5	22.6	22.8	22.9	23.0	23.1	23.1	23.1	23.1
Total incorporated	51	180	283	288	293	297	299	300	304	306	309	313	318
Total unincorporated	1261	1132	1029	1024	1019	1015	1013	1012	1008	1006	1003	999	994
Total county	1312	1312	1312	1312	1312	1312	1312	1312	1312	1312	1312	1312	1312

[a] January of each year.
[b] Not yet incorporated
[c] City of Alviso consolidated into the City of San Jose, March 12, 1968
[d] Area encompassing northern portion of Anderson Reservoir disannexed from Morgan Hill during 1966 and annexed to the City of San Jose
[e] In 1973–74, 51 acres were annexed; 90 were disannexed
[f] An inhabited land transfer from San Jose to Cupertino was effective on June 19, 1979. The area involved totaled 1.19 square miles.

Source: Santa Clara County Planning Department, *Information*, June 1980.

Table 4.2 Agricultural Bearing Areas in Santa Clara County: 1950–79

Categories	Agricultural Bearing Areas (acres)								
	1950	1955	1960	1965	1970	1975	1976	1977	1978	1979
Fruits, nuts, berries	86,105	77,826	66,453	52,419	38,614	20,756	15,922	15,130	13,365	12,434
Vegetables	26,277	22,310	14,220	13,613	15,615	15,617	15,250	14,925	13,030	12,833
Total	112,382	100,136	80,673	66,032	54,229	36,373	31,172	30,055	26,395	25,267

Source: Santa Clara County Planning Department, *Information*, June 1980.

Local Agency Formation Commission, Planning Department, and Parks and Recreation Department)

5. Central city (San Jose Planning Department, and Parks and Recreation Department)
6. A representative affluent suburban community in the western section of the metropolitan area (city of Saratoga)
7. A typical job-rich community in the northern portion of the metropolitan area (city of Sunnyvale)
8. Middle-class South County suburban communities (cities of Morgan Hill and Gilroy)
9. Representatives of minorities and low income families (Mexican American Community Service Agency, Confederacion de la Raza)
10. Environmental interests (Sierra Club, Committee for Green Foothills, People for Open Space)
11. Nonprofit open space acquisition group (Peninsula Open Space Trust)
12. Open space special district (Midpeninsula Regional Open Space District)
13. Private organization representing industries located in Santa Clara County (Santa Clara County Manufacturing Group)
14. Private land development interests (Building Industry Association)
15. Business interests (San Jose Chamber of Commerce).

Our research staff found that because of the similarity of perspectives held by some of the actors regarding the open space and recreation issue, seven teams could reasonably represent the spectrum of actors' views.

Bay Area and Federal Planning Institutions (Association of Bay Area Governments, California Office of Planning and Research, U.S. Department of Interior)

Problem: From a Bay Area perspective, open space is not a single land use issue. Rather, it involves various types of land, many of which are areas of critical environmental concern, such as lands for managed resource production; lands for resource preservation; lands for health, welfare, and well-being; lands for public safety; regional and parks recreation; scenic resources and regional landscape; and sites of historic, cultural, scientific, and educational interest.[10] The regional concern about the preservation of these lands is presented below.

Lands for Managed Resource Production

Agriculture. The San Francisco Bay area has some of the finest agricultural land in the nation, providing important food commodities, specialty crops, and wines of worldwide distinction. However, there is substantial pressure to convert prime agricultural lands to urban uses. Job growth in the Santa Clara Valley and the resulting pressures for additional housing could result in major reductions in agricultural acreage by 1990 unless local policies are amended to provide needed housing in locations other than prime agricultural areas of South County.[11]

Minerals. The regional concern is that mineral resources are needed to meet construction and development goals for the region, and inadequate protection of these lands might preclude their future use. An Association of Bay Area Governments (ABAG) study[12] calls for the preservation for future use of those minerals of strategic concern that are in short supply, essential to sustain life, or crucial for national security; for which there is a continuing high user demand; and that cannot be reasonably obtained elsewhere because of high transportation costs.

Water Supply. An adequate supply of high quality water requires that the region manage and conserve its local surface water and ground-water resources. Local water supplies may be particularly important for agriculture, recreation facilities, and small rural communities. Several open space uses, including recreation activities, are generally compatible with the protection of water supply lands, but some agricultural uses could contribute to pollution of local water supplies.

Timber Resources. Lumber products are valuable building materials in metropolitan areas. The Bay Area, including the Santa Clara Valley, is fortunate to have lands with timber resources. The regional concern is to preserve lands containing or supporting unique timber species, or lands that complement regional needs for wood products.

Energy. The regional concern is to protect lands uniquely qualified to produce an alternative or supplement to existing forms of energy. Geo-thermal resources as well as petroleum and natural gas need to be developed or located and preserved.

Fish and Wildlife. The health of the natural ecology within the region requires that diversity of animal species be maintained. The key to maintaining wildlife, according to ABAG, is the identification and preservation of lands that make up the fish and wildlife habitats. Regional and federal policy recommends preservation of wildlife resources having a key role in a regional scale ecosystem, and of lands that are the habitats for rare or endangered fish and wildlife, and that contribute to species diversity or are necessary to maintain such species at an acceptable level.[13]

Lands for Resource Preservation

Vegetation resources include natural settings containing trees, plants, brush, and grasslands; these serve a function parallel to that of fish and wildlife, and are essential to their life cycles. The regional concern is that undeveloped land containing these types of vegetative resources will be depleted.

Lands for Health, Welfare, and Well-Being

Air Quality. Vegetation-filled open space areas can help to dissipate air pollution, thereby contributing to good air quality. Open space buffers can also filter and absorb noise. The Bay Area needs to identify and protect open space for these purposes.

Water Quality. Land can be used to maintain water quality. Certain types of soils are capable of absorbing effluents from secondary wastewater treatment facilities; other types can capture storm and agricultural runoff before it contaminates surface water supplies. The regional concern is to identify and protect these lands from activities that would impair their absorbency.

Waste Disposal. Satisfactory locations for the disposal of waste materials on land are dificult to find. It is ABAG's concern that such sites be protected for future use, particularly suitable sites for the disposal of hazardous wastes. Disposal sites need to be identified and preserved for present and future regional use.

Lands for Public Safety

The region needs to identify those areas which contain geological features and processes that pose potential hazards to human safety, and to protect the public from such hazards. Of regional significance are those hazards relating to flooding or earthquake activity, since these may have major regional impacts.

Regional Parks and Recreation

ABAG is concerned that the current high demand for recreational open space is only a fraction of the demand expected by 1990, especially for close-in recreational opportunities.[14] There will be an increasingly regional approach to providing recreation facilities; however, there is no single agency responsible for proposing and maintaining regional parks at the nine-county level. With the exception of the three subregional special districts, park planning and maintenance is conducted either at the city and county level or directly by the state and federal governments. There is also a shortage of funds for the acquisition and maintenance of regional parkland.

Scenic Resource and Regional Landscape

The outdoor environment is more than recreational open space. It includes lands that are not directly related to an active recreational experience but are of visual and emotional value to the people. The region needs to protect landscapes that are viewed, used, or appreciated by the public. The Critical Areas Plan states:

> —the landscape concerns have to be seen as part of a larger urban design process that recognizes the many dimensions of landscape experiences and images and relates them to the comprehensive planning process.[15]

Features of land and water areas of Bay Area importance are the following:

—characteristic or unique landscape settings
—major landforms or landmarks
—areas within the viewshed of the bay, scenic highways, regional transportation corridors, communities visited by tourists, and major population and activity centers.

Sites of Historic, Cultural, Scientific, and Educational Interest

These areas are man-made resources, many of which have open space significance. The regional need is to protect areas of cultural and historic significance, special areas for scientific investigations, and areas having the potential for enriching the learning experience, such as interpretive centers, special communities and neighborhoods, and historic sites.

The ABAG *Regional Plan* notes that although agriculture is a major economic force in Santa Clara County, agricultural land has been converted to urban uses at a rapid rate.[16] Nevertheless, the value of agricultural production and average annual employment levels still rank high relative to other counties in the region. Air quality conditions are severe countywide. Water resources in the southern part of San Francisco Bay include salt ponds, sloughs, and estuarine flats. These open areas are immediately adjacent to existing development, and are particularly vulnerable to waste discharges. Remote areas of the county are not anticipated to be developed in the foreseeable future, and environmental conditions may preclude such development. Deterioration of groundwater supplies could result from the development of some portions of the valley where septic tanks already are in use, such as in South County.

A specific open space issue that involves Santa Clara County is the future of the East Bay ridgelands. Regional concern over the future planning and management of this area of 1,300 square miles within Contra Costa, Alameda, and Santa Clara counties led to the preparation of *Ridgelands, a Multijurisdictional Open Space Study*[17] by several agencies. The purpose of the study was to examine existing efforts to protect open space resources of the ridgelands and to recommend additional actions to be taken. Major emphasis was on those actions that could be taken by existing local agencies. The ridgelands study is an example of interjurisdictional cooperation; it provided a unique opportunity for the participating agencies to benefit from a sharing of information, ideas, and perspectives.

A related open space issue, the potential for decline of agriculture, is identified by ABAG as also being an economic development issue. Economic development objectives and policies were adopted by the ABAG General Assembly in 1980.[18] In meeting the objective of retaining the Bay Area's existing industries, the policy to support the continuation of agriculture and food processing industries was adopted. The production and processing of food is one of the largest industry groups in the Bay Area's economic structure. The economic development policies state that the economic contribution of agricultural uses should be recognized and the land that sustains them should be protected.

The daily management of urban activities has been delegated to cities, counties, special districts, and regional councils of governments. The state of California and the federal government concede that the principal responsibility for addressing open space issues should remain in local control.[19] However, several components of the issue of open space are beyond the power of any one level of government to resolve. The parochial orientation of city and county jurisdictions in Santa Clara County belies the fact that recreational decisions of local government frequently have far-reaching impacts throughout the Bay Area.[20] There is at present no formal process to ensure that sensible and efficient steps are taken to meet the open space needs of all San Jose metropolitan area residents.[21]

Solution: ABAG's interest in open space has evolved from the environmental concerns of the late 1960s and early 1970s. *The Regional Plan 1970–1990*[22] outlined general open space goals to discourage urban sprawl and to protect open land. The *Open Space Plan* of 1972 developed a more specific program of identifying the characteristics of the region's remaining open land and established the following land use goals: the protection of resources, the maintenance of the regional ecology, the promotion of health and safety, the provision of outdoor recreation opportunities, and the rational guidance of urban develop-ment.[23] These concerns have been incorporated into the updated *Regional Plan 1980*.[24]

Open space issues are addressed in several sections of the Regional Plan. Various implementation actions could contribute to resolving open space problems. ABAG, in reviewing plans, projects, and applications, and subject to staff resources available, will comment on actions that would have adverse effect on local efforts to preserve land for production of regionally significant crops, lumber, minerals, and energy. ABAG ad-vises local governments that they can remove pressure on agricultural land and other nondeveloped, resource-bearing lands by amending public service policies so as to discourage premature conversion of such lands to urban uses.

The city-centered concept consists of broad land use and develop-ment actions and is called the "urban development strategy," in keeping with recent state and federal policy statements.[25] Part of this strategy is that policies for open space, water, sewage, and transportation should be coordinated to guide the timing, location, growth, and (wherever neces-sary) the limits of urban development. Such policies are to be im-plemented by ABAG in its review of plans and projects.

The open space strategy, the counterpart to the urban development strategy, seeks to protect land areas where development should not occur. It states that planning and management of the regional open space system is a prime responsibility of ABAG. Land preserved as open space for future controlled growth should be left in open uses for as long as possible, or be included in the permanent open space system. ABAG is directed to continue its development of open space resources and needs.

The issues in Santa Clara County, as identified in the ABAG Regional Plan, are primarily urban development issues, such as the jobs/housing imbalance, the lack of adequate public transit, and the prevalence of low density residential development in urban fringe areas. The plan's recom-mendations for development focus on improving the locational balance of job and housing growth, increased utilization of the transportation system, and development of higher density housing in portions of the county. The only recommendation directly concerned with the open space issue is as follows:

> Support the maintenance of Coyote as an agricultural preserve and the strengthening of county policies restricting development in unincorporated areas of the county.
>
> Development options for Coyote and the rest of unincorporated South County should be preserved beyond 1990, and planning for long-range development of this area should be deferred until more is known about the need to convert this productive agricultural land into urban uses.[26]

The review of local plans and projects for consistency with regional objectives is a critical function in a regional planning process that endeavors to retain maximum planning flexibility at the local level.[27] However, ABAG reviews are advisory actions that depend upon subsequent action by federal, state, regional, and local agencies empowered to approve grants, issue permits, and exercise the powers of general purpose units of government. ABAG's recommendations to these agencies are arrived at through its review of regionally significant plans, programs, or projects carried out by other agencies. If a project or plan received by the plan and project review staff is seen to affect the resolution of regional issues, it is deemed to be of regional significance. Review commentary is normally provided only for those projects and plans where there is a very clear relationship to regional policies and where staff decides that there is a pressing need to respond.

An important function of ABAG is to provide a forum to resolve local differences through workable compromises. ABAG sponsors workshops and conferences where local officials, business, industry, special interest groups, and private citizens can discuss programs, regulations, and legislation.

In this role ABAG's Regional Planning Committee heard a presentation by the environmental organization People for Open Space concerning the future of Bay Area farmland in 1980; and an ABAG General Assembly meeting in 1981 included the panel discussion "Housing vs. Farmlands: Does it have to be Either/Or?" [28] No other agency in the region provides such a forum for discussion by several sides representing various positions on an issue of regional concern.

Thus, the solution to Bay Area open space issues will require some form of regionwide management even if that form is comprehensive regional planning by a voluntary association of local governments. If ABAG is to provide regional management consistent with its advisory role, then all of the activities and functions described above will contribute to resolving conflicts concerning how open space resources should be used or conserved in the Bay Area, including Santa Clara County.

ABAG should continue to identify open space areas of regional concern, to provide assistance and guidance to its members, and to protect local efforts to maintain local control over land use. ABAG's decision-making bodies are composed of representatives who are predominantly local control advocates desirous of protecting local prerogatives from being usurped by regional government.[29] ABAG also tries to protect local interests from unnecessary state and federal intervention.

Because open space is only one of several issues of regional concern, ABAG's comprehensive regional planning activities are vital to resolution of the problem. ABAG provides the mechanism for cooperative action among the various levels of government operating in the Bay Area.

The state of California shares ABAG's viewpoint that there is a need for coordinating local government efforts to provide and maintain various classifications of open space. The state's Urban Strategy Program calls for an intergovernmental process of planning for California's open space needs.[30] It is believed that the direct, ongoing provision of adequate open space and recreational facilities in Santa Clara County should remain with the cities, county, Mid-Peninsula Regional Open Space District, and the regional council of governments (ABAG). However, the obligation to establish overall open space goals should be the responsibility of the state. The envisioned state plan is a partnership of the state, local governments, regional council of governments (ABAG). However, the obligation to providing open space belongs to the coordinated efforts of local Bay Area governments, working together through ABAG. The state's preferred role is one of leader and catalyst, working with other government agencies, citizens, and private enterprise to give direction to California's open space needs.[31]

Two basic solutions have been devised by the state to arrest the loss of important agricultural lands.[32] The first mitigation measure proposes the adoption of local land use policies that discourage the needless expansion of development beyond existing urban and suburban areas. A second solution, in effect at the present time, is legislative in nature and requires that certain findings must be made before conversion of agricultural land is permitted.

The state recommends that new urban development should be located according to the following land use priorities:[33]

a. Renew and maintain existing urban areas.

b. Develop vacant and underutilized land within existing urban areas that are presently served by public services.

c. When urban development is necessary outside existing built-up areas, use land that is immediately adjacent.

California is obviously stressing the concept of "infilling." It is recommended that rehabilitation of existing homes and businesses be encouraged, that the leapfrogging of development be curtailed, and that densities be increased wherever feasible. In essence, the state is proposing to create a more compact urban environment that will help protect existing agricultural land. Santa Clara County cities are cognizant of the state's position because of the widespread distribution of the *Urban Development Strategy*, a document that describes California's goals and policies. However, the response to these proposals has been minor to date.

Fortunately, there has been strong state legislative support to pre-serve outstanding natural resources, especially areas of important scenic and ecological value. A more recent interest has been shown in acquiring and developing close-in recreation opportunities that are accessible to large population groups.[34] For example, California has passed legislation that provides economic incentives for the continued use of school playgrounds after a school site has been declared surplus property.[35]

In sum, state and federal governments are pursuing legislation that could provide new incentives for the provision of more open space and recreational facilities in the San Jose metropolitan area.

The Metropolitan View
(Santa Clara County Local Agency Formation Commission, Planning Department, and Parks and Recreation Department)

Problem: An important problem concerning open space preserva-tion is the mounting urban growth pressure that appears to be occurring in most of the 15 cities in Santa Clara County. This pressure for cities to expand has been generated by the attractiveness of increasing the establishment of industry and commerce in order to increase local tax revenues.[36] The desire of the cities to expand industrial and commercial activities has primarily been encouraged by Proposition 13.[37]

During the 1970s local sources of revenue accounted for a declining proportion of all city revenues, and federal and state subventions and grants to cities increased.[38] This shift away from locally controlled revenue sources has meant diminished city control over local budgets. Proposition 13 further eroded the amount of revenues under direct city control by shifting control of the property tax away from cities. Historically, the property tax (specifically the property tax rate) has been the main tool available to local governments for raising revenues. Since the passage of

Proposition 13, however, cities can only indirectly influence property tax revenues through land use decisions.[39]

In the first year after the passage of Proposition 13 (fiscal 1978–79), total revenues for the 15 cities in Santa Clara County grew by $351.9 million (3.9 percent), which represented a percentage reduction in growth over the previous fiscal period (1977–78), during which time city revenues grew by $338.7 million (8.0 percent).[40] In fact, five cities (Los Altos, Los Gatos, Mountain View, Saratoga, and Sunnyvale) experienced actual dollar declines in total revenues in fiscal 1978–79, following the passage of Proposition 13.

Insufficient tax revenues not only contribute to the desire for local governments to expand physically, but also induce competition among the cities for their share of the county's economic growth. This competitive and isolationist stance of the cities further complicates interjurisdictional cooperation on land use issues. The Santa Clara County Planning Department is prevented from being effective in coordinating open space projects that would be beneficial to residents countywide, because of problems in dealing with separate jurisdictions.[41] One example is the proposed Bay Trail, which crosses land owned by several cities, the Midpeninsula Regional Open Space District, and the Santa Clara Valley Water District. Development of the trail is hampered because jurisdictions are concerned only with the piece of it within their own boundaries, and seldom communicate with one another.[42]

There also seems to be a lack of cooperation from the cities to proceed within the precepts of agreed-upon county policy.[43] For example, much of the unincorporated land surrounding the City of Gilroy is zoned by the county for agricultural and open space use. The county intends to maintain these lands in open space or in agricultural production. However, a large portion of these lands is designated by the Gilroy *General Plan* as industrial or residential, and Gilroy can apply to the Santa Clara County Local Agency Formation Commission (LAFCO) with an urban service area amendment or an annexation proposal.[44] If the proposal is approved, these lands can be rezoned by Gilroy for urban development.

Another problem identified by the county also is rooted in monetary concerns. As urban growth pressures have increased in Santa Clara County, so have land values, particularly within urban fringe areas. It has therefore become enticing to owners of open space and agricultural land near urban areas to sell their land for urban development.[45] Much more profit can be realized from the sale of these properties for urban uses than can be gained from leaving the lands in open space or in agricultural production. The pressure to urbanize open space land emanates from both cities and property owners. It can therefore be said that the major problem in preserving open space land is money. The cities want and need more tax dollars, and individual property owners want and need the financial resources that can be gained from the sale and urban development of their properties.

County planning problems concerning open space preservation also involve citizen lack of awareness of the urbanization process. Land use decisions that endanger open space usually take place parcel by parcel, virtually unnoticed by the general citizenry, which often values the open space resource.[46] This incremental process can easily be perceived as having an effect only upon the individual landowner and not upon his or her neighbors or the public at large. Even the decisionmakers may not perceive the significance of the cumulative effects of their rulings unless it is brought to their attention as a controversial issue.

An additional problem is neighborhood opposition to infill.[47] Great numbers of people resist more intensive development within their existing neighborhoods because of its perceived threat to their quality of life, such as undesirable neighbors, more traffic, increased crime, more children in the streets and schools, and other public costs.[48] By preventing more intensive use of existing inlying urban land, many citizens who use and appreciate open space may be unwittingly encouraging the conversion of scarce open space resources into developed urban land at the metropolitan fringe.

While urban development threatens to consume increasing amounts of open space, the county's regional park system (see Figure 4.1) is under continual pressure to expand and improve its recreational services. The problems facing this park system are the following:[49]

a. The financial challenges resulting from Proposition 13, such as difficulties of maintaining existing service and staff levels during a period of escalating costs and limited governmental revenues. The county has enough money for acquisition but not enough money for personnel expenses

b. Obtaining sufficient funds to assure adequate park maintenance has been particularly difficult because of the competition with other programs for limited funds

c. Planning, developing, and managing regional park sites so that their natural and heritage resources are protected, and their potential adverse impacts on adjacent and nearby privately owned lands are minimized. Planning and developing streamside areas for recreation uses is especially desirable because they usually have scenic qualities that provide a pleasant environment for trails and picnic areas. However, they are also important wildlife habitat areas that are environmentally sensitive and can be easily damaged or disrupted

d. Vandalism and crime

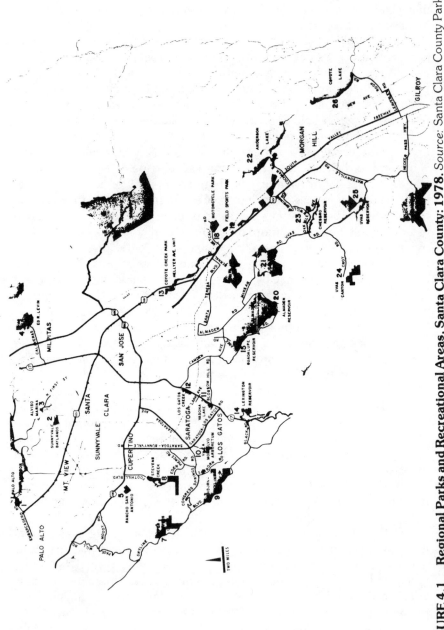

FIGURE 4.1 Regional Parks and Recreational Areas, Santa Clara County: 1978. *Source:* Santa Clara County Parks and Recreational Department, *Regional Parks and Recreation Area* (1978).

e. Changing recreational preferences of the county's expanding population

f. Educating citizens to use the recreation facilities in more efficient ways without destruction of these areas

g. Creating a public awareness to consider the importance of the recreation facilities that exist in the community.

A final problem area deals with the composition of county agencies having authority over the use of open space, such as LAFCO. While open space preservation may be important to LAFCO, it is difficult for the commission to deny a city's request to annex land or to expand an urban service area.[50] This reality stems primarily from the political nature of LAFCO's constituency (two county supervisors, two city representatives, and one public representative). As a political entity, LAFCO is very responsive to lobbying efforts on behalf of the cities. Environmental and other groups that oppose urban expansion are not as effective in influencing LAFCO's decisions as the cities, which propose such expansion and have two representatives on the commission. As a result, a large majority of urbanization proposals are approved by LAFCO.

Solution: One set of proposed solutions calls for the establishment of an institutional structure that will increase regional authority over the use of land at the expense of local government control.[51] For example, one proposal calls for the establishment of a Bay Area agricultural land regulatory commission that would have authority over the conversion of agricultural land within Santa Clara County.[52] Another scheme argues for the establishment of a county-wide interjurisdictional body with real land use control, a strengthened version of the Inter-Governmental Council (IGC).[53] Such a body could implement existing state and council policies that call for infill development prior to further outward expansion. This process would keep political pressure on local decisionmakers from having undue weight in development decisions of metropolis-wide importance. Further, it could effectively monitor growth implications of one city on others, and then act accordingly.

Although this solution would be politically difficult to implement at the present time, the County Planning Department staff believes that a regional government, making appropriate regional decisions, could alleviate the competition among the cities to capture their share of the county's economic growth.[54] This would be accomplished through tax-sharing programs and powers among the 15 cities, and through redistribution of revenues. This solution probably would not be appropriate from LAFCO's perspective, however, and might even require a major crisis situation to be considered.

Another solution suggested by the staff, to alleviate urban expansion and the loss of open space land, involves the introduction of a publicly supported initiative to manage growth.[55] Yet another solution would be to not allow sewer expansion and construction of new or extension of existing major arterials. Since this solution is extremely controversial, its implementation would be met with considerable resistance.

The county staff also suggests the use of an urban limit line in order to control urban growth.[56] The concept involves the delineation of all boundary lines beyond which no urbanization will ever by allowed. This line would be a cooperative agreement between the cities and the county, based on environmental and resource considerations (such as quality of agricultural lands and hazard areas). The urban limit line would be founded on an agreement similar to the urban service area boundaries, and would be administered by LAFCO. It is probable that this solution would be adopted by LAFCO, but only as a long-range concept. It would also be moderately infeasible, since its implementation would require a great cooperative effort on the part of the county and the cities.

With regard to the problem of multijurisdictional conflict, one solution is to promote better communication among agencies working to achieve common goals.[57] With such cooperation, open space use proposals that impact on otherwise nondevelopable land can be pursued without threatening individual jurisdictions. For example, the rights-of-way along Pacific Gas and Electric (PG&E) utility power corridors could be used for trails, with the county functioning as the coordinating agency. Other open space proposals that involve school sites or land running through several cities, should also be investigated by multijurisdictional organizations. An intergovernmental body such as IGC can serve both as a moderator between local authorities and as a monitor of effective open space use of sites. Although this function already exists on paper in Santa Clara County, a stronger commitment for cooperation between local governments is clearly needed. This can perhaps be accomplished through stressing the value to the cities of monitoring each other.

An additional solution to coordination problems is a city-county consolidation of the planning process.[58] While in principle this solution already exists to some extent, through such functions as the Santa Clara County Association of Planning Officials (SCCAPO) and the IGC, it could be more effective with greater regional authority. A similar approach is currently being considered by LAFCO, and involves using the annual General Plan review process as an initial screen for urban service area expansion proposals.[59] During the county's annual General Plan review, cities requesting urban service area expansions would be required to solicit a General Plan amendment request if the parcels proposed for inclusion were in conflict with the county's General Plan land use designation. In this way county officials, such as the Board of Supervisors, would be forced to make decisions regarding urbanization proposals. If the county denies the General Plan amendment, a city could still appear before LAFCO with the urban service area expansion proposal. Thus, LAFCO would receive both city and county views regarding an urbanization proposal. The implementation of this solution would facilitate a much more logical process for making land use decisions. However, the details of how this concept should be utilized still need to be developed.

Another set of proposed actions calls for the county government to find ways of making undeveloped open space land more economically competitive with urban uses.[60] One means of accomplishing this objective is to encourage parcel consolidation wherever possible, for the purpose of achieving the most economic management practices. This solution is feasible, and is in use, but is of limited effectiveness.[61]

A solution advocated by both the planning staff and LAFCO involves contractual arrangements between the county and individual property owners, such as the offering of more tax advantages to urban fringe property owners for retaining their land in open space or agricultural production.[62] Another alternative would be the provision of subsidies to these property owners. The expansion of the Williamson Act program, which gives tax reductions to land kept unurbanized,[63] and use of such concepts as leasebacks are also advocated. Williamson Act contracts have been employed for some time in the ranchland areas, but have not been as successfully utilized in the prime agricultural areas that are most endangered by city expansion. A hindrance to this solution is that programs involving expenditures or losses of county funds are not likely to be undertaken during a time of financial austerity in government.

One solution to the problem of lack of public knowledge about the development process is to have the county institute a program to educate the public about various planning functions and their interrelationships with other actions.[64] This program would need to address such important issues as how current policies were formed and why they are important; how development and preservation actions relate to each other; and how the public can use this information to participate in the decision process concerning land development.

A procedure should also be established to maintain a flow of current information that would be available at a centralized location such as the County Administration Center.[65] A similar education system should be organized to aid decisionmakers in assessing the impact of Proposition 13 on future growth, and to educate political bodies on alternatives to the economic development outlook in post-Proposition 13 California. Since these proposals for information and education programs are generally not regarded as controversial, they could be implemented without much opposition. Concerning the improvement of the metropolis-wide park system, the following actions are outlined:[66]

a. To help obtain sufficient funds for adequate park maintenance, Santa Clara County Charter Measure A was submitted to and approved by county voters in 1978.

Measure A authorized the Board of Supervisors to allocate up to 30% of each year's Measure C monies for County park maintenance. Previously, Measure C funds could only be used for park acquisition and development, and park maintenance funds were provided entirely out of the County's General Fund. Measure A also extended the park acquisition and development program authorized by Measure C from 1982 to 1987.[67]

b. Further efforts that the county adopted are likely to be needed if the county's regional park system is to be maintained at a satisfactory level.

One idea which merits serious consideration involves making greater use of citizen volunteers to help with park clean-up activities. Individual citizens, community organizations, and local business should be encouraged to "adopt a park" and take part in periodic planting, park improvement projects, or clean-up days at that park.

Local businesses could encourage their employees to participate in such events or could donate some of the Proposition 13 property tax savings to help maintain County parks.[68]

c. Realization of many of the regional park proposals will require the cooperation of numerous jurisdictions. The recreation and public facilities programs of the 15 cities in the San Jose metropolitan area and the Santa Clara Valley District have important contributions to make.

A number of examples already exist in Santa Clara County where such interjurisdictional cooperation has occurred and significant beneficial results have been achieved . . . [like] Coyote Creek Park Chain . . . Los Gatos Creekside Park projects . . . and Rancho San Antonio.[69]

d. Many of the streamside park chain proposals shown in the county's General Plan should receive careful study prior to implementation because

In areas with extensive residential development or in environmentally sensitive areas it may be desirable to route segments of parks and trails away from creeks to avoid conflict, or to leave the streamside area in private ownership, subject to appropriate land use controls.[70]

With regard to the problem of the composition of LAFCO, the county planning staff has suggested that studies be conducted regarding alternatives available, such as direct election of commission members.[71] Another solution that would be acceptable to LAFCO would involve an improved and more open information system whereby environmental groups and other interested parties could be more effective in presenting their views to the commission.[72]

The Central City (San Jose)

Problem: San Jose lies in the richly landscaped Santa Clara Valley floor, which has gradually shifted from a purely natural state to one of agricultural land use including vegetable farms, orchards, and vineyards. As late as 1935, San Jose was characterized as "one of California's most charming communities . . . deserving its fame as the Garden City."[73]

The surge of growth that occurred after World War II began to supplant this heritage of nature by transforming hundreds of acres of farmland to urban development. At the same time an increased demand for open space developed. This was due to the compound effects of an increasing population living in and around San Jose, with more leisure time, higher incomes, and a greater interest in outdoor recreation activities.[74] The challenge for San Jose is thus one of making provisions for, and preserving adequate amounts of, open space in and immediately around its centers of population. More basically the problem can be stated as follows:

> How can San Jose continue to grow while at the same time, retaining and restoring those native qualities of beauty and openness which makes it a uniquely pleasant place to live?[75]

Another problem concerns the relationship of open space to the city's land-use planning activities and methods of acquiring open space lands. In order to provide adequate open space, San Jose must have sufficient land and water areas of satisfactory size, properly distributed and developed to serve a variety of recreation and scenic beauty functions.[76] Land that was once relatively inexpensive in San Jose has become very costly and in great demand. As a consequence, open space has been diverted to other uses in order to serve a variety of social and economic needs.

Financial difficulties also abound for San Jose because there are insufficient funds to maintain the present level of parks and recreation service, in particular maintenance and operation of programs and facilities.[77] In addition, there is a lack of financial resources to remedy inequities between neighborhood park facilities and services available to particular population groups, as identified in a 1980 parks planning

study.[78] For example, it was found that Council Districts 2, 3, 5, and 6—
respectively West San Jose, Central City, Alum Rock, and Willow Glen—
have greater recreational needs than resources, whereas the other districts have greater resources than needs.[79] Neighborhoods with few parks
tend to be older and without vacant land, and often house low income
persons who could derive great benefit from additional nearby park
services.[80]

Proposition 13 has resulted in city General Fund deficits. Not only is
a 25 percent reduction in operating costs anticipated for the fiscal year
1981–82, but the ability to fund the operating costs related to proposed
capital improvement projects is uncertain.[81] Yet, urban growth in San
Jose will continue, and park service needs will continue to expand.

The potential loss of existing recreational facilities presents another
set of problems for San Jose.[82] For example, surplus school sites and
private golf courses currently providing urban open space are being
converted to nonopen space uses. The market prices of these properties
are usually too high for the city to purchase them.[83] City acquisition is
normally accomplished 20 to 25 years in advance of projected need,
when the property is affordable and undeveloped.

The city is also faced with the problem of conflicting views about
open space policy, even within its own administration.[84] For example, the
Parks Department, which is charged with providing for public recreational
need, is anxious to see that public access to natural resources, such as
streams, is assured when development occurs. Purchase of creekside land
is often the method of acquisition used by the Parks Department. At the
same time the Planning Department is particularly concerned about the
city's economic viability, and is anxious to expedite development so as to
create an adequate tax base for service provision.[85] The Planning
Department is sometimes antagonized by the Parks Department's view of
provisions for public access to natural resources, when it is wooing
developers who might oppose such provisions.[86] Open space is costly to
developers, and the Planning Department doesn't want to place burdens
on them that might cause them to lose interest in the city. From the Parks
Department perspective, it is shortsighted for the city not to make
provision for recreational opportunities while these opportunities exist.[87]

In order for funds to exist for Parks Department purposes, development that provides city tax revenues appears to be desirable. However,
new development creates an additional round of demand for Parks
Department services. Conditioning traditional-type subdivisions for park
provision does not appear to be at issue.[88]

Solution: In contrast with the county policy of providing large areas
for environmental relief, the city of San Jose emphasizes recreational
opportunities through citywide, district, and neighborhood parks.[89]

Nevertheless, many open space areas in San Jose, such as Coyote Valley, have multiple functions, providing food and fiber, hillsides, floodplains, urban definition, scenic areas, preservation of fragile environmental areas, buffers, and school sites with recreation areas.

In order to preserve open space, the city of San Jose recommends the following measures:[90]

a. Open space zoning. The California Constituion and state enabling legislation give cities and counties the authority to exercise the police power in terms of zoning. This authority has been specified in terms of regulating the use of open space lands, and further specified to include lands with value for recreation, scenic beauty, and conservation of natural resources. In addition, cities can prezone land that they eventually intend to incorporate. Two buttressed devices are the following:

1. Williamson Act. The Williamson Act allows property owners to sign contracts with local governments to maintain land in agricultural or recreational use in exchange for lower taxes. Experience has demonstrated, however, that the act provides no guarantee of permanent open space, and it has involved a high public cost in the form of lost taxes.

2. Cluster zoning. There are two applications of cluster zoning in San Jose: the planned development combining district (PD) and the cluster permit. On a 50-acre site where one dwelling unit per acre is allowable, a 50-unit development could be clustered on 25 acres, leaving 25 acres for open space. That is, the City Council can waive normal zoning requirements for a proposed development as long as the development does not exceed the density standards of the General Plan for the subject area.

b. Land acquisition. Two variations on public land acquisition are described below:

1. Assessment districts. The power to acquire land for public purposes through special assessment districts is provided for in the 1913 Municipal Improvement Act. Assessment districts are often suggested by cities and citizen groups when no other means or funds are available to acquire land. They can be used to acquire local parks or areas of special interest, such as the grove of oak trees in the Almaden Valley, which was acquired by citizens through an assessment district.

2. Land gifts and easements. Local governments in California are empowered to receive gifts of land and to hold and maintain such gifts for public use. They also are specifically authorized to accept gifts of open space easements. The acquisition of easements or development rights can be used to preserve open space that, at the same time, remains in private ownership and use. This method could be employed along utility corridors to link up larger expanses of open space and provide bicycle, hiking, and riding trails.

With regard to financial difficulties for recreational facilities, the San Jose Parks and Recreation Department recommends that the projected operating and maintenance budget cut should be met by eliminating community center programs and by deferring the planned opening of Lake Cunningham (Lake Cunningham has a projected annual operating budget of $43,000).[91] It is also suggested that the establishment of assessment districts for improvements such as planting street trees and landscaping be explored for special areas such as the central business district.[92]

Other city proposals argue that user charges for community-wide facilities such as Lake Cunningham should be instituted (not being recommended at this time is a differentiated user fee for residents and non residents at facilities supported by city taxes, such as the Kelly Park zoo).[93] In addition, it is suggested that a portion of the conveyance tax be used for operating and maintaining new park facilities, in conjunction with providing an overall reduced level of service.[94]

Making up the projected operating budget deficit requires instituting a policy that all new parks will be acquired, developed, and maintained by means of the construction and conveyance tax funds.[95] The Parks Department would continue to receive the same proportion of its total income from these funds, averaging about $6.0 million annually through the mid-1980s. Half of the construction and conveyance tax income would be used for neighborhood and district parks, sport facilities, and school playgrounds. The minimal development policy and user fees for sports complexes would be effected. Citywide and special facilities, such as completion of the river park chains, would be financed by the other half of the funds. The General Fund would be used for existing park system maintenance with a minimum recreation program.

Concerning the potential loss of existing facilities, the city suggests that school sites and golf courses be designated as a private recreation zoning district. Sites presently threatened by development would be preserved for open space and recreational uses.[96] The state Naylor Bill[97] should be modified to allow surplus school sites to be sold for less than 25 percent of market value if they are to be used for public recreational purposes.[98] The current statute does not recognize that both the school district and the city serve the same public (although city boundaries do not correspond to any school district). One public agency should not be making money from another.[99]

San Jose's commitments to specific solutions to its open space and recreation facilities problems is reflected in its estimated $48.6 million proposed parks and recreation plan for the 1981–86 Capital Improvements Program, which emphasizes the improvement of 359 acres for parkland.[100] By 1986 nearly all presently owned park sites would be at least minimally developed, in accord with a city council policy to develop park sites 50 percent so as to spread funds available for improvements and minimize maintenance costs. In addition, renovations of 30 older parks are planned, as well as joint development of 12 school facilities—under agreement that the schools are responsible for maintenance.[101]

Acquisition of 103 acres of land for future park development is also intended, in order to provide future service at a level similar to that which currently exists.[102] Park acreage per 1,000 population in 1980 was 4.7. A reduced ratio of 4.5 is anticipated in 1985, based on General Plan predictions of an 11 percent population increase and assuming fulfillment of planned parkland acquisition. The city General Plan standard for park acreage per 1,000 population is 8.0.

Of the 1981–86 capital resources allocated for parks, 79 percent is proposed for park development, renovation, and reserves for future development, 5 percent for recreation improvements at school sites, and 16 percent for land acquisition.[103]

The following criteria, in order of importance, were used in establishing priorities for park capital improvement program projects:[104]

Self-supporting projects or those involving nominal maintenance and operational costs, such as community gardens, school playgrounds, park renovations, and land acquisition

Carry-over projects from the 1980–81 Capital Improvement Program, Community Development Block Grant Program, and City Council-authorized grants and approved joint participation projects, such as Lake Cunningham.

Projects generally involving minimal development parks, such as Curtner, Thousand Oaks, Branham, Almaden Meadows, Kora, and Meadow Fair park sites.

Sports fields and recreation centers having high public use but additional operational costs, such as Starbird Center, Houge, T. J. Martin, and La Colina parks.

Citywide parks involving additional operational costs, such as Coyote Creek park chain and Lake Cunningham Park.

Responses to an opinion survey of city residents also are likely to be used in refining priorities. Preferences identified in the planning study are as follows:[105]

About 64 percent of survey respondents believe the city should develop neighborhood parks.

About 65 percent favor spending more money on programs and services in existing facilities.

About 32 percent favor developing a number of large citywide parks.

About 74 percent want the city to purchase available land for future park use. Purchase of land for open space is also desired. This response contrasts with those favoring upgrading of neighborhood parks and existing facilities.

Regarding the resolution of open space administrative conflict problems, two promising methods for facilitating action have been proposed and are in use in various parts of the country:[106]

a. Conservation commission. Enabling legislation in other states has provided for the creation of local conservation commissions in conjunction with city and county governments. Such commissions are empowered to conduct inventories and analyses of local natural resources; to coordinate activities among various public and private groups; and to recommend overall land use policy to the local planning agency and legislative body. Such a commission would have the new capability of taking affirmative action to preserve open space and coordinate the work of private groups such as nature conservancies.

b. Land development agencies. The Baltimore Area Regional Planning Council is authorized by state law to establish quasi-public development corporations for the purpose of acquiring land and phasing urbanization. This type of agency, adapted to the needs of San Jose, could be used to acquire priority open space lands and receive gifts of land. It would differ from a commission in that it would be somewhat more autonomous. Such an agency might be in a better position to deal with real estate in the public interest; and landowners wishing to make gifts of land might be more willing to do business with this type of entity.

In addition to these regional approaches, some mechanism is needed to resolve park and recreation planning conflicts within San Jose city government itself.[107] Perhaps the city manager's office could play a mediating role in order to foster a cooperative relationship between the departments responsible for meeting the open space and recreation needs of the city.

The Suburban View (Cities of Sunnyvale, Saratoga, Morgan Hill, and Gilroy)

Problem: The cities surrounding San Jose in the metropolitan area are independent entities, and as such have a local rather than a regional perspective of the open space issue. For example, Sunnyvale, a typical mature, job rich community in northern Santa Clara County, believes that it may be too late to devise an effective open space plan, since there is very little vacant land in the city.[108] Also, Sunnyvale has zoned all of its land in accordance with its General Plan. Consequently, there haven't been any real open space choices to be made, except to rezone some previously designated parcels. The direction of the city's development has essentially been established.[109] Therefore, only one significant issue exists to be resolved: How should the open space be used? This question has numerous applications that are directly related to other, basically economic issues.[110]

Sunnyvale has been reluctant to spend large sums of money for protecting open space areas. Consequently, funding has been both controversial and scarce.[111] During the early 1970s there was an attempt to pass a bond issue for the purpose of acquiring lands for preservation uses. Although the City Council strongly endorsed this effort and worked very hard to get it approved, the measure was defeated at the polls. This setback severely restricted the city's hopes of purchasing any substantial parcels of remaining orchard land. Thereafter, several open plots went to high-bidding developers because they were not strategically located or large enough to be self-sustaining in an agricultural use. In addition, if a property owner was unable to retain his or her land because of an attendant loss of economic viability, the city was unable to act. Thus, the city's lack of financial resources has prohibited it from acquiring any ample-size parcels for public open space and recreational facilities.

The concern for open space in the city has been directed toward quality rather than quantity. City officials have tried to compensate for a paucity of vacant land by utilizing open space to the best possible advantage. Also, the amount of land relegated to open space purposes has been relatively small, because of the heavy competition from other uses, such as housing, which is at a premium in Sunnyvale.[112]

Since it provides a valuable economic resource by contributing to the city's tax base, industry is important to the economic well-being of Sunnyvale.[113] Accordingly, industrial land users are another major competitor in the market for vacant and potential open areas. Thus, some parcels that might have been used for open space purposes are now devoted to the industrial sector. This, in turn, has generated an additional demand for housing for the employees of these businesses. Consequently, structures now cover or threaten to consume much of the land in Sunnyvale. They take the shape of both housing and industry. It is these requirements of a community—for both income and shelter—that demand that city lands be equitably distributed among a variety of supporting functions.

Characteristic of the affluent suburban cities of the west foothills, Saratoga is essentially a built-up, low density, residential community. Although visually accessible to the undeveloped foothills, it has a low proportion of designated parkland to total population.[114] In addition, some large residential areas in Saratoga do not have easy access to a neighborhood park.[115] These areas are located in the northern part of the city, where, in the 1950s, development was permitted on small lots without provision for open space. This problem is the direct result of development that occurred prior to the park procurement program started in 1968.

The Saratoga Community Services and Planning Departments staffs stated that residents have never passed a local park bond issue, indicating a general lack of desire for additional developed parklands.[116] As a result of rapidly escalating land costs and uncertainty concerning future park acquisition funding from the state, Saratoga is very limited in its ability to acquire additional parkland.[117]

One of the greatest problems facing the Saratoga Community Services Department, which provides and maintains parks, is the cost of maintaining existing parks.[118] Funds for the maintenance of parks comprise a very small portion of the city's General Fund and Operating Expenses Budget,[119] yet present costs of park maintenance range from $4,000 to $6,000 per acre annually.[120] These costs have risen in recent years as a result of higher labor and material costs, along with the increasing amount of parkland acreage held by the city. Policy makers have been forced to take high cost of park maintenance into consideration, possibly encouraging them not to acquire additional lands.[121] Whereas park acquisition is a one-time expense, park maintenance is a permanent, escalating operating expense.

Perhaps the most critical problem facing Saratoga's open space resources is the pressure by owners of vacant land to develop their property for single family homes.[122] Undeveloped land is located primarily in two areas, the orchards and the hillsides. At present, a large portion of the orchards is protected, as least temporarily, by the Williamson Act. Saratoga has a policy of encouraging the renewal of Williamson Act contracts as long as possible, in order to prevent premature development of the orchards; however, the future of these lands as an open space resource is becoming less likely, since these lands would be easy to develop because they are flat and would be conveniently served by existing city services.

The other important open space problem for Saratoga is the planning of residential development on the ecologically fragile hillsides. As of April 1980, 225 residential homesites had been approved in this environmentally sensitive area.[123]

Morgan Hill and Gilroy are examples of the relatively less affluent South County suburbs that have substantial amounts of space availabile in their vicinity. Consequently, there is great metropolis-wide pressure on these cities for industrial and residential development.[124]

The General Plans of both South County cities express a concern for the loss of open space for the following reasons:[125]

Natural hazard
Agricultural use of remaining prime soil areas
Preventing urban sprawl
Provision of recreational facilities for residents
Other purposes, such as wildlife habitats and special aesthetic qualities.

Although several outstanding county and state recreational facilities are nearby,[126] Morgan Hill and Gilroy have very limited park resources within their boundaries.[127] These communities find acquisition of new parkland difficult and expensive, despite the dedications obtained from new residential development.[128]

Perhaps even more important than land acquisition costs are the on-going park maintenance and recreation program expenses required to meet the active recreational demands of the relatively young South County communities.[129] In addition, the impact of Proposition 13 makes it more difficult for these cities to finance the facilities and programs needed by their rapidly growing populations.

Solution: Despite its awareness of the limitations of open space planning, Sunnyvale has responded to its residents' demand for open space with a combination of land use strategies. The city employs some of the more general approaches to preservation, such as public acquisition and land use regulations.[130] Public acquisition is a useful tool for the purchase of recreational and scenic properties that can be applied to some or all open space lands. Previously the city employed this technique to obtain an undeveloped site designated for school use. This parcel subsequently remained an orchard until the city developed it for an arboretum.[131] Recently, interest has been expressed in procuring open space lands for the provision of regional parks, such as the Baylands. Sunnyvale's General Plan recommends this use,[132] and the city strongly endorses the concept.[133]

Techniques for the regulation of land uses include zoning and subdivision controls. These are restrictions imposed by local government that have been upheld by courts as appropriate devices for implementing the land use provisions of a city's General Plan. Zoning is often used for retaining open space, since it controls such aspects of development as the use of land and buildings, height and bulk of structures, the proportion of a lot that buildings may cover, and the density of dwelling units in a given area.[134] In this regard Sunnyvale's approach has been to implement a very strict plan review and approval process for both residential and industrial development proposals.[135]

Sunnyvale's Zoning Ordinance requires that usable as well as decorative open space be provided within a project. Recently, open space preservation has been encouraged through the application of density zoning for large scale projects (such as planned developments) where there is a mixture of uses with a variety of yard and lot sizes, heights, types of open space, densities, and housing styles.[136] The city also requires that landscaping be provided in connection with industrial development. In 1980, Sunnyvale imposed a moratorium on industrial construction that led to a lowering of intensity in such projects. This limit, which was enacted partly in response to the jobs/housing imbalance discovered within the county,[137] caused the city to restrict the density of industrial development that could occur citywide. Indirectly, this restriction decreased building coverage and parking, thereby leaving more land available for landscape and open areas.

Subdivision controls establish procedures and regulations for portioning larger parcels of land into smaller ones. This division of land can affect the open space potential of a lot area, neighborhood, or even the entire city. Early in 1981, Sunnyvale imposed a requirement that all new subdivision developments provide dedicated parklands as a condition for project approval.[138] This action was prompted by the recent closing and offer for public sale of several school sites. The city regarded these closures as open space losses, it hoped to offset them by providing supplemental lands.[139]

Other potential sources for either gaining or preserving open space are school properties, depending upon the ultimate disposition of the sites. In Sunnyvale four schools are projected for closure in the immediate future. The playground portions of two closed school properties, the San Antonio and Panama schools, already have been obtained by the city for recreational purposes. Both of these parcels are intensely used by the public. The remainder of these properties are leased by the school district to a private educational institute. In another case the city plans to offer the land for private sale and development.[140] In the near future the Morse Elementary and Madrone Junior High Schools will be available for sale. These properties are continguous, and offer the opportunity for park development. Sunnyvale hopes to obtain at least 10 to 15 acres of these sites, a parcel large enough for the creation of a significant recreational facility.

The city has a policy to acquire higher priority school sites, those in areas where there is now the least amount of open space.[141] Accordingly,

Sunnyvale is actively attempting to purchase as many of these school sites as is economically feasible. City officials are also accommodating expected losses of open space by amending the General Plan (currently in the revision stages) and rezoning particular parcels to lower intensity uses. Future additional open space needs will be met by the city in cooperation with the county on a regional park system, which will include the Baylands Park, the Sunnyvale Mountain Park, and the salt ponds at the northerly limits of the city. Planning for these regional open space lands and their recreational potential is already under way.

In addition, Sunnyvale advocates other techniques of open space preservation. Certain publicly owned lands, such as utility corridors, water areas, and flood zones, should not be developed.[142] In particular, the city encourages public utility rights-of-way to be landscaped and beautified for open space.[143] Parklands and greenery easements should be established at waterline rights-of-way along Stevens Creek and other waterways. This effort should be accomplished in coordination with other interested jurisdictions, such as the Santa Clara Valley Water District and the City of Mountain View.[144] Some of these techniques already have been used in such projects as the PG&E and Hetch-Hetchy rights-of-way for strip park and trail development. Two other approaches to open space preservation have been tried by the city: conservation in the form of bike paths, and a community garden program that is no longer active.

Some public and private areas should be permanently protected from development for reasons of public health, welfare, and safety. These include those portions of the Baylands requiring preservation in order to maintain vital ecological balances. Natural hazard areas also should be excluded from construction and other intensive land uses. Examples of these areas are properties exposed to floods, fires, and landslides, as well as land near earthquake fault lines. Man-made hazard zones, such as the air flight pathways under Moffett Field Naval Air Station, should also remain undeveloped for reasons of public safety. This land is currently developed in an appropriate low intensity conservation use: an 18-hole municipal golf course. Other noise-impacted parcels that should remain vacant are the strips alongside freeways and expressways. These areas are best used as landscaped open space buffer zones between more intensive land uses and the freeways.[145]

Other useful tools for preserving open space are economic incentives to private landowners. The only existing case of this in Sunnyvale is an orchard that was placed under a Williamson Act contract.[146] A voluntary agreement was entered into between the property owner and the appropriate jurisdiction that the orchard would be kept in an agricultural use for a specific period of time. This has allowed the land to be taxed on its agricultural value, an amount significantly lower than that of more intensive uses. In addition, Sunnyvale has expressed a willingness to have those sections of the Baylands owned by the Leslie Salt Company placed in this type of designation. Little progress is expected on this issue, however, since the Leslie Company seems hesitant to commit itself to such an agreement.[147]

Control and regulation of urban development processes represent a final method used by Sunnyvale in the preservation of open space land. This method includes mechanisms designed to restrict the outward expansion of an area, regulate the direction and timing of growth, and implement public service curtailments.[148] Two of these techniques have been employed by Sunnyvale in an attempt to direct its growth rate. An urban service boundary has been established by the city and approved by LAFCO. No future changes are anticipated in the urban service boundary, with the exception of several areas intended for annexation.[149] The city's General Plan and Capital Improvements Program have already been designed to accommodate these projected additions of land. LAFCO has not pressured Sunnyvale to protect these parcels from development, since they lack the potential for open space use.[150]

Curtailments of public service are being contemplated by Sunnyvale for managing urban growth. Since the city has now reached the maximum capacity of its sewage treatment facility, it is attempting to slow industrial development and regain control over the future direction of its community.[151] Consequently, the city has enacted a three-year moratorium on the issuance of new building permits.[152] However, the moratorium is not comprehensive in scope, since it does not prohibit construction or halt all development activity. For example, those areas that the city intends to annex are exempt from the ban; and projects that have already received plan approvals will not be subject to the restriction.[153] Building will therefore continue to occur at a semiregular pace until all of the previously accepted projects are completed. Thus, the moratorium really applies to new developments that would generate a demand for sewage treatment that the city could not accommodate.

In Saratoga open space means more than designated parks. It includes mountain areas located outside the incorporated city limits, but visually and psychologically attached. It also includes the extremely low density residential development in parts of the city and the nine school sites that provide visual and usable open space. Saratoga's proximity to three large county parks also reduces its need for additional parks. These include Villa Montalvo, a 175-acre park used as an arboretum and wildlife reserve; Stevens Creek, a 655-acre multipurpose park; and Sanborn County Park, part of a 1,000-acre undeveloped regional corridor along Skyline Boulevard.[154]

Saratoga's policies try to provide the community with both active and passive recreational facilities in city parks. However, since much of the city has been developed, only one vacant parcel of land remains that would be suitable for park use.[155] Although the Community Services Department of Saratoga would like to purchase this property, it has not done so because park acquisition funds are very limited. The city has been unwilling to take action until the site is threatened with development.[156] Saratoga park supporters hope that acquisition funds can be raised, should this occur.

One method Saratoga has for raising funds for park acquisition is its conveyance tax. When a house is built or resold, approximately $1,000 is obtained by the city.[157] In addition to its policy of using local bond issues to acquire and develop land for parks. Saratoga has a park dedication fee as part of its subdivision ordinance.[158] Despite the high cost of land and the limited development occurring, these dedication fees have contributed some funds for park acquisition.

Because of the problems Saratoga is having in maintaining and improving its parks, a number of special interest community-based groups have emerged to lend a helping hand. The city is increasingly relying on contributions from these user groups to help defray maintenance costs. An example is the 3.2-acre baseball diamond in Congress Springs Park, which was developed and is maintained by the Saratoga Little League. As part of the agreement, the Little League was given the right to build and operate a concession stand.[159] The Saratoga Athletic Facilities Foundation was formed by persons interested in providing additional facilities for baseball and soccer.[160] The city is also working with this group to provide a master plan for the park and to arrange for its maintenance upon completion. Other groups, such as the Saratoga Rotary Club and the Foothill Faculty Club, have made similar arrangements with the city.

With regard to controlling hillside residential development, Saratoga voters passed Measure A, the Northwest Hillside Initiative, "to conserve the City's rural character, maintain public safety, preserve scenic beauty, avoid excessive traffic, and minimize excessive public costs."[161] Supporters of this initiative saw the character of their community changing because of the pressure to develop land and to allow lower standards for higher densities that they claimed were out of step with Saratoga's tradition. They also felt that current practices allow "piecemeal, high-density development [that] degrades the beauty of Saratoga Hills, increases landslides and traffic congestion, and imposes higher service costs on the city as a whole."[162]

Although Saratoga's Measure A faced heavy opposition from many landowners and developers, it was passed by a significant margin.[163] The measure imposed a moratorium on further development in the hillside area until a specific plan can be completed for the entire hillside area. Consequently, about 144 of the 225 residential homesites already approved for the area must again go through the subdivision process.[164]

Like other communities in the San Jose metropolitan area, the cities of Morgan Hill and Gilroy do not see open space as a single issue. Rather, they view open space in terms of the trade-offs of benefits from preserving land for a desirable purpose, against the costs associated with parkland acquisition, or against the opportunity costs of tax revenues lost by not allowing development.[165]

An expression of these possible trade-offs in open space policy is made in both South County cities' General Plans, which indicate the interim nature of agricultural land use.[166] In addition, these communities have zoned some of their best agricultural land for industrial development.[167] At the same time, negative reactions to the rapid population increase and the limited potential in property tax revenues from housing that is a result of Proposition 13 have induced both cities to adopt growth management policies for regulating the timing and volume of new residential development.[168]

Thus, like Saratoga and Sunnyvale, Morgan Hill and Gilroy are attempting to increase their control of the trade-off options they have in framing open space policy for the benefit of their own residents without the interference of other units of government in the San Jose metropolitan area. Unlike the other, more developed suburban communities, Morgan Hill and Gilroy have a wide range of options to determine their future character.

Environmental Groups (Midpeninsula Regional Open Space District, People for Open Space, Sierra Club, Committee for Green Foothills, Peninsula Open Space Trust)

Problem: The increasing conversion of undeveloped areas to urban land uses is a real threat to California's economy and environment.[169] This urbanization process is consuming open space needed to produce food; to supply natural resources, such as water; to provide recreational facilities; to preserve natural areas and wildlife; and to shape urban regions.[170] It is estimated that if this process continues for another decade, one-fourth of the state's best land could be removed from agricultural use.[171]

The Bay Area is also suffering a loss of open space, lands that are active, useful, and productive agricultural areas.[172] The amount of land lost to urbanization in the Bay Area each year is about 19,000 acres, an area two-thirds the size of San Francisco.[173] About three-fourths of this loss may be attributed to urban growth in the form of subdivisions and its effects on adjacent lands, such as parcelization—breaking up large properties into small ones.[174]

Approximately 375,000 acres, or 20 percent of the present Bay Area crop land and rangeland, is projected to be lost by 1995.[175] At the same time Bay Area projections made by public agencies and business interests indicate that during the 1980–2000 period, there will be a 20 percent population increase and a corresponding need for more, not less, regionally produced food and open space.[176]

There are three basic reasons for preserving agricultural lands.[177]

Importance in the state (regional) and county economy
Preservation of areas where specialty crops are grown
Necessary production of food and fiber.

Since 1945, Santa Clara County has seen the building over of 170,000 acres of outstanding agricultural soil.[178] As Table 4.2 indicates, the total county agricultural bearing acreage declined by more than 50 percent during the 1970s. As shown in Tables 4.3 and 4.4, during the 1974–78 period total farmland declined from about 380,000 acres (45 percent of the county total) to 262,000 acres (31 percent of the county). Thus only a fraction of the original total of the county's agricultural land remains in production, primarily in South County—the area under the greatest pressure for urban development in the region.

In the 1960s and 1970s the lands in Santa Clara County were becoming urbanized at a rate of nearly 4,000 acres per year, with most development taking place on prime agricultural land.[179] As one observer of Santa Clara County development pointed out:

> Some of the finest agricultural lands ... are in places where urban development is most desirable and where people want to live. However, the simple facts are that while it is not imperative for industry or subdivisions (or ranchettes) to occupy the best farmland, it is imperative that these lands be reserved for agriculture. There is no point in attempting to farm second rate land.[180]

At present urban development is threatening the very rich agricultural land of Coyote Valley, 40 percent of which is within San Jose city limits.[181] In addition, Morgan Hill has plans for a large industrial park in the north part of town, and Gilroy plans to transform acres of cropland to housing industry.[182]

An additional problem concerning open space preservation is that trends in rangeland and cropland management indicate a decline in wildlife habitat. Since less than 10 percent of a farm or range is required for habitat, maintaining this cover should be feasible.[183] However,

Table 4.3 Bay Area and Santa Clara County Farmland: 1974

	Area	
Farmland (acres)	Bay Area	Santa Clara County
Vegetables	49,047	14,245
Field crops	288,876	17,743
Fruit, nuts	119,991	20,410
Total cultivated	457,914	52,398
Range and pasture	1,729,343	327,955
Total farmland	2,187,257	380,353
Percent of total land area	49%	45%

Source: People for Open Space, Endangered Harvest: The Future of the Bay Area Farmland (San Francisco: November 1980).

because of changes in farm and range ownership and economics, many areas previously set aside have been brought into production.[184] These changes have emerged because corporate ownership has different priorities than family ownership. Family or individual ownership usually represents a long term commitment to the land, and good soil conservation is therefore more likely to be practiced. In contrast, corporate ownership seeks incremental profitability every season for every acre. Consequently, swales, fences, trees, and other unusual appurtenances are modified or removed, then farmed, resulting in the destruction of wildlife habitats. An example of this phenomenon can be found in the Dakotas, where a once numerous pheasant population has been all but

Table 4.4 Total Agricultural Areas in Santa Clara County: 1978

Crop	Acreage	Percent of Total Agriculture	Percent of Total County
Ranching, livestock	225,000	85.7	26.8
Vegetables, berries	13,280	5.1	1.6
Orchards, vines	13,000	5.0	1.5
Field crops	7,840	3.0	0.9
Nursery, seeds	3,260	1.2	0.4
Total	262,380	100%	31.2%

Source: Santa Clara County Planning Department, General Plan (November 1980).

eliminated.[185] These trends suggest that the traditional mutually supportive relationship between farmer and wildlife may no longer be possible.[186]

The apparent inability of the public sector to systematically guide urban development represents another open space problem. Open space issues in Santa Clara County are fraught with contradictions. In such county documents as *An Urban Development/Open Space Plan* and the revised *General Plan,* policies to preserve open space have been adopted. Yet, as Table 4.1 shows, they haven't prevented its loss. The San Jose metropolitan area continues to generate urban sprawl because of the intense pressure for subdivision on land use decisions, which are ultimately political, not planned.[187]

LAFCO actions have been very important with regard to open space. County plans that sought to preserve open space have been ineffective; cities have annexed land almost at will, disregarding land use designations and other factors. The spirit of the Knox-Nisbet Act,[188] which created the local agency formation commissions to control urban sprawl, has not been reflected in its effectiveness. The purpose of LAFCOs, as stated by the California Legislature in creating them, is to

> encourage and provide planned, well ordered, efficient urban development patterns with appropriate consideration of preserving open space lands within such patterns.[189]

Solution: Environmental groups, especially People for Open Space (POS), have advocated a greenbelt for the Bay Area, a part of which would be the ridgelands. This nonprofit organization is dedicated to helping conservationists and other civic leaders in the Bay Area develop common policies and exchange information about regional planning and the open space preservation needs of the region. POS is primarily concerned about the preservation of agricultural lands.[190]

One solution to wilderness and agricultural open space protection is the greenbelt approach. The establishment of a successful greenbelt appears to require the involvement of the federal government, the state, and the local agencies and policymakers.

A promising greenbelt example is the Pinelands management plan in New Jersey. Under this plan, land use zones were designated and mapped for agricultural use, wilderness preserves, rural use, and urban and metropolitan use. For areas that were considered sensitive and intolerant of any development, a scheme of development credits was enacted. A person owning land prior to 1979 and restricted from further development received a "development credit" with an insured base value. These credits could be sold for developable lands in other zones commensurate with the stated carrying capacity of the zone.[191] Despite a few legal challenges, the plan has had success in its initial application and acceptance by farmers.[192]

The Committee for Green Foothills, Sierra Club, and POS have participated in several years of discussion and lobbying for a similar approach for the ridgelands. However, some of these organizations are concerned about the compensation component of the Pine Barrens program, and have expressed a reluctance to support similar legislation.[193]

Several other solutions are being tried to preserve agricultural land in the Bay Area. One effort in Marin County, which combines zoning regulation and compensation to preserve agricultural land, is similar to the activities of the Peninsula Open Space Trust (POST), a private trust set up in 1977 to assist the Midpeninsula Regional Open Space District in acquiring undeveloped land. The Marin County effort established a private foundation, the Marin Agricultural Lands Trust (MALT), which seeks permanent agricultural land use by the purchase or through the dedication of development rights. This foundation is the result of a coalition between conservationists and farmers with a shared goal but dissimilar approaches and philosophies.[194]

In Marin, conservationists from the Sierra Club and POS worked over a 10-year period with local conservationists and farmers. The first step was to implement 60-acre minimum zoning. After the zoning was in place, many dairymen felt a new sense of security and stability, and began to reinvest in their businesses. However, the mounting pressure to develop agricultural land convinced conservationists and farmers that a more complete preservation effort was needed. True, a series of policies including price support measures and relaxation of standards for treated water to be used agriculturally helped in the commitment. Still, something more was needed to stop the consumption of available farmlands. Consequently, MALT was established. It remains to be seen whether MALT will be able to obtain sufficient resources to secure enough land to maintain dairy farming viability.[195]

With the support of the Sierra Club, Committee for Green Foothills, and POS, Santa Clara County has zoned two large agricultural areas for agricultural use only.[196] The environmental groups realize that the zoning is a holding action with little long term hope for protection. However, the zoning does provide a mechanism for slowing undue parcelization and securing time for implementation of a system of preservation.

The Committee for Green Foothills and other groups[197] support a bill that would establish an agricultural lands study committee to examine agricultural land use in the San Francisco Bay area. The bill states:

The committee shall undertake a study to ascertain the public interest in agricultural lands in the San Francisco Bay area . . . include information concerning the impact of agricultural land conversion on food production, food markets, agricultural employment, energy use, social values connected with rural living and natural resources.[198]

The committee would be required to report its findings and recommendations for protecting agricultural land use to the state legislature.

The Midpeninsula Open Space Regional District provides a viable solution to the problem of diminishing wilderness areas. By acquiring large tracts of open space that can be managed with good conservation techniques, it helps to maintain the ecological balances so important to wilderness areas.[199] Income obtained from lease-back agreements with ranchers can contribute to capital improvements and other programs needed to maintain these open areas.

Other environmental groups seek preservation of wilderness open space through state and federal acquisition. The Sierra Club has long stood for acquisition, but considers the Bay Area a special case requiring immediate attention. While not endorsing the ridgelands proposal, it nonetheless has encouraged discussion on the feasibility of greenlining the federally designated area.[200] The proposed greenlining approach would combine acquisition, regulation, and compensation to protect open space.

Recreational wilderness open space and agricultural lands do not make up all the open space of the Bay Area, nor do they represent the only concerns of the environmental groups. But these two categories form the common bond connecting the diverse groups. Therefore solutions sought by these groups require a further definition of agricultural lands. An important reason for this need is that public policies could be abused if others than farmers benefit from them (for instance, owners given publicly supported incentives to keep their land open even if they do not farm).

An additional environmental solution is the British Columbia model, whereby the Provincial Agricultural Land Commission designates agricultural lands for farming use only, based on a soils capability description.[201] This regulatory action has been coupled with programs of low interest loans, leasebacks with options to buy, and a price support system smoothing out the fluctuation of the market that occurs with agriculture goods.

Another proposal of the environmental groups to preserve open space is to foster metropolis-wide agreement on actual limit lines for urban areas based on an ultimate population carrying capacity of the region.[202] Some areas are not suitable for development, and should be inventoried and designated accordingly. Although the carrying capacity of the San Jose metropolitan area is constrained by the available resources, there is no defined limit to its urban expansion. This situation should be corrected, so as to create a better long term balance between development and regional resources.

A system of development credits, similar to that indicated in the Santa Clara County *General Plan*,[203] would be one useful way to preserve prime agricultural land under pressure for development, such as areas in the South County. Like the New Jersey Pinelands management plan discussed earlier, this system would establish boundaries delineating where open space is to be preserved and where development can occur, and would enable an agricultural owner to receive economic gain from the permanent commitment of the land to farm or other open space use through a transfer of development rights. A formula would be agreed upon for bestowing the credits on farmers, and a marketplace for transferring them to developers would be created. Although the task force mentioned in the *General Plan* to study the use of these transfers in South County has not yet been organized, the environmental groups see great promise for this preservation system.

With regard to land acquisitions, clearer tax laws would make it possible to tell potential donors of open space land where they would stand with the Internal Revenue Service. The environmental groups believe that the Internal Revenue Service has not clearly defined a land donation for a "public purpose."[204]

Finally, the environmental groups have made proposals for some form of regional planning and land use management. At the Bay Area scale POS recommends the formation of an agricultural land commission that would prepare a plan for agricultural protection, submit the plan to the public for a vote, and have authority to review local government actions to insure compliance with the plan.[205] At the San Jose metropolitan area level, the environmental groups suggest that the operations of Santa Clara County, cities, and LAFCO should be tied into the same general plan. This could be done by a joint powers agreement or a contract among these jurisdictions.

The Social View (Mexican American Community Services Agency, Confederacion de la Raza)

Problem: The Mexican American community represents about 18 percent of the Santa Clara County population and approximately 22 percent of San Jose's residents.[206] In San Jose the Mexican American population has shown a tendency to concentrate in what is known as the

East Side, stretching roughly from McKee Road to Hellyer Avenue, and in the central part of the city. Various environmental factors have created a negative milieu in these neighborhoods, causing adverse and pervasive socioeconomic conditions such as inadequate and poor housing, lack of jobs, educational underachievement, high school dropout rates, and an ongoing conflict with the justice system.[207]

The rapid transition from an agricultural based economy prior to World War II to a major center for high technology and aerospace manufacturing has caused Santa Clara County to undergo a change from a rural area to one of the largest metropolitan areas in Northern California. With a highly mobile population, the San Jose metropolitan area is straining to develop stable community institutions able to meet the needs of displaced agricultural workers. Most of these workers are Mexican Americans who have had a difficult time making the transition from a rural to an urban technological setting.[208]

For Mexican Americans open space represents all of those images of recreational and wilderness areas held by others, but with an additional thrust toward an agrarian orientation. In light of the various negative social issues faced by the community, in tandem with the present government cutbacks of social services, open space comes close to becoming categorized as an amenity. However, open space can and should be advocated as a means of injecting a positive influence into the negative milieu in which many Mexican Americans now find themselves. A better environment for the young through the provision of open space and recreational activities may contribute to lowering the crime rate and the other negative consequences of their environment.[209]

The Mexican American Community Services Agency (MACSA) and the Confederacion de la Raza identified several problems associated with the issue of open space and the Mexican Amercian community.[210] As Table 4.5 illustrates, in 1975 there were inequities in the spatial distribution of the current and planned recreational facilities in the City of San Jose. While the distribution of parks and facilities should at least be proportional to the population in a district, there should also be some weight given for a district's population density. Parks and other open spaces are an attractive alternative to overcrowding. People can gain relief from daily tensions that are exacerbated by crowded living conditions. In order to take account of this, a population density factor was calculated for each district in Table 4.5. Alum Rock, Cambrian/Pioneer, West Valley, and Willow Glen exceed the average density factor for San Jose. Therefore, these districts should have more community parks and planned facilities than would be indicated by distribution according to population alone.

In addition to the density factor, neighborhood socioeconomic

Table 4.5   Distribution of Population, Land, Parks,

District	Population		Area		Density
	Number	%	Acres	%	(1)/(3)
	(1)	(2)	(3)	(4)	(5)
Almaden	24,100	4.3	3680	4.8	6.5
Alum Rock[b]	92,400	16.4	10160	13.3	9.1
Alviso[b]	1,800	0.3	2740	3.6	0.1
Berryessa	43,500	7.7	6610	8.7	6.6
Cambrian/Pioneer	50,600	9.0	5060	6.6	10.0
Central[b]	83,400	14.8	7450	9.8	11.2
Edenvale	26,100	4.6	11310	14.8	2.3
Evergreen	26,100	4.6	6710	8.8	3.9
S. San Jose	40,900	7.3	7350	9.6	5.6
West Valley	100,600	17.9	7950	10.4	12.7
Willow Glen	73,300	13.1	7300	9.6	10.0
Totals:	562,800	100.0	76320	100.0	7.4

[a]Column 14 includes community centers, swim facilities, baseball fields, soccer fields, lighted softball fields, and tennis courts.

[b]District with a high proportion of Mexican American families.

characteristics, such as average family income, and age structure should be considered. Higher income and age groups allow for a broader range of leisure activities than is available to lower income families with many small children.[211] For these reasons low income neighborhoods in the San Jose metropolitan area are very much in need of recreational facilities. In fact, a San Jose study that considers these socioeconomic factors finds that low income districts, such as Alum Rock and Central City, are among the most deficient areas in terms of recreational resources.[212]

Another problem is that often in the past, recreation programs and administrators failed to take into consideration the cultural and ethnic differences that exist in many of the communities they serve.[213] For example, until recently the park system did not provide bilingual leadership or associated bicultural programs.[214] The majority of these parks

and Recreational Facilities in San Jose, by District: 1975

Neighborhood Parks								Planned Facilities	
(Area)				(Number)				Number	%
Developed		Undeveloped		Developed		Undeveloped			
Acres	%	Acres	%	Number	%	Number	%		
(6)	(7)	(8)	(9)	(10)	(11)	(12)	(13)	(14)a	(15)
45	6.5	44	6.5	3	3.9	5	11.5	4	5.9
60	8.7	50	7.3	8	10.4	3	7.0	8	11.8
8	1.2	0	0.0	1	1.3	0	0.0	0	0.0
12	1.7	77	11.4	2	2.6	7	16.3	5	7.2
36	5.2	0	0.0	4	5.2	0	0.0	—	—
111	16.1	0	0.0	17	22.1	0	0.0	9	13.2
73	10.6	92	13.6	10	13.0	11	25.6	13	19.2
11	1.6	76	11.1	3	3.9	6	14.0	7	10.3
189	27.4	330	48.6	8	10.4	3	7.0	4	5.9
100	14.5	10	1.5	12	15.6	5	11.6	8	11.8
45	6.5	2	0.0	9	11.6	3	7.0	10	14.7
690	100.0	681	100.0	77	100.0	43	100.0	68	100.0

Sources: Data in col. 1 from San Jose, *The General Plan—1975, City of San Jose* (1975); data in cols. 3, 6, 8, 10, and 12 from San Jose Parks and Recreation Department, *Inventory of Parks and Special Facilities* (1976); data in col. 14 from San Jose Parks and Recreation Department, *Project '75* (1975).

showed only a minimum of sensitivity to the recreational needs of the Mexican American youth.[215]

An additional recreational problem involves the limited usability of many parks.[216] Vandalism periodically limits the amount of services the parks can provide, in addition to making them unsightly and therefore undesirable. From another perspective, public safety is of concern. Evening use of such facilities as tennis courts is curtailed by fear of being attacked. In a broader sense, open space is not adequate in terms of providing a desirable living situation and providing and heightening a concept of community.[217]

Transportation to recreational facilities represents another open space problem to the Mexican American community. [218]While there are numerous parks within the San Jose metropolitan area, many of the outlying regional parks and open space areas are not easily accessible to the Mexican American population. This is because of the large distances between regional open space facilities and Mexican American neighborhoods; the increasing cost of private transportation; and the limited public transit available to residents of those neighborhoods. Many Mexican American families do not own an automobile.

Solution: In advocating any plan, the soical groups are primarily concerned with the allocation of open space and recreational facilities. Rather than comparing community centers with playgrounds, or allocating resources solely according to population density, the broad range of community needs should be taken into account when formulating a recreational plan.[219] As discussed earlier, there is a multitude of social, economic, and environmental characteristics that should be considered in order to make a realistic assessment of need: age structure, juvenile delinquency rates, population density, median income, housing characteristics, population stability, occupation, education, employment rate, and ethnicity.[220] All of these factors should be considered in determining specific recreational features, such as acreage, type of facilities, leadership, attendance, costs, and types of programs.[221]

The ideal situation provides planning for parks and open space on the neighborhood level, considering the special needs of that community.[222] The Hispanic community is closely knit and highly identifiable, connected by means of a powerful consortium of agencies serving its special needs.[223] A planning process actively seeking the participation of these actors in identifying community needs is a necessary first step.

On a more specific level the social groups recommend the following:[224]

a. Minimize transportation costs and maximize convenience by improving the mass transportation system linking Mexican American neighborhoods with regional park and recreational facilities, including weekend service
b. Emphasize inexpensive activities and facilities compatible with the low incomes of the population
c. Provide bilingual leadership and bicultural activities that relate to the recreational preferences of the Mexican American community
d. Demonstrate sensitivity to the Mexican American agrarian orientation by increasing the amount of agriculturally oriented activities, such as community gardens
e. Utilize school sites as active open space areas in disadvantaged neighborhoods

f.   Improve maintenance of park facilities and implement programs to decrease vandalism and crime.

In order to meet the needs of the Mexican American community more effectively, service providers should begin to respond to the preferences of the recipients. Specifically, more understanding of the Mexican American culture should be incorporated into the planning of open space and recreational facilities.[225] Unfortunately, decisions often lack the correct insights into the problems affecting the Mexican American community.[226] The San Jose metropolitan community therefore should provide a way to facilitate more interaction and communication between users and providers of open space and recreational services, for the benefit of the entire region.

The Private Sector (San Jose Chamber of Commerce, Building Industry Association, Santa Clara County Manufacturing Group)

Problem: The private sector does not support the use of mandatory controls for the provision of open space as a part of the development process.[227] It fully recognizes the social, economic, and environmental benefits to be derived from the preservation of open space and agricultural lands.[228] However, it also believes that people can best determine their own needs and priorities. While we all have needs for a variety of services, such as parks, police, and transportation, we should determine which needs are of such high priority that members of the public are willing to allocate their dollars in order to satisfy them. As Proposition 13 demonstrated, the public is less willing to pay for as many services today as it has been in the past. Therefore, the allocation for public open space should be determined by the degree to which the public is willing to pay taxes to support that particular use.[229]

Public regulation of open space and urban development is indivisible by the very nature of the two concepts. Open space precludes land from becoming urbanized. In the course of development, open space and agricultural lands are depleted. As the Building Industry Association points out:

> ...The community development process must interrelate economic growth, housing requirements, service provisions and budget considerations. We must remain cognizant of this interrelationship and avoid the pitfalls of single purpose planning. ABAG's sole orientation toward

environmental planning during its early years contributed to the economic requirements of the region being sadly ignored.[230]

Excessive regulations are counter productive. Past regulations (i.e., large lot zoning, growth moratoria, land use constraints) are largely responsible for the jobs housing imbalances we experience today. The new wave of regulations (rent control, inclusionary zoning, condo conversion restrictions) now seek to allocate the housing shortage ... new regulations are designed to correct the problems created by the old. . . .[231]

Partly because of the public constraints on private development, the price of land has increased fivefold since 1975.[232] In addition, developers are increasingly being asked to pay for open space and services as a part of their projects.[233] The private sector is generally opposed to the levying of fees or to requiring that a certain amount of open space be provided by developers. Fees should be levied community-wide in order to be equitable. The marketplace should dictate what percentage of open space people prefer. People who want open space should purchase higher priced units to secure those amenities associated with open space, or should purchase units with open space in lieu of some other amenities. Residents of low cost housing cannot afford to subsidize open space on their site and remain in low cost units at the same time. Requiring the provision of open space on small development sites of two or three acres creates disparities and the following problems for developers and residents:[234]

a. Such small developments are not of sufficient scale to provide for recreation facilities.
b. Unregulated recreational use becomes a nuisance.
c. Not enough units are provided, resulting in the underutilization of recreational space.

Although many cities encourage urban infilling with higher densities, no mechanism exists to ensure that this actually takes place. Developers are continually confronted with the situation where they provide a density requested by city staff in their plans, only to see the Planning Commission or City Council decrease their density of development, succumbing to political pressures for lower densities from local residents.[235]

A major problem facing the private sector is the urban service area boundary (USAB), which creates land shortages by precluding areas outside it from development, and thus artificially inflates the land values inside the USAB.[236] "The price of land and the affordability of homes, is directly related to the supply of residentially developable land, and the ability to construct units on such land in an expeditious manner."[237] As an example, Figure 4.2 shows the bid-rent curve of households for land in a metropolitan area with its business and employment center at 0. Line A–B represents the land price structure in an unrestrained market situation, where land values drop with distance from the city center. Line C–D displays the land price structure constrained by the USAB. Since the land outside the USAB is removed from the market, the price of the available land within the USAB is bid up. At point M property values drop, since this begins the area precluded from development. Thus it can be seen that the USAB inflates land values inside the urban service area by creating an artificial shortage of land.

Another problem is that the land use controls presently employed by county and local governments are chaotic. Land use decisions are being made on the basis of how much influence the applicant has, as in the cases of Exxon and Syntex in Evergreen, IBM at the Stile/Rule Ranch, and the Wiltron-Morgan Hill Business Park and Advanced Micro Devices in Gilroy, or through default by local government, as in the case of Coyote Valley.[238] In the latter case, the county refuses to plan outside the urban service area, and the City of San Jose refuses to acknowledge that the Coyote Valley exists.[239]

Solution: According to the private sector, the government cannot reflect individual needs through the utilization of land controls that create distortions in the marketplace. It believes that the role of the government planner should be one of accommodating development and making sure that urban services and facilities are available for development to occur, and to control those externalities associated with development.[240]

The private sector therefore recommends that market-oriented planning for open space and development outside the urban service area should be accomplished as follows:[241]

a. Streamline the permit and development process. Redundant and unnecessarily time-consuming procedures in the permit and develop process should be eliminated. For example, once a building plan has been approved, there is no reason why that same plan should be required to go through the same process all over again on a different development. "The use of a 'master permit' and 'super stamp' process would greatly expedite plan checking and the issuance of building permits."[242]

b. Environmental analysis and urban suitability study. Prior to opening the urban service areas, environmental analysis should be conducted for the lands that might be available for development.[243] Such a study would identify those areas that will be most environmentally suited for open space, agricultural, and urban uses. Some of the factors that might be included in such a study are geology, vegetation, wildlife, soils, hydrology, and scenic qualities.

Although many of these environmental factors have already been

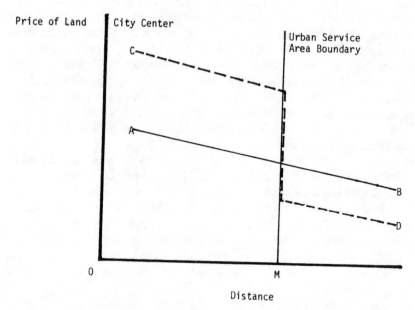

Price of Land

City Center

Urban Service
Area Boundary

C

A

B

D

0

M

Distance

FIGURE 4.2. Effects of Urban Service Area on Land Values in the San Jose Metropolitan Area. *Source:* William Alonso, "A Theory of the Urban Land Market," in *Readings in Urban Economics,* ed. Matthew Edel and Jerome Rothenberg (New York: Macmillan, 1972), pp. 104–11.

Point 0—Central city center.
Point M—Urban service area boundary.
Line A–B—Land values without an urban service area boundary.
Line C–D—Land values with an Urban Service Area Boundary.

compiled by the county and city planning staffs, no one has structured the information into a meaningful form. Such a study could be performed either by the county planning staff or by consultants to the county at a modest cost. Funding could come from either the public or the private sector.

    c. Zoning for development or nondevelopment. Areas identified as being the most environmentally suitable for open space, agricultural, and urban uses should be zoned for either development or nondevelopment. Only appropriate uses should be permitted in each of the zoned areas.

    d. Windfall fess for developable land. When these zoning areas are established, windfall fees should be imposed upon those areas that experience a substantial increase in property value because they were chosen by the public for development. Such fees could be used for the following purposes:

1. To purchase open space or agricultural lands. These lands would experience a drop in property values because they would be excluded from development. Consequently, they would become more affordable to public and private agencies and groups. Agricultural lands purchased by a government agency could be leased back for farming. This would help to preserve the agricultural land and bring in revenue at the same time[244]
2. To pay for public services
3. To pay for planning services for those areas that have been singled out for urban development.

e. Removal of the urban service area boundary (USAB). The urban service area should only be an area where the public has a commitment to provide services; it should not serve as a boundary to development. Beyond the USAB development should be allowed, but should also be required to pay for extension of services, or pay user fees that larger industrial users and developers could afford. Development within the urban service area would still be based upon a capital improvements program.

f. Area plans. Area plans should be generated for land identified as being suitable for urban development. These plans could be provided by local jurisdictions if the areas to be developed are within their sphere of influence, or by the county or private developers. Such plans could be paid for with public funds or, if the funds were not available, the developer could be required to pay for a planning consultant to provide plans to the responsible agency involved. These area plans should encourage the following:

1. Mixed land use, so that people could live, work, and play where they reside, eliminating energy-wasting commuting and inefficient land use patterns
2. Cluster development for higher densities and more open space
3. An investigation of the possibility of density transfers from open space or agricultural lands.

Specific plans will have to be provided by the developer prior to allowing development to proceed inside these planning areas. Development should be permitted only if it meets certain performance standards for the provision of urban services.

Within the urban service area, the remaining vacant developable land should be carefully studied for its highest and best use. This study should consider regional housing and employment problems. For example, the industrially zoned vacant land in northern San Jose should probably be rezoned to residential or mixed use development in order to help alleviate the jobs/housing imbalance. Mechanisms should be established to help insure that urban infilling takes place at higher than present densities, and to encourage mixed use and cluster development.

The private sector believes that this planning approach will result in the integration and preservation of open space in an urban setting, and in the creation of efficient mixed use, large scale developments, primarily financed by private interests.[245] It feels that this approach is a rational method for providing both open space and development in an environmentally responsible manner. If something is not done soon to alleviate the high cost of housing and building, unplanned development will occur to meet rising social pressures.

SUMMARY

There appears to be a substantial difference in views regarding the nature of the open space and recreation problem in the San Jose metropolitan area. One set of perceptions of the problem sees too little public control and too few financial resources to stop the expansion of urbanization that threatens to consume the region's natural open space environment, especially agricultural land. Other views of the problem express a concern that too much public control over urban development has removed an excessive amount of land from the marketplace, bidding up the cost of industrial and residential development, and in turn artificially constraining the economic development of the metropolitan area. Still other perceptions refer to the poor quality and inaccessibility of recreational facilities for low income neighborhoods.

The corresponding solutions also vary substantially, from extreme public control of urban development, such as establishing a permanent USAB beyond which no urbanization will ever be allowed, to an abandoning of the urban service area concept and allowing interaction in the marketplace to guide the metropolitan land development process. Even among actors with similar views, such as the environmental groups, tools proposed by each organization to counter the problem of encroachment of urban sprawl have differed.

While the multiple advocacy process exposed and sensitized the actors to one another's differences, it also revealed their similarities in values and interests. For example, representatives of the private sector claim to be very supportive of the creation of open space and recreational areas on both the state and local levels. The San Jose Chamber of Commerce has consistently endorsed open space measures, and supports private group and individual efforts to obtain funds for open space.

At the same time, environmental groups claim that they are not anti-business, anti-housing, anti-city, or anti-poor. It is not their efforts to preserve open space that have created the jobs/housing imbalance; rather, unplanned regional growth has done so. They realize that housing is an important metropolitan need, and that homebuilders should be allowed to supply a product needed throughout the metropolis.

Another area of general agreement is that higher density housing with improved public transportation and mechanisms for infilling will result in more livable places and projects, and relieve some of the outward pressure for urban growth.

There was also almost universal agreement regarding two basic problems related to the open space issue. One is the lack of funds, not only to acquire open space land but also to maintain what had been acquired. It has evoked a variety of responses. The policy groups whose geographic area of concern exceeded city boundaries had a broad perspective and were concerned with regional planning. Jurisdictions that actually allocated funds were mostly concerned with the local fiscal constraints.

The other major problem was the lack of a regional institution with the power to enforce sound regional planning in the Bay Area or in the San Jose metropolitan area. Most of the actors believed that coordinated general plans and zoning of the entire Bay Area according to the intrinsic nature of the land and needs of the people would counter the present-day urban growth by accretion, and save the prime soils, protect the ridgelands and bay, and provide adequate parks and recreation. Regional government could then zone for development or nondevelopment. Those areas zoned for development would pay a windfall fee that would be used to purchase open space or agricultural lands, and to pay for public services and for area plans for urban development areas.

For many people open space is not a pressing issue. Crime and the cost of housing have a higher priority. When budget money is reduced, parks and recreation allocations are among the first items to be cut because their benefits are difficult to quantify. Police and fire protection are more obvious needs. In the same way, agricultural land and hillsides are lost to urbanization because the economic benefits of jobs and housing are considered more important.

During the interactive process of multiple advocacy, the actors, in their search for solutions to the open space problems, became open to suggestions and new ideas. They also developed a sense of cooperation. As a private sector representative indicated:

> . . . the public and private sectors should work together cooperatively in addressing the underlying problems of providing for open space and urban develpment.[246]

This public-private collaboration in the development process has already been tried, with successful results. Examples are the Peninsula Open Space Trust's "facilitated development" coalition work with developers in the El Toro Mountain project in San Bruno, and San Jose's cooperation with IBM in developing the Stile/Rule Ranch in the southern part of the city. In the light of Proposition 13 and declining budgets, all actors concerned with the issue of open space and recreation facilities may have to pool their resources in order to support the environmental amenities desired by the metropolitan community.

NOTES

1. President's Commission on National Goals, *Goals for Americans* (New York: Prentice-Hall, 1960), p. 239.
2. James E. Carter, *1980 President's National Urban Policy Report* (Washington, D.C.: U.S. Government Printing Office, 1981).
3. Ibid., pp. 9–18.
4. California, *Urban Development Strategy for California* (Sacramento: Office of Planning and Research, 1977), p. 28.
5. California, *State of California Planning and Zoning Laws and The Subdivision Map Act* (Sacramento: Office of Planning and Research, 1979), p. 53.
6. Santa Clara County, *An Urban Development/Open Space Plan for Santa Clara County* (San Jose, Calif.: Santa Clara County Planning Department, 1973), p. 1.
7. Santa Clara County, *General Plan* (November 1980).
8. An urban service area is the area in which a city agrees to place its new development. Ibid., p. 19.
9. Ibid., p. 23.
10. These views are based on interview with Chris Hartzell, planner, Association of Bay Area Governments, February 1977; interview with Linda Morse, planner, Association of Bay Area Governments, February 1981; Association of Bay Area Governments, *Areas of Critical Environmental Concern* (May 1976); interview with Staff, California Office of Planning and Research, March 1981; California, *Urban Development Strategy;* and interview with staff, U.S. Department of the Interior, April 1981.
11. Association of Bay Area Governments and the Metropolitan Transportation Commission, Joint Policy Committee, *Santa Clara Valley Corridor Evaluation Summary* (March 1979), pp. 5, 6, 11–13; and California, *Urban Development Strategy*, p. 11.
12. Association of Bay Area Governments, *Areas of Critical Environmental Concern*.
13. See also U.S. Department of the Interior, *San Francisco Bay National Wildlife Refuge* (1970), p. 1.
14. Interview with Morse.
15. Association of Bay Area Governments, *Areas of Critical Environmental Concern*, p. 65.
16. Association of Bay Area Governments, *Regional Plan 1980* (July 1980), pp. 3–1 to 3–8.
17. Association of Bay Area Governments, *Ridgelands, a Multijurisdictional Open Space Study* (May 1977).
18. The overall governing body of the ABAG is the General Assembly, composed of one representative from each member city and county. It meets twice a year to adopt the

budget and overall work program, review major actions of the Executive Board, and adopt regional policies and plans. The Executive Board, composed of up to 38 elected officials from member cities and counties, directs ABAG's ongoing operations. See Association of Bay Area Governments, General Assembly, *Economic Development Objectives and Policies* (December 1980).

19. Interviews with staff, California Office of Planning and Research; and staff, U.S. Department of the Interior.
20. Ibid.
21. Ibid.
22. Association of Bay Area Governments, *Regional Plan 1970–1990* (1970).
23. Association of Bay Area Governments, *Regional Open Space Plan: Phase II* (1972).
24. Association of Bay Area Governments, *Regional Plan 1980*.
25. See, for example, California, *Urban Development Strategy*.
26. Association of Bay Area Governments, *Regional Plan 1980*, p. 3–6.
27. For example, the A-95 review process requires regional institutions, such as ABAG, to review local government grant proposals to the federal government with respect to regional policies.
28. See Association of Bay Area Governments, Regional Planning Committee, *Meeting Minutes*, December 10, 1980; and Association of Bay Area Governments, General Assembly, *Meeting Minutes*, March 27, 1981.
29. Rob Elder, "ABAG Suddenly Bay Area's No. 1 Political Topic," *San Jose Mercury*, February 19, 1978, p. 2.
30. California, *Urban Development Strategy*, pp. 11, 27–28.
31. Interview with staff, California Office of Planning and Research.
32. Ibid.
33. California, *Urban Development Strategy*, p. 10.
34. Association of Bay Area Governments, *Financing Open Space for the San Francisco Bay Region* (1973), p. 42.
35. California Assembly Bill 8591 (Naylor Bill) was adopted and became effective on January 1, 1981. This bill requires school districts to offer surplus playgrounds to a city or county at a below-market rate. The purchase price will be equal to what the district originally paid for the site, adjusted somewhat for inflation. The purpose of this law is to continue to make each school's open space available for ongoing public use, if the local jurisdiction is willing to pay the reduced price.
36. These views are based on interviews with Kim Vogl, planner, Santa Clara County Local Agency Formation Commission, February, April, and May 1981; interviews with Donald Weden, associate planner, Santa Clara County Planning Department, January, April, and May 1981; and interviews with Felix Errico, planner, Santa Clara County Parks and Recreation Department, January and April 1981.
37. Proposition 13, the Jarvis-Gann Property Tax Initiative, was passed in California in 1978 in order to limit local real estate tax revenues available to cities. Since nonresidential land uses generate relatively high real estate tax revenues and usually require limited public services, they are often considered more desirable than residential development by local governments. Ibid.
38. Santa Clara County Planning Department, *The Fiscal Impacts of Proposition 13 on Local Governments in Santa Clara County* (December 1980), pp. 12–80.
39. Cities can do this by encouraging land uses that generate relatively high real estate taxes, such as commercial and individual activity. See Ibid., p. 8.
40. Ibid., pp. 4–9.
41. Interviews with Weden.
42. Ibid.
43. Interviews with Vogl.

44. In response to the uncontrolled urban growth and the increasingly fragmented local government formation, the California Legislature passed the Knox-Nisbet Act in 1963, creating County Local Agency Formation Commissions, with powers and duties as follows:
    1. To discourage urban sprawl
    2. To encourage orderly development and formation of local agencies
    3. To make studies and furnish information
    4. To approve or disapprove wholly, partially, or conditionally proposals for
       a. Incorporation of cities
       b. Formation of special districts
       c. Annexation of territory to cities
       d. Spheres of influence (in Santa Clara County, Urban Services Areas)
    See California Government Code, sec. 54774.
45. Interviews with Vogl.
46. Interviews with Weden.
47. Ibid.
48. See, for example, Paul Davidoff and Mary E. Brooks, "Zoning out the Poor," in *Suburbia: The American Dream and Dilemma*, ed. Philip C. Dolce (New York: Anchor Press, 1976), pp. 135–66.
49. Interviews with Errico.
50. Interviews with Vogl.
51. Interviews with Weden.
52. This is similar to the proposal for a Bay Area Agricultural Land Commission presented in People for Open Space, *Endangered Harvest: The Future of the Bay Area Farmland* (San Francisco: November 1980), p. 69.
53. The IGC was established in 1976 to promote the solution of multijurisdiction problems in Santa Clara County. It is a voluntary advisory organization representing the cities, county, and special districts in Santa Clara County.
54. Interviews with Vogl.
55. Ibid. Such growth control initiatives have been passed in such Santa Clara County cities as Morgan Hill.
56. Ibid. An existing urban service area is defined as "the area in which a city designates where and when urban development should occur." Land within an urban service area should not exceed the acreage required during the next five years, based on current industrial/commercial and population growth figures. See Santa Clara County Local Agency Formation Commission, *Guidelines and Policies* (February 1978), p. 18.
57. Interviews with Weden.
58. Ibid.
59. Interviews with Vogl.
60. Interviews with Weden.
61. Ibid.
62. Ibid., and interviews with Vogl.
63. The California Land Conservation Act of 1965 (Williamson Act) provides that a County Board of Supervisors or a City Council may establish agricultural preserves. Once they are established, affected property owners may sign contracts with the appropriate jurisdiction to maintain land in agricultural or recreational use in exchange for preferential taxation.
64. Interviews with Weden.
65. Ibid.
66. Santa Clara County, *General Plan*.
67. Ibid., p. 47.

68. Ibid.
69. Ibid.
70. Ibid.
71. Interviews with Vogl and Weden.
72. Ibid.
73. San Jose, *The General Plan: Open Space Element* (April 1973), p. 2.
74. Based on interviews with John Guisto, chief of parks planning, San Jose Parks and Recreation Department, February, April, and May 1981; Interviews with Dennis Korabiak, planner, San Jose Planning Department, February and April 1981; and interview with Carolyn Kramer, planner, San Jose Planning Department, April 1981.
75. San Jose, *The General Plan*, p. 4.
76. Interviews with Korabiak.
77. Interviews with Guisto.
78. San Jose Planning Department and the Parks and Recreation Department, *An Analysis of Parks and Recreational Needs for the City of San Jose* (November 1980), pp. 96–136.
79. Ibid., pp. 96–124; and Philip J. Trounstine, "Study Shows 4 Council Districts Lagging Parks," *San Jose Mercury*, January 13, 1981, pp. 1B, 5B.
80. Ibid.
81. San Jose Planning Commission, *Report to the City Council on the 1981–86 Capital Improvement Program* (April 15, 1981).
82. Interviews with Korabiak and Kramer.
83. Interviews with Guisto.
84. Ibid.
85. Interviews with Korabiak and Kramer.
86. Ibid.
87. Interviews with Guisto.
88. Ibid. California state law permits municipalities to impose a requirement to provide for parkland in connection with residential development. See California, *State of California Planning and Zoning Laws and the Subdivision Map Act*, pp. 120–21.
89. Ibid.
90. San Jose, *General Plan*, pp. 27–29.
91. Interviews with Guisto.
92. Ibid.
93. San Jose Planning Commission, *Report to the City Council*.
94. Ibid.
95. Interviews with Guisto.
96. Ibid.
97. Assembly Bill 8591. See note 5.
98. Interviews with Guisto.
99. Ibid.
100. San Jose Planning Commission, *Report to the City Council*.
101. Ibid.
102. Ibid.
103. Ibid.
104. Ibid.
105. San Jose Planning Department and the Parks and Recreation Department, *An Analysis of Parks and Recreational Needs*, pp. 10–11.
106. San Jose, *General Plan*, pp. 32–33.
107. Interviews with Guisto, Korabiak, and Kramer.
108. About 6 percent (801 acres) of the developable property within Sunnyvale's sphere of

influence is vacant or in an agricultural use. Based on Sunnyvale, "Housing and Community Revitalization Sub-Element" of the "Community Development Element," *1972 General Plan of the City of Sunnyvale* (February 1980), p. 2.3–15; and interview with Edward C. Moore, planning officer, City of Sunnyvale, April 1981.

109. Open space as a topic for debate has emerged only since 1965. Sunnyvale's pattern of development was well-shaped by that time. Based on interview with Moore.

110. Because land values are so high, they make any open space decision costly. This factor has influenced the city's policy toward open space and land development within its boundaries. The council feels that it should avoid acquiring open space where the monetary costs are excessive. However, it also wants to maintain, where possible, plans for preserving open space lands. Ibid.

111. The city has limited financial resources available for open space purchases. Its policy inclinations have reflected this constraint. Ibid.

112. Ibid.

113. Because of the great influx of industries into Sunnyvale, the city has been able to establish a firm economic base that benefits both government and its citizens. See Sunnyvale, *1972 General Plan of the City of Sunnyvale* (February 1980), p. XII-2.

114. Saratoga Community Services Department, *Saratoga Parks 1st Ten Years,* (Saratoga, Calif.: January 1979), p. 1.

115. Williams and Mocine, *Saratoga Basic Data Report* (Saratoga, Calif.: May 1974).

116. Based on interview with Barbara Sampson, director of community services department, City of Saratoga, May 1981; and interview with Vicki Rudin, Planner, planning department, City of Saratoga, May 1981.

117. Ibid.

118. Interview with Sampson.

119. For example, in 1973 funds for park maintenance comprised only 3.7 percent of Saratoga's budget and represented a per capita expenditure of $0.56. See Williams and Mocine, *Saratoga Basic Data Report,* p. 39.

120. Saratoga Community Services Department, *Saratoga Parks 1st Ten Years.*

121. Interview with Sampson.

122. Ibid.

123. Interview with Rudin.

124. This pressure has led to a substantial increase in the consumption of incorporated lands by these South County communities. During the 1950–80 period, the amount of incorporated land in Gilroy and Morgan Hill increased by 373 and 350 percent, respectively. See Table 4.1.

125. Gilroy, *General Plan* (1979), pp. II-2 to II-6, III-2 to III-9, IV-2 to IV-9, VI-2 to VI-5; and Morgan Hill, *General Plan Policy Document* (1980), pp. 31–33, 75–83.

126. Santa Clara County Parks and Recreation Department, *Regional Parks and Recreation Area* (1978).

127. Interview with Michael Dorn, director, Planning Department, City of Gilroy, February 1981.

128. Ibid. See footnote 88.

129. Ibid.

130. See People for Open Space, *The Case for Open Space* (San Francisco: 1969), p. 7.

131. Interview with Moore.

132. Sunnyvale, *1972 General Plan,* p. VIII-2.

133. Interview with Moore.

134. Sunnyvale, *1972 General Plan,* p. XI-1.

135. Additional requirements for landscaping and open space in residential developments were incorporated into the city's *1972 General Plan.* These requirements are reflected

in the stringent standards applied to the provision and maintenance of privately landscaped areas. Based on interview with Moore.

136. Sunnyvale, *1972 General Plan*, p. XII-1.
137. See, for example, the findings of Santa Clara County Industry and Housing Task Force, *Living Within Our Limits: A Framework for Action in the 1980's* (November 1979).
138. See California, *State of California Planning and Zoning Laws*, pp. 120–121; and note 88.
139. Interview with Moore.
140. Ibid.
141. Ibid.
142. Santa Clara County Local Agency Formation Commission, *Guidelines and Policies*, p. 24.
143. Sunnyvale, *1972 General Plan*, p. VIII-2.
144. Ibid., p. VII-2.
145. Interview with Moore.
146. California Land Conservation Act of 1965.
147. Interview with Moore.
148. Sunnyvale, *1972 General Plan*, p. 21.
149. These would include a number of county islands, as well as one parcel located along Mary Avenue between Sunnyvale and Mountain View. Based on interview with Moore.
150. Based on interview with Moore.
151. Richard Cowart, ed., *Land Use Planning, Politics and Policy* (Berkeley: Extension Publications, University of California, 1976), p. 94.
152. Interview with Moore.
153. Ibid.
154. Williams and Mocine, *Saratoga Basic Data Report*, p. 79.
155. Interview with Sampson.
156. Ibid.
157. Ibid.
158. Williams and Mocine, *Saratoga General Plan Report* (Saratoga, Calif.: May 1974), p. 18.
159. Saratoga Community Services Department, *Saratoga Parks 1st Ten Years*. p. 11.
160. Ibid., p. 12.
161. California, *The Growth Revolt: Aftershock of Proposition 13?* (Sacramento: Office of Planning and Research, 1980), p. 33.
162. Ibid., p. 13.
163. The measure passed, 4,652 to 3,956. See Ibid.
164. Ibid.
165. Interview with Michael Dorn.
166. Gilroy, *General Plan*, p. II-3; and Morgan Hill, *General Plan Policy Document*, p. 33.
167. Interview with Michael Dorn.
168. See Gilroy, *Residential Development Ordinance* (1979), ordinances nos. 79–28 and 80–21; and Morgan Hill, "Residential Development Control System," *Municipal Code* (1978), Title 8, ch. 66.
169. These views are based on interview with Steven Sessions, land manager, Mid-peninsula Regional Open Space District, February 1981; interviews with Larry Orman, executive director, People for Open Space, February and April 1981; interview with Clara Mae Lazarus, Sierra Club, February 1981; interviews with Cynthia Wordell, Committee for Green Foothills, February and April 1981; and interview with Ellie

Huggins, Peninsula Open Space Trust, February 1981.

170. Edward A. Williams, *Open Space: The Choices Before California* (San Francisco: Diable Press, 1969).
171. Ibid., p. 138.
172. People for Open Space, *Endangered Harvest*, pp.9–12.
173. Ibid., p. 9.
174. Ibid., pp. 9, 49.
175. Ibid., pp. 64, 65.
176. Population projections indicate that between 1980 and 2000, the population of the Bay Area will increase by about 1.1 million (22 percent). See, for example, Bay Area Council, *Housing: The Bay Area's Challenge of the 1980's* (San Francisco: Bay Area Council, December 1980), p. 10.
177. Williams, *Open Space: The Choices Before California*, p. 136.
178. People for Open Space, *Endangered Harvest*, p. 25.
179. Alfred Heller, ed., *The California Tomorrow Plan: The Future Is Now* (Los Altos, Calif.: William Kaufmann, 1972), p. 70.
180. Williams, *Open Space: The Choices Before California*, p. 134.
181. People for Open Space, *Endangered Harvest*, p. 53.
182. Ibid.
183. People for Open Space, *The Functions of Bay Area Farmland*, Background Report no. 2, Farmlands Conservation Project (October 1980).
184. Ibid.
185. Ibid., p. IV-5.
186. Interview with Frank Hall, biologist, California Fish and Game Department, February 1981.
187. Interviews with Vogl and Weden.
188. The Knox-Nisbet Act (1963) California Government Code, sec. 54774.
189. Ibid., sec. 54774.5.
190. See People for Open Space, *Endangered Harvest*.
191. New Jersey Pinelands Commission, *New Jersey Pinelands Draft Comprehensive Management Plan* (June 1980).
192. Interview with Terrance Moore, executive director, New Jersey Pinelands Commission, February 1981.
193. Interviews with Orman, Lazarus, and Wordell.
194. Interview with Orman.
195. Ibid.
196. Santa Clara County, *General Plan*.
197. Interview with Wordell. For example, the Bay Area Farmlands Committee was formed to lobby and promote this legislation.
198. California Assembly Bill 2060 (1981).
199. Interview with Sessions.
200. Interview with Paula Carrell, Sierra Club, April 1981.
201. Gordon Graham, presentation on the British Columbia Provincial Agricultural Land Commission, Sonoma Farmlands Conference, April 1981. See also People for Open Space, *The Endangered Harvest*, p. 68.
202. Interviews with Wordell and Lazarus.
203. Santa Clara County, *General Plan*, p. 13.
204. Interviews with Lazarus, Huggins, and Wordell.
205. People for Open Space, *The Endangered Harvest*, pp. 69–71.
206. Santa Clara County Planning Department, *Advanced Final Count of 1980*, San Jose, Calif.: Santa Clara County Planning Department (April 1981).
207. These views are based on interviews with Rosa Maria Hernandez, executive director, Mexican American Community Services Agency. February and April 1981; interviews

with Jose Villa, executive director, Mexican American Community Services Agency, February and May 1977; interviews with Manuel J. Sandoval, executive director, Housing Services Center, February 1980 and April 1981; and interviews with staff, Confederacion de la Raza, April 1979 and April 1981.

208. Ibid.
209. Interviews with Villa.
210. Interviews with Hernandez, Villa, Sandoval, and staff, Confederacion de la Raza.
211. San Jose Planning Department and the Parks and Recreation Department, *An Analysis of Parks and Recreation Needs*, pp. 101–07.
212. Ibid., pp. 96–136.
213. Interviews with Hernandez and Villa.
214. Interviews with Hernandez.
215. Ibid.
216. Interviews with Sandoval and staff, Confederacion de la Raza.
217. Interview with Villa.
218. Ibid.
219. Seymour M. Gold, *Recreation Planning and Design* (New York: McGraw-Hill, 1980), ch. 1, 15.
220. Ibid.
221. Interview with Villa.
222. Ibid.
223. For example, the Mexican American Community Services Agency and the Confederacion de la Raza.
224. Interviews with Hernandez, Villa, and Sandoval.
225. Ibid.
226. Ibid.
227. These views are based on interviews with James I. Tucker, executive director, economic development and communications, San Jose Chamber of Commerce, June 1980 and March 1981; interviews with Steven G. Speno, executive vice-president, Building Industry Association, February and April 1981; interviews with staff, Santa Clara County Manufacturing Group, April 1981.
228. Ibid.
229. Ibid.
230. Building Industry Association, "Urban Service Programming," (March 17, 1981), p. 1.
231. Building Industry Association, "Affordable Housing Presentation," (March 17, 1981), p. 1.
232. Interviews with Speno.
233. Interviews with Tucker.
234. Interviews with Speno.
235. Interviews with Tucker.
236. Ibid.
237. Building Industry Association, "Affordable Housing Presentation," p. 3.
238. Interviews with Tucker.
239. Ibid.
240. Interviews with Speno.
241. Interviews with Tucker, Speno, and staff, Santa Clara County Manufacturing Group.
242. Building Industry Association, "Affordable Housing Presentation," p. 6.
243. See Ian McHarg, *Design With Nature* (New York: Doubleday, 1971).
244. Interview with Maurice Abraham, urban development director, George S. Nolte and Associates, March 1981.
245. Interviews with Tucker and Speno.
246. Building Industry Association, "Affordable Housing Presentation," p. 1.

5

PROVISION OF LOW AND MODERATE COST HOUSING

The difficulty of providing affordable low and moderate cost housing has long been a national problem. This problem, as indicated in Table 5.1, has worsened since 1970 because of housing cost increases disproportionate to the annual rate of inflation.

The Bay Area, the San Jose metropolitan area in particular, has experienced this problem more acutely than most of the nation because these areas have been generating jobs at a substantially faster rate than they have been constructing new housing. The San Jose metropolitan area, a rapidly growing center for electronic manufacturing employment, brings this problem into sharp focus. In 1975 there were 501,600 jobs in Santa Clara County and 411,500 housing units.[1] During the 1975–80 period about 200,000 new jobs were created countywide, while only 62,300 new homes were constructed.[2] This gap between the number of jobs generated and the number of housing units constructed has created an enormous shortage of housing that affects people at every economic level, and particularly low income families. This jobs/housing imbalance is expected to worsen, impacting the social, environmental, and economic functioning of this metropolitan community.

The average monthly cost of shelter increased from $241 in 1975 to over $750 in 1979,[3] with the average price of an existing single family home in the San Jose metropolitan area reaching $127,960 by December 1980.[4] (See Table 5.2.) In the rental housing market, which is the most viable alternative for low income households, housing shortages are most critical. In 1980 the average vacancy rate was 1 percent or less, and the average rental price for a one bedroom apartment varied between

Table 5.1 House Price Increases Compared with Increases of Other Prices and Income, United States: 1968–77

			Compound Annual Rates			
Item	1968-1977	1968-1970	1970-1972	1972-1974	1974-1976	1975-1977
1. New houses (1967 kind)	8.3%	5.6%	5.6%	9.9%	10.0%	11.1%
2. Existing houses (NAR)	8.9	7.4	8.2	9.1	8.6	10.8
3. Weighted average for (1) and (2)[a]	8.7	6.9	7.6	9.3	8.9	10.9
4. CPI[b]	6.4	5.6	3.8	8.6	7.4	6.1
5. GNP deflator[c]	6.2	5.2	4.6	7.9	7.2	5.4
6. Housing component of CPI[d]	6.9	6.8	4.2	8.0	8.5	6.8
a. Rent	4.6	3.7	4.1	4.7	5.3	5.7
b. Homeowner expenses	7.6	10.3	4.4	7.9	8.4	6.2
7. Disposable personal income	9.2	8.1	8.5	10.7	9.4	9.9
8. Same, per capita	8.3	6.9	7.1	10.0	8.9	9.0

[a]Rates of price increases for new and existing houses were averaged for each period by using weights for each type derived from the dollar volume of existing home sales and the computed dollar volume of new home sales (number of homes times average sales price). The weights for existing houses are 78 for 1968–77, 75 for 1968–70, 76 for 1970–72, 78 for 1972–74, 81 for 1974–76, and 80 for 1975–77. The weights for new homes are the reciprocals of these numbers.

[b]All items, including the housing component, shown separately under (6). The weight of the housing component in the total CPI has increased in recent years. Computed from "old" CPI.

[c]The GNP deflator is a broader measure of price changes than the CPI. It reflects price movements for investment goods, export and import goods and services, and government purchases of goods and services, as well as those for competition.

[d]Total housing component, including rent, home ownership expenses, fuel and utilities, and household furnishings and operation.

Source: Leo Grebler and Frank G. Mittlebach, *The Inflation of House Prices* (Lexington, Mass.: D.C. Heath and Company, 1959).©1959 by D.C. Heath and Company.

Table 5.2 Prices of New and Existing Homes in Santa Clara County: 1966–80

Year	Median Price[a] of New Homes	Percent Change From Previous Year	Average[a] Price of Existing Homes	Percent Change From Previous Year
1966	$24,000	—	$22,910	—
1967	25,600	+ 6.7	24,780	+ 8.2
1968	24,800	− 3.1	25,690	+ 3.7
1969	26,700	+ 7.7	27,780	+ 8.1
1970	24,500	− 8.2	27,650	− 0.5
1971	24,300	− 0.8	28,660	+ 3.7
1972	29,200	+20.0	31,160	+ 8.7
1973	33,800	+15.8	34,390	+10.4
1974	42,000	+24.3	38,510	+12.0
1975	48,600	+15.7	44,760	+16.2
1976	54,800	+12.8	54,500	+21.8
1977	71,400	+30.3	71,410	+31.0
1978	76,900	+ 7.7	77,120	+ 8.0
1979	100,300	+30.4	101,150	+31.2
1980	124,700	+24.3	127,960	+26.3

[a]Prices given for December of each year shown.

Source: Median price of new homes from records of Santa Clara County Planning Department (April 1981); average price of existing homes from records of the San Jose Real Estate Board (June 1981).

$350 and $400 per month.[5] While the typical family had to pay less than 20 percent of its income for housing in 1970, by 1979 more than 40 percent of its income was needed, because salaries did not increase as rapidly as inflationary housing costs.[6] (See Figure 5.1.)

Thus, in the San Jose metropolitan area, housing problems are especially severe for moderate and low income households. Housing is extremely expensive, and new housing is generally located far from the employment centers in the northwestern sector of the county. In addition, because of the rapidly growing demand for housing, and the limited number of federally supported rental units available, landlords have been able to raise rents substantially.

This chapter will explore ways in which the competing interests concerned with the low cost housing problem might be able to resolve their differences for the benefit of the metropolitan community.

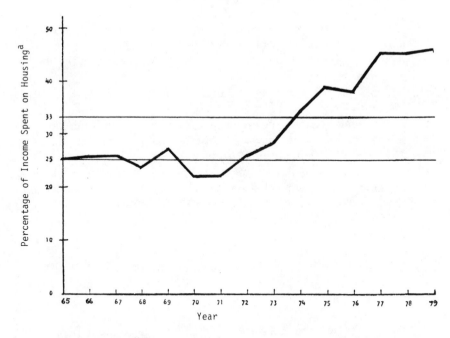

^aMonthly cost of owning a median priced home ÷ median monthly household income.

FIGURE 5.1. Monthly Housing Costs as a Percentage of Gross Monthly Income in Santa Clara County: 1965–79. *Source:* Records of Santa Clara County Planning Department (June 1981).

ACTORS' VIEWS

After examining the issue of providing low and moderate cost housing in the San Jose metropolitan area, our research staff identified and interviewed representatives of the following actors:

1. Federal government (Department of Housing and Urban Development)
2. State of California (Housing Finance Agency)
3. Bay Area regional planning agency (Association of Bay Area Governments)
4. Metropolitan planning interests in the San Jose area (Santa Clara County Planning Department and County Board of Supervisors)
5. Central city (San Jose Planning Department and City Council)
6. A representative affluent suburban community in the western part of the metropolitan area (town of Los Gatos)

7. A representative middle class, suburban community in the eastern portion of the metropolitan area (City of Milpitas)
8. A typical job-rich community in the northern section of the metropolitan area (City of Sunnyvale)
9. Middle class South County suburban communities (Cities of Morgan Hill and Gilroy)
10. A representative minority organization with a definite commitment to solving problems of low and moderate income families (Mexican American Community Service Agency)
11. Low cost housing development corporation (Community Housing Developers, Midpeninsula Coalition Housing Fund, and South Santa Clara County Housing Development Corporation)
12. Housing counseling agency for low income families (Housing Services Center)
13. Real estate interests (San Jose Real Estate Board)
14. Business interests (San Jose Chamber of Commerce)
15. Public education interest (Center for Educational Planning and Santa Clara County Office of Education).

Our interviews with these actors indicated a clustering of perceptions regarding the nature of and solutions for the housing problem in the San Jose metropolitan area. Consequently, we were able to cover the range of actors' views with five teams.

Regional and Federal Planning Institutions (Santa Clara County Planning Department, and Office of Education, County Board of Supervisors, Association of Bay Area Governments, California Housing Finance Agency, and U.S. Department of Housing and Urban Development)

Problem: Regional actors stated that the problem of providing low and moderate income housing is the result of a disparity between the supply of and demand for affordable housing.[7] As of December 31, 1978, it was estimated that Santa Clara County had 56,510 households requiring housing assistance (of which more than 80 percent were renter households).[8]

Regional and federal actors generally concur on recognition of the problem, and tend to view the reasons for its existence as concomitant to factors beyond their control. Among the factors the U.S. Department of Housing and Urban Development (HUD) officials identified as the cause of rising demand was the substantial in-migration of workers precipitated by the industrial boom in the county.[9] Job growth between 1960 and 1975 occurred at three times the national average, with another 200,000 to 300,000 projected for 1990.[10] Most of these jobs will be generated by the burgeoning electronics industry or its spinoffs. In addition, the people born during the postwar baby boom have reached adulthood; and changes in life-style, such as the growing number of single-person households, single parents (mostly mothers), and elderly people living alone, have caused the demand for housing to increase dramatically by increasing both the total population and the number of individual households requiring individual housing units.

Complicating the problem of skyrocketing demand is the short supply of all types of housing. Growth in the housing stock has not kept pace with the population growth of the 1970s. Although an additional 139,000 housing units are forecast to be built during the 1975–90 period, they will not adequately satisfy the demand.[11]

Some of the principal reasons for this shortage are the following:

a. The supply of land, which was once regarded as inexhaustible, is now greatly limited. Many of the desirable areas of the country are completely built up. Desirable areas that are still available have experienced dramatic price increases. On the other hand, many areas that are still available are no longer considered desirable, since they are generally farthest from employment centers. Long commutes and the cost of energy are principal causes of their loss of desirability.

b. Local jurisdictions also play a part in the shortage. Since 1970 they have come to realize the social, fiscal, and environmental costs of unhampered development, and have responded by limiting growth and emphasizing growth management. In addition, large areas of the county have been planned for industrial development, thus preventing the land from being used for residential purposes.

The problems of jurisdictional fragmentation and the pursuit by local jurisdictions of their perceived self-interest have had the same effect on assisted housing. Those cities, especially in North County, that managed to capture the most profitable development (in terms of the highest tax base) are often those most resistant to accepting their "fair share" of assisted housing. HUD can withhold funds from these cities, but this provides little leverage.

In the community development block grant (CDBG) applications for federal funds, HUD requires that communities attempt to address at least 15 percent of their housing needs. Because of community resistance, this is rarely done. Every year HUD has money left over that has been allocated for this type of housing assistance in the Bay Area but has not been claimed by local jurisdictions. Some of this money is given to communities that are willing to take more than their fair share of assisted housing. However, because of HUD's site and neighborhood standards, which attempt to avoid impaction of low income housing by encouraging scattered site housing, less money is allocated to these communities than they hoped for. San Francisco is the best example, with little vacant land left except in already impacted areas. Meanwhile, cities such as San Jose are turning some funds back because they don't want to commit additional subsidized housing to impacted areas such as the city's East Side, and aren't able to gain acceptance for assisted housing in other neighborhoods. Thus, much of this unspent money is returned to Washington or spent in other areas of the nation that do not have impaction problems and are willing to build subsidized housing.

c. The state of the economy and the nation's attempts to deal with it are having a detrimental effect on the housing industry. Rampant inflation and the rising costs of land, labor, and materials have bedeviled the industry for the last few years. Federal manipulation of interest rates and the money supply has fallen most heavily on the housing industry.

This combination of low supply and high demand has caused new home prices in Santa Clara county to soar from a median of $24,500 in 1970 to $48,600 in 1975 and to $124,700 in 1980 (see Table 5.2). Prices of existing homes have increased likewise. For example, Table 5.2 shows that between 1975 and 1980, the average sales price of existing homes rose from about $44,760 to $127,960, and increase of 186 percent.

Another problem consists of those difficulties facing primarily households on the lower end of the economic ladder that have relied on rental housing. Rental housing is experiencing all of the problems common to other housing, plus some uniquely its own.

First, the rapidly increasing demand for rental housing, as the shortage of affordable homes forces more people out of the owned housing market, puts tremendous additional pressures on the rental housing stock.

Second, the supply of rental housing has fallen far short of the need, and below the supply of owned housing. In some areas there has been an actual decrease in the supply of existing rental housing as units are converted into condominiums to capitalize on the demand for owner-occupied housing and the related tax advantages and huge profits for the converters. New construction of multifamily rental housing has been almost nonexistent as building costs, land costs, and money costs have outpaced the rents that people can or will pay.

Thus, today we see the traditional upward mobility in housing for the more affluent, and the movement of the less affluent down to less adquate housing and their finally being forced out at the bottom. Gentrification and displacement are the new threats of the 1980s. The American dream of home ownership has all but disappeared.

The Association of Bay Area Governments (ABAG) defines the major reasons for the low cost housing problem in terms of the following:

a. Article 34 of the California Constitution, which requires local public approval for public housing, and is used by many communities to block assisted housing developments in their neighborhoods

b. Limited public subsidies to cover the growing gap between the rising cost of housing and the incomes of low income families

c. Uncertainties in the amount and type of the federal funding commitments to low cost housing programs

d. Long delays and uncertain outcomes of project review by various levels of government

e. Low vacancy ratios, which are rapidly bidding up the cost of low cost housing, especially in the rental market

f. Local community and neighborhood opposition to the construction of high density, low cost housing.[12]

The county reports that the present General Plans, combined with the growth pressures in Santa Clara County, resulted in a serious housing shortage from April 1975 to April 1979.[13] The countywide housing shortage increased to an estimated 35,000 units in April 1979. If present housing plans remain unchanged and recent job growth trends continue, the projected housing shortage in 1990 could climb as high as 115,000 units.[14]

Santa Clara County states that a housing growth management approach is being used by many jurisdictions that limits residential development while encouraging job growth. This partial growth management approach greatly contributes to the growing housing shortage and higher housing costs by limiting housing supply while housing demand is still increasing because of job growth, changes in demographic trends, and speculation in the housing market. Fiscal concerns and the desire to preserve local neighborhood character play major roles in guiding local growth management and planning. Both these concerns result in the imposition of limits on new housing.[15]

The "Housing Element" of the Santa Clara County 1980 *General Plan* fully states the county's view of the problem:

The people of Santa Clara County are facing a serious housing crisis. Growth in the county's housing supply has not kept pace with the unprecedented industrial growth that has been occurring in the county over the last few years. Prices are rising much faster than average family income leaving a large segment of the population unable to afford to purchase a home. Affordable housing is harder to build because of high land costs, skyrocketing interest rates and the rising costs for materials and labor. People are being forced to live far from their jobs, often outside of the county . . . . Rental housing is scarce and existing supply is threatened by condominium conversion and lack of new construction. Discrimination is becoming more prevalent against minorities and families with children, since landlords can more easily pick and choose their tenants in a tight housing market.

The housing problems that Santa Clara County is experiencing now are not few. Affordable housing for the low income family has always been a need that government is called upon to address. The difference today is that the problem is so much worse that it has affected the middle income households who represent the backbone of the Santa Clara County working force. Young professionals just out of college, young people trying to leave home or live on their own, seniors looking for smaller housing, and single-parent households will not be able to find suitable, affordable housing in this county unless all of the cities and the County take an active role in providing for the housing needs of existing residents looking for change and future employees looking for work.[16]

Solution: Both state and federal agencies see their roles as providers of the funds that allow local jurisdictions to implement projects, based on "fair share allocations."[17] The state views its role as providing leadership and statewide direction, reportedly through mandated actions and funding.[18] HUD's most successful program, the Section 8 Rental Assistance Program, is aiding families in 4,000 household units in Santa Clara County.[19] In its first three years of activity, the California Housing Finance Agency (CHFA) has financed 541 units in the county.[20] These figures are an indication of the limitations of regional assistance, which needs massive funding to alleviate a problem of the magnitude that has developed in the county.

The regional perspective covers a spectrum of strategies to alleviate the housing shortage, ranging from ABAG's long standing Bay Area-wide effort to obtain community acceptance of low cost housing to the state's emerging policies of financial assistance. ABAG and the Santa Clara County Planning Department appear to have the clearest perceptions of the low income housing problem. However, the actions of both these agencies are severely limited by the relatively autonomous local governments.

Because it is a voluntary regional association, ABAG cannot mandate the implementation of its policies. Its only regulatory authority lies in its A-95 review function as a regional clearinghouse for federal assistance.[21]

Through this mechanism it helps to partially attain one of the primary objectives identified by the regional actor: the dispersion of assisted housing so as not to further impact low income areas.[22] Similarly, despite its limited authority, the County Planning Department has attempted to persuade the autonomous suburban communities to accept an increased number of low and moderate cost housing units.[23]

Notwithstanding the limited authority of regional and federal planning agencies, they offer the following solutions to help alleviate the housing problem:[24]

a. Increase regulatory powers or implementation mechanisms of regional institutions with regard to low cost housing.
b. Implement legislative reorganization and amend Article 34B to make it easier to provide low cost housing developments in local communities.
c. Work through housing development corporations and other nonprofit organizations (not subject to Article 34 referendum).
d. Educate the metropolitan population to accept high density subsidized housing in their communities.
e. Provide fiscal incentives through local governments, such as density bonuses and mortgage bond programs.
f. Expand financing options, such as state subsidies tied to below market rate financing.
g. Work with local government to promote the following:
   1. Below market rate schemes for low cost housing
   2. Land banking of publicly acquired areas
   3. Land write-downs for selling public lands to builders of low cost housing
   4. Rezoning land to increase residential densities and convert vacant industrial areas to new residential neighborhoods
   5. Use of vacant school sites.

It should also be recognized that the need for low cost housing in the San Jose metropolitan area is great and that the federal resources available for such housing have been very limited. At the same time, the fiscal and monetary policies of the national government, which have decreased the supply of money and increased the interest rates, have been discouraging the construction of new housing units and exacerbating the housing shortage. The regional, state, and federal planning institutions suggest that the national government recognize the sensitivity of the housing market to its policies, and increase its commitment to housing, including the creation of a mechanism to insulate low income housing from the pressures of the marketplace.[25]

The Central City (San Jose)

Problem: Typical of other central cities, San Jose has many poor and minority residents. More than 30 percent of the city's residents earn less than 80 percent of the median income of Santa Clara County, and approximately 22 percent are Mexican American, many of whom live in the barrios of central and eastern San Jose.[26] The crisis in the housing market, which has increasingly affected all residents, has had a profound effect on housing conditions and opportunities for the poor and minority groups.

The City of San Jose must identify the housing needs of the poor and determine appropriate responses, balancing the demands on scarce resources. It is the city that ultimately determines, through its land use controls and zoning powers, the type of housing that is allowed within its jurisdiction and in what locations.[27] Thus, it is the city that must develop a housing strategy that encompasses the needs of its own residents and neighborhood groups, and also reflects a perspective that recognizes regional needs and the larger social and economic context of the problem.

One of the most pressing problems facing San Jose residents is the rapidly rising cost of housing.[28] Costs have increased dramatically while the supply of developable land has diminished. All communities are affected, but the impact is greatest among low and moderate income families, who are priced out of the home ownership market and are left to compete for the limited and diminishing supply of rental housing.

The high demand for and low supply of low cost units within the tight housing market result in overcrowding. In 1970, 9,899 (7 percent) of the city's units were considered overcrowded. A unit is considered to be overcrowded when it is occupied by more than one person per room.[29]

In the 1979 Housing Assistance Plan (HAP),[30] about 62,300 low income households were identified, 32,700 of which were found to be needing housing assistance. Of these, 9,699 were female-headed and 15,045 were ethnic minority. About 24 percent of those needing assistance were elderly or handicapped. Both low income households and substandard housing units are concentrated in the central and eastern portions of the city, such as the Alum Rock neighborhood. As Table 5.3 indicates, in 1978 these neighborhoods contained a majority of the city's 10,681 substandard housing units.

These low income, substandard areas were further impacted in the late 1960s by the development of federally assisted housing projects.[31] The early projects were poorly maintained and managed, and generated social problems in areas already experiencing poor and overcrowded schools and generally deteriorating services. Only after the 1974 housing and community development legislation that, among other things, re-

Table 5.3   San Jose Housing Conditions: December 1978

Planning Area	Total Housing Units	Substandard[a] Housing Units	Percent Substandard
Almaden	8,033	112	1.40%
Alum Rock	24,986	2,465	9.86
Alviso	406	140	34,50
Berryessa	12,818	192	1.50
Cambrian-Pioneer	17,546	438	2.50
Central	28,671	3,847	13.41
Edenvale	31,253	459	1.46
Evergreen	9,113	116	1.27
North San Jose	1,404	59	4.20
South San Jose	13,264	953	7.18
West Valley	35,454	807	2.27
Willow Glen	24,760	1,090	4.40
Other	207	3	1.50
Total	207,915	10,681	5.13%

[a]Physically substandard in terms of structural decay or absence of plumbing facilities.
Source: San Jose Property and Code Enforcement Department, *Housing Condition Survey* (1978).

established local review of all assisted housing projects, was San Jose able to put forward a housing strategy that reflected its commitment to the goal of dispersing low cost housing. It stated in the 1974 General Plan that the city should promote increased housing opportunities for lower income households in a wide range of locations throughout the city, thereby avoiding undue concentrations of assisted housing in areas already containing a high proportion of low income persons.[32]

A major problem in implementing dispersion goals is neighborhood resistance.[33] While most people recognize the value of dispersion in principle, the response of "but not in this neighborhood, not near me" has hindered the development of low income housing even more than have land costs and availability.

San Jose's overall housing needs can be described in the following categories:[34]

a. The need for safe and decent housing with sufficient services. Physically substandard housing is a serious problem in the city and is generally concentrated in the central and east areas. These same areas also need public improvements. Improving housing conditions and public facilities is essential to neighborhood stability.

b. The need for fair housing opportunities for low income persons and dispersion of low income households. Housing discrimination has been a problem throughout the city. It includes the outright refusal to rent or sell to certain persons and the practice of imposing higher prices or rents on minority group members. This problem is worsening with the tighter housing situation.

c. The need for an adequate supply of affordable housing. It is estimated that 32,700 low income households are in need of housing assistance. The problem of meeting these needs is aggravated by the continued rising cost of housing. Emergency housing is another critical need for the city's low income population.

d. The need for neighborhood preservation and rehabilitation. The rehabilitation of houses is usually the least costly way to maintain the available low income housing stock. Preserving neighborhoods and preventing blight is an incentive for owners to maintain their houses.

e. The need for economic development. A major need in San Jose is to develop jobs readily accessible to the unemployed population concentrated in the central and eastern areas. Closely related is the need for diversification of the city's economic base and provision of more jobs in low-skill commercial and manufacturing establishments. It is important that the city develop ways to utilize the existing labor force and to train the potential labor force. Because of the high cost of housing, industry is having recruiting problems. Positions need to be filled from the existing labor pool. The city should approach this as an opportunity to capture a greater number of job openings for its residents, especially the unemployed.

Solution: San Jose has a complex approach to meeting the low income housing needs of its residents. The city's overall housing program is developed in the "Housing Element" of the General Plan.[35] The *Housing Assistance Plan*[36] further specifies strategies and programs focused to have a meaningful impact on low income housing problems.

To improve housing conditions, San Jose has an extensive housing rehabilitation program. In 1980 more than $1.8 million in CDBG funds were available to qualified owners to bring single family and small apartment units up to building code standards.[37] The city combines grants and financing from both federal and state programs to augment the rehabilitation program, including HUD's Section 8 substantial rehabilitation funds and Section 312 low interest rehabilitation loans, and CHFA's home improvement loans.

These funds are spent predominantly in the neighborhood strategy areas (NSA), so designated because they contain high concentrations of substandard units, low income and minority households, and many public assisted housing units. The five neighborhoods currently designated as NSA's are Mayfair, Gardner, Northside, Olinder, and Alviso.

An important General Plan policy that will significantly facilitate the rehabilitation program states that code regulations and enforcement should not impose disproportionate hardships on those who need low priced housing.[38] Implementation would mean that code standards for funded rehabilitation projects would be amended while standards for public health and safety are maintained.

The improvement of housing conditions is coordinated with other aspects of neighborhood revitalization and preservation. In 1980 some $1.9 million in CDBG funds were used for capital improvements, including streets and sewers.[39] The purpose is to improve the living environment and to stabilize conditions in low income neighborhoods, as well as to provide incentives for individual homeowners to improve their properties.

Social and recreational facilities are also supported by CDBG funds.[40] These services include community centers, child care centers, information and referral services, housing counseling, libraries, parks, and special facilities and improvements for the elderly and handicapped.

Funds from federal and state sources also help low and moderate income families to become homeowners. Programs such as the federal Section 235 mortgage payment subsidies and the state-insured home ownership programs are a beginning. In this type of program, below market rate (BMR) loans are made to qualified persons either directly from the public agency, if legally permitted, or through cooperating private lending institutions. It is through the expansion of BMR programs that the city hopes to address housing accessibility to moderate income households.[41]

The city is also working with private sector financial institutions in developing their own BMR loan programs that will be especially geared to areas that have had a history of declining property values or have been deemed to be mortgage deficient—that is, areas that were ignored by lending institutions in the past.[42] Some private institutions have also organized counseling centers to teach low and moderate income households the techniques of home buying and home ownership.

Home ownership programs are like general assistance programs, though the income supplement is earmarked only for housing services. Unless more affordable homes become available, this approach can have only a minimal impact, particularly for the low and very low income households. It is therefore the policy of San Jose to encourage the development of assisted housing units whenever possible, either for ownership or for rental.

In 1980, San Jose had about 820 units of HUD sponsored Section 221d3 rental units and approximately 1,937 units built through HUD Section 236 funds, an extension of the earlier federal rent subsidy program.[43] Section 8 new construction funds, which provide economic incentives for builders of low cost housing units, are the basis for existing and currently proposed projects.[44] The San Jose Greens apartment complex in the Cambrian-Pioneer area has 79 units under construction. The Mayfair I redevelopment project, consisting of 100 Section 8 units designed for the elderly, is scheduled to be completed in 1981. The Moreland apartment project, located on the site of the Moreland School in the West Valley area, is in the planning stages and will consist of 148 family units. The Arbor Apartments, completed in June 1979, have 122 units.

The existing Section 8 program, which is also like an income supplement program, allows the low income tenant to find his or her own rental unit, and then supplements the difference between the rent and a figure representing 25 percent of the tenant's income. The Santa Clara County Housing Authority manages this program for the city. There were 1,578 households participating in the program in 1979, and 1,010 more units were allocated in 1980.[45] While greatly increasing the housing services purchasing power of participants and the number of units available to low income households, it cannot determine the location of these units. Ideally, this program should promote the dispersion of low income households, but because of the rental range imposed on participants and some elements of choice on the part of the participants, these units are often found in or near low income and minority areas.

This raises the question of fair housing and dispersion, which has been a major part of San Jose's housing strategy since 1974. In the same year that federal guidelines for the HAP called for a locational element, San Jose amended the "Housing Element" of the *General Plan* to direct assisted housing to a wide range of locations of the city and to avoid its undue concentration in areas containing a high proportion of low income persons. The HAP now defines particular areas in which new assisted units are or are not approvable. In the not-approvable areas the housing plan focuses on rehabilitation and neighborhood revitalization approaches.

This policy is being implemented in numerous ways.[46] One way is to educate the community to accept low income housing without the usual stereotyped notions about such housing. Another is to acquire land in a wide variety of areas through land banking. It is through such funds that San Jose was able to acquire the Moreland School site in March 1979.

The city has now placed CDBG funds into land banking, for without this procedure there will be no way to develop the dwindling supply of parcels appropriate for assisted housing.

One tool that the city adopted to meet the challenge of neighborhood recalcitrance was an amendment to the city's General Plan in December 1978. This amendment allows density flexibility for government-assisted housing. Where such projects are approved and the proposed density is found to be compatible with surrounding land use, an alternative density can be established by the City Council as part of action taken on a planned development application.[47]

San Jose has also cooperated with state and regional agencies in promoting housing dispersion for low income units. In September 1979, the City Council approved the state's "fair share" housing allocation system, which assigns assisted housing goals to jurisdictions based on a formula of available jobs and current low income residents.[48] The City Council also approved ABAG's *Bay Area Housing Opportunity Plan*,[49] which promotes additional assisted housing in jurisdictions where there are unmet needs. This plan, which would amend HAP goals, has not yet been accepted by HUD.

The city has also taken significant measures to facilitate development processing of assisted units and to reduce construction taxes on such units.[50] The simultaneous processing of various permits required for a project and the conveyance of authority to the planning director for acting on Planned Development Combining District permits and tentative maps greatly streamlines the review process. The administration is also working on design criteria that will clarify expectations early in the process, preventing costly delays and misunderstandings.

The question of economic development, while not directly a dimension of the housing strategy, is central to improving the capabilities of low income people to buy better housing services.[51] Both in its economic development strategy and in its redevelopment program, San Jose is attempting to increase the supply of jobs accessible to low income people and to retrain the existing low income labor force. The city has also used its CDBG monies in revitalizing the downtown and the Alum rock commercial areas. In 1980 the city's Housing Steering Committee recommended that more CDBG funds go to neighborhood revitalization rather than to downtown development.[52] This recommendation was made not only in response to community concerns but also because the momentum for downtown development had begun to accelerate. Supported by the Santa Clara Valley Corridor Study[53] and existing public and private investment, San Jose is confident that the program will continue toward its goals.

Two programs that San Jose stresses as keystones to the improvement of housing for low and moderate income people are mortgage financing through the sale of tax exempt revenue bonds and the development of financial capacities to increase the land banking program.[54] Both programs are inhibited legally and by a lack of funds. The promotion of both programs requires a great deal of public education and understanding of their value, not only for low income households but also for promoting the local construction industry. The city has taken significant steps to initiate action in support of these programs, and is committed to do so through its most significant policy documents.

The Suburban View (Cities of Sunnyvale, Los Gatos, Milpitas, Morgan Hill, and Gilroy)

Problem: The suburban communities may be grouped together in terms of the increasing homogeneity in their attitudes towards housing. Essentially, they view the low and moderate income housing problem in terms of the vast increase in all housing prices in the San Jose metropolitan area during the 1970s.[55] Though this problem is nationwide, it has been especially acute in this area because of the explosive growth of industrial employment in Santa Clara County, in particular the North County. More and more people work in the county and would also like to reside there, creating a tremendous demand for all types of housing. As a result, the issue of low and moderate income housing is no longer based on historical prejudices about the very poor and minorities. The issue in Santa Clara County is the provision of housing for those people, plus housing for a great many middle class, blue collar and white collar workers.

As a suburban example, the cost of owning a home in Sunnyvale increased dramatically. The federal census reported the median value of an owner-occupied unit at $17,300 in 1960 and $29,200 in 1970.[56] In 1979 it was reported that the median price of a Sunnyvale home was $91,976.[57] These figures represent an increase in cost of 215 percent from 1970 to 1979 for owner-occupied homes in Sunnyvale.

Demand for existing housing can best be measured by the vacancy rate. A 1979 survey estimated a 1 percent vacancy rate for single family dwellings.[58] This represents a high demand; a 5 percent vacancy rate is considered healthy.

From 1970 to 1979 income in Sunnyvale increased by 56 percent, while the cost of housing rose by 215 percent.[59] Less than 15 percent of the people who live in Sunnyvale could afford to purchase a home there today, if one employs the typical rules of thumb of 10 percent down, monthly payments at 1 percent of the remaining mortgage, and four times the gross annual income as an affordable housing expenditure.[60] Even under the new rules of thumb of 20 percent down and 3.5 times the gross annual income as an affordable expenditure, most Sunnyvale home-owners could not purchase there now, as shown in Table 5.4.

Of 4,771 low income owner-occupied households in 1975, 3,263 had affordable housing costs. This situation existed largely because these owners purchased their homes in the 1940s and 1950s. Although their incomes were low, their housing costs were also low. Typically, these owners can not afford to rent or to move, and thus have remained in their homes. However, when the house is sold, it will be at the market rate, and thus not be in the affordable range for most families. Thus, it is difficult to estimate how many owner-occupied units in Sunnyvale are truly affordable to low and moderate income residents. The reported housing costs today would not remain constant if such units were sold.

Overpayment has traditionally been said to occur when a family pays more than 25 percent of its gross income for housing. The best data on overpayment are in the *1975 Special Census of Santa Clara County.* Although the information is obsolete, given current market conditions, the problem of overpayment has undoubtedly increased. Of all homeowners in 1975, 17 percent (2,192 households) paid more than 25 percent of their income toward housing. Of this group 69 percent (1,508) were in the category of low to moderate income.

The 1960 and 1970 U.S. censuses reported median rents of $107 and $150, respectively, in Sunnyvale, demonstrating a 41 percent increase in 10 years. However, a phone survey taken in June 1979 of 76 apartment complexes representing 9,305 units revealed that the average rent was $317, an increase of 111 percent over 1970.[61]

Demand for apartments can best be measured by vacancy rates. Apartment vacancy rates declined from a high of 13.0 percent in 1971 to 3.1 percent in 1976. Current estimates are 1 percent countywide and 0.3 percent for Sunnyvale.[62] As is the case with home purchasing, a 5 percent vacancy rate constitutes a competitive rental market.

Although the 111 percent increase in rents is less than the 215 percent increase in ownership costs, it is still substantial when compared with incomes, which increased only 56 percent during the same period. Also, the renter population is composed of relatively more low income persons, including persons on fixed incomes.

In 1975, 37 percent of renter-occupied households in Sunnyvale paid more than 25 percent of their income for rent.[63] Of these, 94 percent (3,327 households) were low income. This is twice the percentage of owners who overpaid. It is unknown how many renter households overpaid in 1979, since rents can vary widely in the same complex, depending upon when a tenant moved in. Similarly, it is unknown how many people wanted to live in Sunnyvale but could not afford to rent

Table 5.4 Affordability of Sunnyvale Housing: 1965–79

Item	1965	1975	1979
Price	$23,800	$45,700	$91,979
Monthly mortgage payment of 1% after 20% down payment	$ 190	$ 366	$ 736
Gross annual income required if "3½ rule" met	$ 6,909	$13,309	$26,764
Percentage of Sunnyvale resident households that could purchase a home	88%	53%	20-25%

Source: Sunnyvale, 1979–1982 Application for Community Development Block Grant Funds (1979); Sunnyvale, Housing and Community Sub-Element (March 1980).

there or had to move because rents became too high. Nonetheless, a 1979 housing survey indicated that none of the rentals surveyed would be affordable to a prospective household living on Social Security.[64] Only at maximum occupancy (for example, four people in a two bedroom unit) would the average rents be affordable to a low income household. Since most apartments are not rented at maximum occupancy, it is estimated that at the very most, 25 percent of all unassisted rental units would be affordable in 1979 to new low and moderate income households.

By 1985, 7,078 more units should become affordable to low and moderate income households if the city is to meet its HUD-ABAG allotted "fair share."[65] These housing needs are not typically met by the market and thus, in the state's view, are the responsibility of each jurisdiction. A good faith effort is expected toward meeting the "fair share" allocation. but since the residential buildout figure of the city, even at increased densities, would provide only 4,987 new units,[66] and since not even the majority of these could be low and moderate income, this figure is not likely to be attained. Certainly, city action alone could not attain it.

In addition to the 590 subsidized low cost units, Section 8 rental assistance is currently being used by an estimated 120 families in Sunnyvale.[67] Thus, an estimated 710 families are receiving some kind of housing assistance.

Section 8 new construction funds are being used in Sunnyvale for four planned projects. One, containing 40 assisted units for families, is scheduled for 1981 completion. The other three are planned to contain 70 units of assisted family housing and 100 units of assisted elderly housing. Sunnyvale's goal is 1,350 units available for lower income households by 1982, as set forth in its 1979–82 application for CDBG funds from HUD[68] (see Table 5.5). Some increase in Section 8 rental assistance may also be hoped for.

However, assistance needs in Sunnyvale are clearly far greater than this. Table 5.5 shows that in 1975, the number of households eligible for assistance was 10,237. Of these, 669 (7 percent) were actually receiving assistance. No current figures measuring need exist, but between 12,000 and 15,000 is a conservative estimate of the number of eligible households. Thus, even if its 1982 goals are met, Sunnyvale's assisted households will still equal only 10–12 percent of its needy households.

The town of Los Gatos, a small, generally affluent community with a relatively high proportion of elderly citizens (14.7 percent), sees the housing problem in terms of the needs of its own residents.[69] The town's housing market is not as well balanced as would be desired. It has a considerable number of high income housing units and, at the other end of the spectrum, a very low income population who cannot keep up with housing prices.[70] Although Los Gatos' main objective is to provide housing for residents of all income levels,[71] many residents are being

Table 5.5 Sunnyvale Housing Assistance Needs and Goals: 1982

Housing Category	Number of Housing Units
Eligible for rental assistance:	10,237 (1975)
Receiving assistance:	669 (7%)
Estimated eligible in 1980	12,000–15,000
Receiving assistance in 1980	710
1982 goals (CDBG application):	
Assistance for construction of new homes:	23
Assistance for construction of new apartments:	
(210 are planned for 1980)	405
Rehabilitation of homes:	330
Rehabilitation of apartments:	108
Existing units:	484
Total	1,350
Estimated 1982 Section 8 rental assistance:	125
Total	1,475

Source: Sunnyvale, 1979–1982 Application for Community Development Block Grant Funds (1979); Sunnyvale, Housing and Community Revitalization Sub-Element (March 1980).

forced to leave the community because of the high cost of existing housing.

Most of the senior citizens in Los Gatos are on fixed incomes, and many of them have sold their homes and are renting apartments. As rents increase, they are not able to meet housing costs.[72] Senior citizens who have not sold their homes live in older houses, and are often unable to afford the increasing costs of repairs, maintenance, and taxes.[73]

In 1970 the population of senior citizens was 2,672; of them 452 had incomes below the poverty level.[74] Inflation is increasing the number of seniors who are in need.

The 1980 HAP for Los Gatos states that 45.3 percent of all seniors in Los Gatos are in need of housing assistance.[75] Even though the HAP shows that 51.4 percent of small families (with four or fewer persons) require housing assistance in Los Gatos, the community's concern is focused on the elderly, who constitute one of the most vocal sectors of the electorate, and only very marginally on the needs of low income households in general.[76]

At the same time Los Gatos, like Sunnyvale, has a very limited amount of land available for residential development. Only small, very expensive parcels remain and, in the absence of large subsidies, are not likely to add to the supply of low cost housing.[77]

Milpitas developed as a middle income, blue collar residential community, with a large percentage of young families. During its early and middle development phases (mid-1950s through the early 1970s), Milpitas was a leader among the South Bay area communities in providing housing, both assisted and unassisted, that was affordable to low and moderate income households.[78] In accordance with the family-oriented character that has been established in the city, due partly to its location outside the primary urban employment and service centers, the majority of those units were owner-occupied, including both low density, single family homes and high density townhouses and condominiums. Furthermore, Milpitas is still one of the submarkets of the San Jose metropolitan area with the lowest housing prices.[79]

The city is entering its last residential growth stage, infilling large and small areas encircled by existing developments. As housing prices continue to rise countywide, developers have been able to sell more expensive housing in Milpitas, a community that traditionally has had some of the least expensive housing in the county. In 1980 new, single family housing units in the city ranged from $74,000 to $134,000, and were beyond the reach of most low income families.[80] Yet, because Milpitas has allowed a relatively high level of assisted housing in the past, it does not see itself as having a low income housing problem. As one planning staff member put it: "Milpitas does not have any problem on the subject of low and moderate housing because as the statistics show, Milpitas is a community with a high proportion of medium income population and more houses than jobs are provided."[81]

The South County cities of Morgan Hill and Gilroy still have substantial acreage of relatively moderately priced, potentially developable land. For this reason these cities are often viewed as the housing reserve for the San Jose metropolitan area, especially for low income families.[82] Yet, most of the new housing built in Morgan Hill and Gilroy, as in the rest of Santa Clara County, is targeted for a select market. In Morgan Hill " . . . the increase in residential units are weighted heavily in favor of moderately expensive to expensive single family homes. This makes it more difficult to achieve the goals set by the Housing Element of the General Plan."[83] According to Morgan Hill City Council member Beth Wyman, most of the recent residential building permits being processed are for the construction of higher priced homes.

Gilroy is also concerned about this housing problem. As stated in its *General Plan:*

> . . . currently, new development . . . not only caters to a relatively narrow range of family characteristics and life styles, it also caters to a narrow range of income levels. If the community goal of a pleasant living environment offering all residents freedom of choice with respect to location, house types, and housing cost is to be realized, a variety of public and private efforts will be required to address the housing needs of Gilroys's residents.[84]

Data since 1977 indicate that an even greater percentage of current home buyers in the South County had more than one income or were previous homeowners with past earned equity.[85] These trends suggest that the prospect of future home ownership will be limited to the affluent, or to those who have managed to buy a first house and thereby capitalized on the rapidly increasing home values.

In Morgan Hill, of the 1,471 households responding to the income question in the 1975 Santa Clara County Special Census, 52 percent of the renter households identified as very low or low income[86] were paying more than 25 percent of gross income for shelter.[87] For owner households identified as very low or low income, 58 percent were overpaying for shelter.[88] In total, 40 percent of all renter-occupied households and 24 percent of all owner-occupied households were overpaying.[89]

In Gilroy, 37 percent of all renter-occupied households and 14 percent all owner-occupied households were paying more than 25 percent of their gross monthly income for shelter in 1975.[90]

The *1975 Special Census*[91] identified the number of low income households needing housing assistance. Households were considered to need assistance if their shelter costs were greater than 25 percent of gross monthly income, or they lived in deteriorated housing conditions, or they were overcrowded (more than 1.01 persons per room). For Morgan Hill and Gilroy the number of households requiring assistance were 1,306 and 1,372, respectively—a number far exceeding the resources available to help such households.[92]

Solution: The suburban cities believe there is little they can do to solve the metropolis-wide housing problem. Although they developed in different ways, they each express a desire to preserve a status quo, not to change the basic character that has evolved in their communities.[93]

Sunnyvale officials would like to take a leadership role in addressing Santa Clara County's housing problems, including those of low and moderate income families. One example of this was the four month moratorium on new industrial development that was adopted in December 1979.[94] Before the moratorium expired, the city rezoned almost half of its industrial-designated vacant land to residential. Another example is the new "Housing Element" of the Sunnyvale General Plan, adopted in March 1980.[95] This element sets forth strong, coordinated policies for improving both the supply and the affordability of housing.

The policies include many of the innovative strategies being discussed throughout the county, such as land banking, the use of CDBG monies for land acquisition, inclusionary zoning to implement a below market rate (BMR) housing policy, retention of BMR prices by deed restrictions and contracts, tax exempt revenue bonds to provide low interest mortgage money to eligible households, and the option of forming a nonprofit housing development corporation.

Sunnyvale officials also feel that the city must work in cooperation with private developers and landlords to assist low and moderate income households.[96] The "Housing Element" includes specific policies directed at the education of and cooperative work with private interests to bring about some relief in housing costs.

On the other hand, Sunnyvale officials believe that they must recognize certain constraints in planning for change. They cite the fact that their "fair share" allotment of 7,028 units exceeds the residential buildout capacity of the city, even with a moderate increase in allowed densities.[97] Even if all new units were built for low and moderate income families, this figure could not be reached.

They also recognize the community's general desires regarding the character of Sunnyvale. They assume the following:[98]

a. That the citizens of Sunnyvale desire to maintain the existing character of the city, with a reasonable modification to density or intensity of use
b. That there are environmental and fiscal, as well as social, constraints that limit and control the ultimate living and working environments in Sunnyvale
c. That Sunnyvale cannot totally balance jobs and housing if the above assumptions are valid
d. That housing is a regional problem requiring cooperation beyond Sunnyvale's borders.

In other words, though they are willing and able to tackle the problem of low and moderate income housing through diverse strategies, they do not expect to be able to solve it. At most, one-tenth of the need for assisted housing can probably be met through directly assisted units, and the success of efforts to induce more private landlords and developers to keep costs low, perhaps through use of various subsidy and assistance programs, is unknown.

The Town of Los Gatos is also trying to increase the supply of low and moderate cost housing. For example, in 1979 the town adopted a home ownership BMR program similar to the one in Palo Alto. The program requires that all developers who want to build 10 or more units have to provide 10 percent of the units at a below market price to moderate income families.[99] The price of the BMR program units is controlled for the first buyer and for future buyers. The initial price is limited to rules set by the City Council.[100] In essence, the BMR buyer pays for the construction and financing cost.

In addition, the town is involved in other programs to provide low cost housing, such as land banking to provide low cost housing sites, low interest loans for housing conservation, mobile home repair grants, and energy grants.[101] However, these policies and programs largely address the specific needs of senior citizens.[102] The "Housing Element" states: "Solving the housing problems of very low income . . . and low income (50–80 percent of the median) families is the responsibility of the state or federal government."[103]

While Los Gatos and Sunnyvale must constrain development because they have little land left, Milpitas hopes to encourage commercial and industrial development, as well as relatively high priced housing.[104] Since many of the housing units built in Milpitas during the past were low and moderately priced, Milpitas believes it has already met its metropolis-wide housing responsibilities. It feels that in its present infilling stage, it should provide medium and high priced housing to achieve a balance, and should limit the amount of subsidized housing.[105]

Morgan Hill and Gilroy have substantial land for residential growth but, like Milpitas, they do not feel they can or should solve the North County's industrial growth problems.[106] Morgan Hill has already passed a growth control ordinance, Measure E, that aims to limit population growth to 30,000 by the year 2000.[107] Guidelines state that 40 percent of the units approved must be affordable to low and moderate income households.[108] Gilroy has adopted a similar growth management policy.[109] However, growth control forces market prices to increase as housing shortages continue. Thus, while South County would have the greatest potential for solving the housing shortage problem, the policy of these cities is to promote a mix of housing prices, and to care for their communities, not to serve as a safety valve for the rest of the county's problems.

It appears that the suburban cities see their metropolitan role as providers of primarily middle and upper middle income housing, as opposed to low income housing, which requires heavy subsidies and generates local citizen opposition.

Low Cost Housing Advocacy Perspective (Community Housing Developers, Housing Services Center, Mexican American Community Services Agency, the Mid-Peninsula Coalition Housing Fund, and the South Santa Clara County Housing Development Corporation)

Problem: Although private, nonprofit organizations offer different functions in dealing with the problem, they all share a deep social commitment to pursue every avenue to ameliorate housing deficiencies for low income groups. In their view the major housing problem in the San Jose metropolitan area is that there is a severe housing shortage due to the housing/jobs imbalance that has been developing in Santa Clara County.[110]

The housing shortage has serious economic and social consequences for low income families, since it has manifested itself most obviously in housing price increases. As mentioned earlier, during the 1975–80 period the average price of an existing single family home in the San Jose metropolitan area increased from $44,760 to $127,960 (186 percent). (See Table 5.2.) There are many areas throughout the county with an even higher average price—for example, Los Gatos, with an average sales price in 1980 of about $196,300.[111]

In the rental housing market the housing shortage is even more critical. During 1980 the San Jose metropolitan area had an average vacancy rate of 1 percent, and had an average rental price for a one bedroom apartment of between $350 and $400 per month.[112] Unfortunately, because of the economic climate, and to a lesser extent the political climate and fear of rent control, only 11,000 new rental units were constructed in the county between 1975 and 1980.[113] Of the 146,000 rental units in the county, 3,500 (about 2 percent) have fallen victim to condominium conversion.[114] The exorbitant price of the scarce rental units, combined with the exclusion of children from over 70 percent of the rental units in the county, make the housing situation extremely critical for people on fixed incomes, young families with children, and lower income members of the community.

In 1979–80 the combined HAPs for all the cities in Santa Clara County identified 72,800 low income households as needing housing assistance.[115] Yet, there are few resources available to aid these households. As was reported about the Santa Clara County Housing Authority in the *San Jose Mercury* (April 1980):

> . . . Last November the Housing Authority closed its doors. There was a crush of applicants and a dwindling supply of housing the Authority could afford . . . [it] simply stopped taking applications until it could catch up with its backlog, at the time close to 1,500 cases . . . .[116]

During this time there were only about 400 subsidized senior citizen housing units being constructed in the county, and no units for low income families.[117]

Low cost housing advocacy groups and private development corporations encounter problems in trying to deal with governmental bureaucracy.[118] HUD approvals take so long that they have detrimental consequences for those to be housed and for the developer. Development corporations find themselves in the double bind of trying to deal with HUD's dispersion goals.[119] While HUD won't disburse any money for impacted areas, corporations cannot afford land in areas that are not impacted, and prices in such areas usually exceed HUD's limits on land acquisition costs.

The South County Development Corporation has to deal with the county bureaucracy, which requires that options on land be totally refundable. However, sellers are not willing to operate within this mode.[120] Midcounty corporations find scarce land and zoning requirements to be major problems, because of low density goals that preclude the economic feasibility of low cost housing.

The Housing Services Center and Mexican American Community Services Agency (MACSA) feel that the major obstacle to the provision of low and moderate income housing is the lack of commitment on the part of both the City of San Jose and the county in developing programs or providing funds to achieve this end.[121] Philosophically, San Jose and the county espouse this goal, but in practical terms they have committed few resources to alleviating the shortage of low and moderate income housing.

Thus, the most salient housing problems perceived by these actors are the financial constraints of the local and national economic situation, the levels of bureaucracy involved in setting up programs, and the perceived selfishness and ignorance of community and neighborhood residents in rejecting low cost housing.

Solution: The housing advocates see the housing shortage as being so critical for low and moderate income families that they are willing to sacrifice locational goals of dispersion as long as they can help provide safe and affordable housing to needy families.[122]

Housing advocates feel that they have the potential ability to educate people, familiarizing them with successful projects so that they will become more open to accepting assistance in their community.[123] They feel that they can raise the consciousness of policymakers and increase community involvement in this issue. For example, Community Housing Developers is actively pursuing an educational program to combat the stereotypes of low and moderate income housing.[124] Workshops and presentations have been conducted for community organizations and an educational brochure has been designed. Outreach programs are also planned for neighborhoods where future projects are proposed. By contacting the residents prior to the project design stage, each housing group can hear their concerns regarding a proposed project and can respond by providing information or by orienting the project design to address those concerns.

The Housing Services Center and MACSA believe that the City of San Jose, Santa Clara County, and private industry should aid in the development of low and moderate income housing, and that local government in particular should devise appropriate means for assisting in that effort.[125] They feel that the county has a stronger commitment to the development of low cost housing than do many cities in the San Jose metropolitan area, as demonstrated by its advocacy of land banking and of density bonuses to developers who are willing to make units available to persons of low and moderate income. Efforts that the advocates feel could be undertaken by the city to help alleviate the situation include, but are not limited to, the use of land banking, the approval of high density residential development for low cost housing, the creation of a bond whose revenue would be used for the development of low and moderate income housing, incentives for developers to construct such units through the underwriting of financing costs or the cost of interest, the levying of a tax on certain types of construction that could be used to create a fund for financing low and moderate income housing.

The housing advocates also believe that there should be more effort expended in developing self-help housing programs. In this respect the Housing Services Center plans to expand its efforts into assisting in the development of housing cooperatives.[126] It is already involved with one such project on Story Road, where it is helping the tenants to organize a tenants' union and is providing them with information on how to finance home ownership. It is the opinion of the center's director that cooperative purchases of housing will grow as the price of housing continues to escalate.[127] In his estimation the efforts of private citizens to provide for their housing needs through self-help programs, such as private rehabilitation efforts, will be far more effective than governmental programs. The role of government, as he sees it, is in creating policies that are supportive of private developers and nonprofit organizations that wish to build low and moderate income housing, in providing funding, and in conducting research and gathering data related to housing. He feels that the government should not have an ownership role when it comes to providing low and moderate income housing. In his opinion home ownership is best left in the hands of those people directly impacted by such housing programs.

The low cost housing advocates would like to work in cooperation with community groups. For example, some of the housing advocates believe that religious institutions would be likely partners in housing development, because in many cases they have excess land that could serve as suitable sites.[128] Land acquisition in such situations would not be a major obstacle to overcome in order for a project to succeed. In addition, the site would probably be located in the same neighborhood as the religious institution, so that a positive relationship would have been formed with the nearby residents. This existing relationship could contribute significantly to the eventual neighborhood acceptance and support of the project.

In sum, the housing advocates are trying to maximize housing opportunities for low and moderate income families through a variety of styles and innovative techniques.

The Private Sector (San Jose Real Estate Board, Santa Clara County Manufacturing Group, and the San Jose Chamber of Commerce)

Problem: For a growing number of Californians, the American dream of owning a home has become a nightmare, as rising prices have driven the cost of home ownership well beyond the reach of more and more potential buyers.[129] In the San Jose metropolitan area the situation is especially severe, with the average price of homes being pushed well beyond the $100,000 mark—substantially above the national average.

This inflationary spiral, combined with current interest rates, has had a particularly significant effect on low and middle income buyers, who often find themselves unable to afford even the most modest single family housing. In fact, of the new families formed in the Bay Area during 1980, experts predict that fewer than 20 percent will be able to afford a conventional single family house.[130]

One of the consequences of excess demand is that property values escalate at a rate that is inflationary in and by itself. Buyers seem to be willing to pay almost any price for a piece of property. In addition, many executives in the electronics manufacturing industries are concerned that if housing conditions continue to deteriorate, then, given the corresponding diseconomies of traffic congestion, air pollution, and higher operational costs, they may be forced to move their entire operations to another city or state.

The ever increasing job market in the Bay Area has placed a high demand for housing on the San Jose metropolitan area. The demand for new housing is beyond the ability of San Jose area developers to provide. Even the prices for the most modest homes are escalating rapidly. Material and labor costs have kept pace with inflation, which requires a continued reevaluation of housing costs. Land costs are such that it has become fiscally impossible to meet any segment of demand except high income demand. Because the high income housing market remains steady, developers have had little choice but to build for the affluent.

Additional pressure on the housing market in Santa Clara County has been created by family breakup. The high divorce rate in the county has created a need for two homes for one former family. The abundance of employment opportunities, including nonskilled jobs, has created an atmosphere of hope, so that even though housing is scarce, people have remained in the area. The high cost of housing stock in the county has mandated that low and moderate income families remain in the older, central districts.

The HUD sections 235 (low income home ownership program) and 236 (low income rental program) of the 1968 Housing and Urban Development Act have not been keeping pace with housing needs.[131] Section 8 funds authorized by the Housing Act of 1974 are turned back by local communities every year because of the negative general concept of assisted housing. Consequently, federal subsidized housing has not been successful in meeting low and moderate cost housing needs.[132]

The only developers in the Santa Clara County area still able to sell their products are, except in rare cases, builders with low priced homes that qualify for government mortgage programs, and large firms that have previous commitments for low interest conventional loans that they can pass on to the buyers.[133] The two federal mortgage programs help buyers in the below $100,000 price range. In 1980 the Federal Housing Administration loaned up to $100,000 at 14 percent, and the Veterans Administration loaned up to $67,000 at the same rate of interest to qualified veterans. These programs might provide an opportunity for the moderate income buyer if prices begin to fall.[134]

Government programs such as the HUD 235 (mentioned above) and HUD 234 (mortgage insurance for purchase of condominiums) may provide the only other work for builders of low and moderate cost housing. Consequently, this economic crisis may result in more time and attention being given to low and moderate income housing. Normally the amount of bureaucratic red tape necessary to complete a government program negates the profit gained. However, it it is the only option available, there should be an abundance of contractors and developers willing to operate within these constraints.[135]

In general, private industry perceives overregulation at every level of government as increasing expenses and making the cost of housing prohibitive.[136] Unnecessary environmental regulations, strict building code requirements, large lot zoning, and maximum density regulations are cited as examples of these types of barriers.

Solution: Government housing is not a solution; management is seldom professional, and regulations such as means of eviction create a less than desirable atmosphere.[137] Low and moderate cost housing should be inclusionary in nature. Placing people in government complexes has not worked in the past, and will not work in the future. If an individual is given the opportunity to live in a positive environment, he or she will be more likely to fit in with that environment.

One technique being used to make home ownership once again obtainable is condominium conversion, in which apartments are renovated and sold as condominiums.[138] The converted apartment avoids many of the costly factors affecting new construction, such as land shortages, inflated labor and materials cost, downzoning, extended government delays and costs, and major environmental regulations.

The buyer profile for condominium conversions covers a broad social and economic spectrum. Young singles and families turn to condominiums as a first step toward ownership of a single family house, while retirees use them as a way to stabilize housing costs against perpetual rent increases.

From a city or county standpoint, converted units generally supply more than twice the property tax value that they did as rentals, with no additional costs to government. With all these factors in their favor, one would think that conversions would be welcomed. Instead, they have met with serious opposition because renters are often displaced. To avoid such controversy, price discounts, usually 5 to 10 percent below the public price, are offered to previous tenants. Where possible, low interest loans are also arranged.

The future of condominium conversions depends upon the incentives provided for the construction of new rental housing. What is needed is a way to make the construction and operation of rental housing profitable again.

Moderate and low cost housing has to be provided so that new entrants to the job market have an opportunity to live where they desire. Inclusionary zoning, government programs, and land banking are all possible solutions. The main objective should be to allow a feasible means of home ownership that provides a profit incentive for the builder and the lender.[139] Condominiums and low interest loans appear viable.

Air pollution and energy consumption continue to rise because employment centers in North County do not have a sufficient number of available housing units. Therefore, as much residentially suitable land as possible in the North County that is zoned industrial should be rezoned to permit residential use.[140]

Except in some special cases, it is still most often the city or county government that decides the design and location of new housing developments. Today realtors, bankers, and builders view government as presenting a variety of building codes, creating layers of land use regulations, condemning older homes, and questioning traditional cost-benefit relationships in new construction. In addition, processing time for government programs has often been prohibitively expensive.

The local governments must assume a strong leadership role to deal with the housing crisis. Local government plans should develop criteria for selecting growth and no-growth areas, and should clearly identify areas designated for residential growth.[141] This process will have to consider the natural, social, and economic conditions in each area, and will have to take into account the needs for a mix of ages, social and cultural groups, and income levels.[142] In addition, the private sector must be given incentives to rehabilitate and develop the inner cities. The following solutions are recommended by the private sector representatives:[143]

a. Develop and finance a land banking program.
b. Expand supply of residential land by increasing urban service areas.
c. Enforce an ordinance to ensure that a percentage of all new housing units is affordable to low and moderate income families. There is not enough housing available to satisfy the demand generated by persons with low and moderate incomes, and for those somewhat above this

level. In present housing markets, developers can make larger profits by providing housing for the more affluent segment of the population. In view of land shortages and other constraints, there is no pressure from competition to motivate them to respond to the needs of the less affluent. General Plan housing elements and zoning regulations should be amended to provide that any development of a certain size must include a certain percentage of low cost units.

d. Enact an ordinance to permit the development of alternative methods to reduce housing costs. Innovative housing programs have been instituted elsewhere to provide housing opportunities for those people too poor to afford housing at current market values, but too affluent to qualify for subsidy programs. A special ordinance to waive fees and certain zoning and building requirements, the utilization of land banking programs, and other requirements could support this program. Developers are willing to build "basic shelter" homes if they feel that people will purchase them.

e. Streamline the housing approval process. Among the housing projects that should be given priority in processing are those that provide needed, affordable housing, including greater density in existing residential areas.

f. Bring commercial and industrial activities into the City of San Jose. If carried out, this would significantly address the imbalance between housing and jobs. This should reduce the land cost of new housing and shorten the job commute. Ultimately, by aiming toward equilibrium between housing supply and demand, housing rents and prices should level off.

g. Cities must decide if they honestly wish to provide low and moderate cost housing. While they all realize that there is a problem, each community tends to feel that another area should take responsibility. Until local governments decide that they are going to become involved, the private sector can do little to support their efforts.

The implications of the proposed solutions are twofold: first, they can remain profit oriented while still meeting an important community need; second, the costs to the taxpayer are kept to a minimum.

The only solution requiring more than local support is the land banking suggestion. However, it is interesting to note that the targeted funds are discretionary, and already allocated. In essence, no new expenditures are required. This is politically wise, and helps to combat the current economic crisis. Land banking by the county would also afford the opportunity for meeting open space objectives.

New commercial and industrial development will help broaden the tax base, thereby reducing service costs. Combined with the reduction of community expenses, it will have a positive impact on low and midcost living expenses.

The profit motivation provided by incentives for innovative building methods should generate more housing opportunities.[144] This should satisfy the developer and, at the same time, meet a community need. The same can be said for streamlining the housing approval process.

It must be remembered that profit has to occur to justify private sector involvement in the present housing shortage.[145] The developer, contractor, banker, and realtor provide the jobs that in turn provide the salaries that enable as many people as possible to afford housing. The result of ignoring that profit would be to put even more people in need of subsidized housing. However, by providing incentives for construction, more jobs are created and fewer families require housing assistance. This is politically wise, and economically and socially acceptable.

The prevailing viewpoint among most of the corporate executives in Santa Clara County is that they do not belong in the home building business.[146] When they assume this position, they are often asked what will happen to the viability of their firms if they can't attract needed workers because housing prices in the county are too high. They are also asked if it would not be better for them to take actions such as limiting industrial expansion, so that fewer new workers are attracted to this area, thereby lessening the competition for an extremely limited supply of housing. The fact is that corporate executives realize that if present housing trends continue, the viability of their firms will be threatened. This is demonstrated by their investments of time and resources in such projects as the Industry and Housing Management Task Force.[147] However, these same executives feel that local and state governments should take the initiative in leading us out of the present housing crisis, mentioning that government officials are being paid to do this.[148] They believe that as long as local cities subject developers to unnecessary environmental regulations, strict building code requirements, and large lot size zoning ordinances, there will be a housing crisis. They are willing to help solve the housing crisis in the county, but they want to feel that the local cities are doing everything possible to provide more housing opportunities for people with modest incomes. At present they do not believe the cities in the county are making that effort.[149]

SUMMARY

It is apparent that there was a considerable similarity of views among the various groups and organizations. Our most important finding was that all of the actors seemed to share a common perspective about the nature and urgency of the problem. It was also instructive to learn of a general attitude of innocence about the problem held by each of the actors. Consequently, the perspectives conveyed by our advocate planners tended to blame someone else at every level, and to assign responsibilities to others.

The benefit of the multiple advocacy process seemed to come from the real world actors' recognition of this situation. It helped to sensitize them to the concerns and objectives of the other groups. For example, it was very constructive to have the view of the private sector represented since it has the economic potential of really making some changes that will help resolve the housing problem. While a representative of the real estate industry pointed out that it is not profitable for builders to produce publicly assisted housing, a planner from the City of San Jose indicated that many developers are finding it profitable to specialize in assisted housing. This is particularly the case for large scale developers who create a specialized unit within their market to address this need.

More of the actors amplified and clarified their positions, and were able to obtain a better understanding of the concerns of others. For example, while the view was expressed that private industry has had difficulty finding a profitable way to enter the low income housing market, it was also pointed out that in the future many more private developers may be willing to participate in the low cost housing market because of decreasing sales in conventional housing markets. This may point to the need for educating the private sector to opportunities made available by state and federal subsidies.

While the actors had similar perspectives about the nature of the low cost housing problem, they had a wide spectrum of views about solutions, ranging from massive national government subsidies to reliance on changes in local housing markets. Of all the actors considered, the low income housing advocacy groups had the strongest ideological commitment to solving the problem. Perhaps the City of San Jose was the governmental entity most willing to accept its responsibility for dealing with the situation, since it had the largest low income family constituency. ABAG was theoretically committed, but appeared to be too far removed from the problem and had very limited authority to deal with it effectively. Although concerned about the problem, the suburban communities and the private sector believed that little could be done to improve the situation in the absence of substantial low cost housing market changes.

Despite these differences, some common themes emerged with regard to solutions. One is the need to make low cost housing more financially viable. An integral part of this effort is to reduce the red tape and bureaucratic procedures involved in obtaining approval for low cost housing.

The need to redefine government's commitment to alleviating the housing problem was also strongly expressed. This applies to all levels of government, and also implies that there must be some coordination between entities. Thus, it should be profitable to build low cost housing in any city, and not just in outlying or impacted areas. This brings us to the need for some control or increased power to be relegated to a regional agency. ABAG or some other entity should have the ability to induce cities to accept their "fair share" allocations. An example is a proposed low income project in Los Gatos, where HUD was able to persuade local officials to consider mostly family units instead of a project exclusively for the elderly.[150] In addition, regional guidance could help alleviate the metropolis-wide jobs/housing imbalance.

Yet, it appeared from the suburban viewpoint that outlying cities are very unwilling to relinquish their prerogatives, and that the viability of such a regional approach is highly questionable. Though each city and area has a different perspective, the effect of the various outlooks appears to be basically the same: low and moderate income housing units will not increase in any substantial way. The increase of housing supply that can be expected will probably be aimed more at middle income families, for whom a small decrease in cost can mean a lot, than at the lower end of the income spectrum, where heavy subsidies are necessary for each unit.

This finding is not really unexpected. Much of the recent discussion of the county jobs/housing imbalance has revolved around the fact that demand for housing will not decrease until industrial employment in the San Jose metropolitan area decreases. Though some steps in this direction have been made, such as Sunnyvale's recent moratorium on industrial growth, restrictions on economic development have both good and bad aspects, and must be approached with care.

Organized pressure against further industrial development is growing, however. Some groups are reaching the conclusion that in terms of pollution, effects on the environment, and overall quality of life, the county is close to buildout.[151] These pressures are reflected in city viewpoints, and suggest that in the absence of new public subsidies for low cost housing, the supply of all housing, including but not limited to low and moderate income housing, will probably increase much more slowly in the future.

The regional character of the problem may bring about more cooperative efforts by all the cities in the San Jose metropolitan area. However, the suburbs will probably strive for tight control of their environments in order to maintain the physical and social conditions they have. As more and more low income people move out (or never move in), high income residents are likely to strive to keep their cities as they prefer them. This usually means low in density and high in average income. City

Council members may be under increasing pressure to bow to these interests or lose the next election, as is the nature of the democratic process. But as the metropolitan population becomes more homogeneous, suburban city viewpoints are also likely to become more similar.

Another important focus of the strategies discussed, involved educating communities to accept low income housing. Developers also need to know more about programs that are available.

Finally, there seems to be a basic need for coordination in finding a solution to the housing problem in the San Jose metropolitan area. By pooling their limited resources, both public and private agencies may be able to maximize the efficiency of their operations. By being receptive to each other's concerns, the region could begin to address the issue of providing low and moderate cost housing. In the end our metropolitan society must ask itself to what extent it is willing to commit its resources for the benefit of its least fortunate members.

NOTES

1. Santa Clara County Industry and Housing Task Force, *Living Within Our Limits: A Framework for Action in the 1980's* (November 1979); Santa Clara County Planning Department, *Advanced Final Count of 1980* (April 1981).
2. Estimated from data presented in ibid.
3. Scott Lefaver, "Will Success Spoil Santa Clara Valley?" *Planning* 46 (April 1980): 22–25.
4. Interview with Steven McKinney, senior planner, Santa Clara County Planning Department, February 1981.
5. Elias Castillo, "Hunt for Low Income Housing Getting Worse and Worse," *San Jose Mercury News*, April 9, 1980, p. 18; see also records of Century 21 Realtors, San Jose April 1981.
6. Lefaver, p. 22.
7. These views are based on interview with Susanne Wilson, supervisor, Santa Clara County, February 1980; interview with Stephen McKinney, February 1980; interview with Dr. Lester Hunt, Santa Clara County Office of Education, February 1980; interview with Daniel Lopez, housing director, Association of Bay Area Governments, February 1980; California Housing Finance Agency, *Annual Report 1978–79* (September 1979); interviews with Michael Flo, family housing coordinator, and Steven Sachs, community development coordinator, U.S. Department of Housing and Urban Development, April 1980.
8. Association of Bay Area Governments, *Bay Area Housing Opportunity Plan* (October 1979).
9. Interviews with Flo and Sachs.
10. Santa Clara County Industry and Housing Management Task Force, *Living Within Our Limits*.
11. Ibid.
12. Interview with Lopez.
13. Interview with McKinney.
14. Santa Clara County Planning Department, *Draft of the Housing Element Problem*

Statement: A Background Report for the General Plan Revision Project (January 1980, as revised).

15. Ibid.
16. Santa Clara County, *General Plan* (November 1980), p. 34.
17. See, for example, U.S. Department of Housing and Urban Development, *Principal Program Areas* (May 1978); and California Housing Finance Agency, *Annual Report 1978–79.*
18. California Housing Finance Agency, *Annual Report 1978–79.*
19. Interview with Mitchell Sperling, planner, U.S. Department of Housing and Urban Development, May 1980.
20. San Jose, *Community Development Plan and Program: July 1979–June 1982* (October 1979), p. 2.
21. This gives regional institutions such as ABAG the opportunity to comment to the federal government about the regional implications of federal grant proposals made by local governments.
22. See Association of Bay Area Governments, *Phase I of the Regional Housing Element* (1971) and *Bay Area Housing Opportunity Plan.*
23. Santa Clara County Planning Department, *Housing* (February 1980).
24. These views are based on interview with Susanne Wilson, supervisor, Santa Clara County, February 1980; interview with Stephen McKinney, February 1980; interview with Dr. Lester Hunt, Santa Clara County Office of Education, February 1980; interview with Daniel Lopez, housing director, Association of Bay Area Governments, February 1980; California Housing Finance Agency, *Annual Report 1978–79* (September 1979); interviews with Michael Flo, family housing coordinator, and Steven Sachs, community development coordinator, U.S. Department of Housing and Urban Development, April 1980.
25. Ibid.
26. Santa Clara County Planning Department, *Advanced Final Count of 1980;* and San Jose, *Community Development Program.*
27. Richard P. Fishman, ed., *Housing for All under the Law* (Cambridge, Mass.: Ballinger, 1978), ch. 1.
28. Based on interviews with Margaret Cohen, planner, Housing Division, City of San Jose, February 1980; Thomas McEnery, City Councilmember, City of San Jose, February 1980.
29. San Jose, *General Plan,* Housing Appendix (1978), p. H-46.
30. San Jose, *Housing Assistance Plan* (1979).
31. Interviews with Cohen and McEnery.
32. San Jose, *Housing Assistance Plan,* p. 54.
33. Interviews with Cohen and McEnery.
34. Ibid.
35. San Jose, *General Plan.*
36. San Jose, *Housing Assistance Plan.*
37. Ibid.
38. San Jose, *General Plan.*
39. San Jose, *Housing Assistance Plan.*
40. Ibid.
41. Interviews with Cohen and McEnery.
42. Ibid.
43. San Jose, *Housing Assistance Plan.*
44. Interviews with Cohen and McEnery.
45. San Jose, *Housing Assistance Plan.*

46. Interviews with Cohen and McEnery.
47. Ibid.
48. Ibid.
49. Association of Bay Area Governments, *Bay Area Housing Opportunity Plan*.
50. Interview with Gary Schoennauer, director, San Jose Planning Department, June 1981.
51. Interviews with Cohen and McEnery: see also San Jose, *General Plan*, pp. 27–29.
52. Ibid.
53. Association of Bay Area Governments and the Metropolitan Transportation Commission, Joint Policy Committee, *Santa Clara Valley Corridor Evaluation* (March 1979).
54. Interviews with Cohen, McEnery, and Schoennauer.
55. These views are based on Sunnyvale, *Housing and Community Revitalization Sub-Element* (March 1980); interviews with Lee Bowman, director of planning, Town of Los Gatos, and Ruth Cannon, Councilmember, Town of Los Gatos, February 1980; interview with James R. Connolly, deputy city manager, City of Milpitas, March 1980; interview with Beth Wyman, council member, City of Morgan Hill, March 1980; Gilroy, *Residential Development Ordinance* (November 1979).
56. U.S. Department of Commerce, *Census of Housing* (1960, 1970).
57. Records of the San Jose Real Estate Board, June 1981.
58. Santa Clara County, *Postal Vacancy Survey* (1979).
59. Sunnyvale, *1979–1982 Application for Community Development Block Grant Funds* (1979).
60. Ibid.
61. Sunnyvale Planning Department, *Housing Survey* (June 1979).
62. Sunnyvale, *1979–1982 Application for Community Development Block Grant Funds*.
63. Santa Clara County Planning Department, *1975 Special Census of Santa Clara County* (1976).
64. Sunnyvale Planning Department, *Housing Survey*.
65. This is based on the HUD-sponsored ABAG allocation for low and moderate income housing in Bay Area communities. See Association of Bay Area Governments, *Phase I of the Regional Housing Element*; and Sunnyvale, *1979–1982 Application for Community Block Grant Funds*.
66. Ibid.
67. Ibid.
68. Ibid.
69. Interview with Jill Cody, director of community programs, Town of Los Gatos, April 1980.
70. Ibid.
71. Los Gatos, *General Plan*, "Housing Element" (1979), p. 11.
72. Rose Weiss, *Analysis of Affluence in Los Gatos* San Jose, Calif.: Economic and Social Opportunity, Inc., April 1975.
73. Interview with Cody.
74. Ibid.
75. Los Gatos, *Housing Assistance Plans Guidelines: June 1980–83* (1980).
76. For example, the Los Gatos BMR program that requires that 10 percent of the units on a project be for moderate income families gives priority of eligibility to senior citizens.
77. Interviews with Bowman and Cannon.
78. Interview with Connolly.
79. Ibid.

80. Milpitas Planning Department, *Housing Survey* (April 1980).
81. Interview with Stephen M. Burkey, assistant planner, Milpitas Planning Department, March 1980.
82. Interview with Wyman.
83. Morgan Hill, *Background Data Report for the General Plan Update* (November 1979).
84. Gilroy, *General Plan* (November 1979), Residential Environment Chapter.
85. Morgan Hill, *Background Data Report*.
86. As defined by the U.S. Department of Housing and Urban Development, very low income households are those earning less than 50 percent of the county median household income of $15,540 ($7,770) in 1975; low income households are defined as those earning between 50 and 80 percent of the county median household income ($7,770 to $12,432) in 1975. Based on interview with Sperling.
87. Santa Clara County Planning Department, *1975 Special Census of Santa Clara County*.
88. Morgan Hill, *Background Data Report*.
89. Ibid.
90. Santa Clara County Planning Department, *Draft of the Housing Element Problem Statement: A Background Report for the General Plan Revision Project* (April 1979).
91. Santa Clara County Planning Department, *1975 Special Census of Santa Clara County*.
92. Santa Clara County Planning Department, *Draft of the Housing Element Problem Statement*.
93. These views are based on Sunnyvale, *Housing and Community Revitalization Sub-Element* (March 1980); interviews with Lee Bowman, director of planning, Town of Los Gatos, and Ruth Cannon, Councilmember, Town of Los Gatos, February 1980; interview with James R. Connolly, deputy city manager, City of Milpitas, March 1980; interview with Beth Wyman, council member, City of Morgan Hill, March 1980; Gilroy, *Residential Development Ordinance* (November 1979).
94. Sunnyvale City Council, *Moratorium on Addition of New Industry* (December 1979).
95. Sunnyvale, *Housing and Community Revitalization Sub-Element*.
96. Interview with staff, Sunnyvale Planning Department, April 1980.
97. Ibid.
98. Ibid.
99. Los Gatos, *Below Market Rate Program Guidelines* (May 1979).
100. Ibid.
101. Interview with Cody.
102. For example, the BMR program gives priority for eligibility to senior citizens.
103. Los Gatos, *General Plan*, "Housing Element," pp. 11–13.
104. Interview with Connolly.
105. Interview with Burkey.
106. Interview with Wyman.
107. Morgan Hill, "Residential Development Control System," *Municipal Code* (1978), Title 8, ch. 66.
108. Morgan Hill, *General Plan*, "Housing Element," (July 1979).
109. Gilroy, *Residential Development Ordinance* (November 1979; 1980)
110. These views are based on interviews with Rosa Maria Hernandez, executive director, Mexican American Community Services Agency, February and April, 1980; interview with Zoe Lofgren, executive director, Community Housing Developers, February 1980; Manuel J. Sandoval, executive director, Housing Services Center, February 1980; interview with Robert Moulton, executive director, Midpeninsula Coalition

Housing Fund, March 1980; and interview with Olivia Sequin, director, South Santa Clara County Housing Development Corporation, March 1980.

111. Records of the San Jose Real Estate Board, June 1981.

112. Castillo, "Hunt for Low Income Housing Getting Worse and Worse"; and records of Century 21 Realtors.

113. Ibid.

114. Ibid.

115. Interview with McKinney.

116. Castillo, "Hunt for Low Income Housing Getting Worse and Worse."

117. Interview with McKinney.

118. Interviews with Lofgren and Moulton.

119. Ibid.

120. Interview with Sequin.

121. Interviews with Hernandez and Sandoval.

122. These views are based on interviews with Rosa Maria Hernandez, executive director, Mexican American Community Services Agency, February and April, 1980; interview with Zoe Lofgren, executive director, Community Housing Developers, February 1980; Manuel J. Sandoval, executive director, Housing Services Center, February 1980; interview with Robert Moulton, executive director, Midpeninsula Coalition Housing Fund, March 1980; and interview with Olivia Sequin, director, South Santa Clara County Housing Development Corporation, March 1980.

123. Interviews with Lofgren, Moulton, and Sequin.

124. Interview with Lofgren; interview with Linda Smith, acting executive director, Community Housing Developers, April 1980.

125. Interviews with Hernandez and Sandoval.

126. Interview with Sandoval.

127. Ibid.

128. Interviews with Lofgren, Moulton, and Sequin.

129. These views are based on interviews with Robert Johnson, Daniel Mack, Mary O'Leary, and Gary Rogers, San Jose Real Estate Board, February 1980; interview with Kenneth Kidwell, chairman, Eureka Federal Savings and Loan Association, April 1980; San Jose Chamber of Commerce, "Position Paper Criticizing Industry Management Task Force Report, Living Within Our Limits" (January 1980); interviews with staff Santa Clara County Manufacturing Group, April 1980.

130. Bay Area Council, Housing: The Bay Area's Challenge of the '80's (San Francisco: Bay Area Council, December 1980).

131. Interviews with Johnson, Mack, O'Leary, and Rogers.

132. Ibid.

133. Ibid.

134. Interview with Kidwell.

135. Interviews with Johnson, Mack, O'Leary, and Rogers.

136. San Francisco Examiner (September 17, 1978) cited a report by Sanford Goodkin showing that nearly 20 percent of the cost of a new house can be directly attributed to government regulation.

137. These views are based on interviews with Robert Johnson, Daniel Mack, Mary O'Leary, and Gary Rogers, San Jose Real Estate Board, February 1980; interview with Kenneth Kidwell, chairman, Eureka Federal Savings and Loan Association, April 1980; San Jose Chamber of Commerce, "Position Paper Criticizing Industry Management Task Force Report, Living Within Our Limits" (January 1980); interviews with staff Santa Clara County Manufacturing Group, April 1980.

138. Interviews with Johnson, Mack, O'Leary, and Rogers.

139. Ibid.

140. Ibid.

141. Ibid.

142. Ibid; also interviews with Steven G. Speno, executive vice-president Building Industry Association, February and April 1981.

143. Ibid.; and Bay Area Council, *Housing*. Also see Steven G. Speno's testimony on behalf of the private sector, Association of Bay Area Governments, Regional Planning Committee, *Meeting Minutes*, March 11, 1981.

144. Ibid.

145. San Jose Chamber of Commerce, "Position Paper Criticizing Industry Management Task Force Report."

146. Interview with staff, the Santa Clara County Manufacturing Group, April 1980.

147. Santa Clara County Industry and Housing Task Force, *Living Within Our Limits*.

148. Interview with staff, Santa Clara County Manufacturing Group, April 1980.

149. Ibid.

150. Santa Clara County Association of Planning Officers, *Meeting Minutes*, December 3, 1980, p. 4.

151. Santa Clara County Industry and Housing Task Force, *Living Within Our Limits*.

6

SURFACE
TRANSPORTATION FACILITIES

During the past decade the expanding Bay Area economy generated employment opportunities at a substantially faster rate than new housing, and reasonably affordable housing has been located at increasing distances from centers of employment.[1] This widening supply-spatial gap has bid up the cost of housing and resulted in increasing traffic congestion and air pollution in the region.

The San Jose metropolitan area, the fastest growing and most geographically dispersed major urban district of the Bay Area, suffers acutely from this transportation problem. For the past thirty years, most of the electronics-related employment opportunities in the Bay Area have developed in the northern portion of Santa Clara County, near the research centers of Stanford University and NASA, while the bulk of the housing has been provided increasingly in the southern part of the county, where land is most readily available and is relatively less expensive.

Some planning thought was given to this issue during the early 1970s in Santa Clara County, resulting in establishment of a County Transit District with a fleet of 516 buses servicing the metropolitan area.[2] However, it was not until 1976, when the Bay Area's land use and transportation agencies, the Association of Bay Area Governments (ABAG) and the Metropolitan Transportation Commission (MTC), began to collaborate to develop a comprehensive transportation plan for the San Jose metropolitan area, *Santa Clara Valley Corridor Evaluation*, that the issue was taken seriously throughout the county.[3]

Not only did the Bay Area-wide planning institutions raise the level of planning consciousness in the San Jose metropolitan area, but they also managed to have their regional transportation planning proposals accepted with minor revisions in 1979 by the diverse communities and interests comprising Santa Clara County.[4] In the wake of a long series of rejections of ABAG-sponsored plans by county and local governments,[5] ABAG's ability to obtain an almost unqualified acceptance of its plan by a subunit of the Bay Area considered to have values and development patterns substantially different from much of the area, represented a remarkable success. Indeed, because of our tradition of strong local government, few regional planning agencies in the United States have been able to plan for, let alone solve, a major metropolitan problem.[6]

This chapter will examine how a regional view of the urban transportation issue was accepted in a subunit of the region, and will discuss the trade-offs made between regional and local objectives concerning this issue.

ACTORS' VIEWS

Based on preliminary research, the following actors were found to represent the groups and organizations involved in the issue of providing surface transportation facilities in the San Jose metropolitan area:

1. Central city (City of San Jose Planning Department and Public Works Department)
2. Community group representing South San Jose residents who have very long commutes to North County industries and who feel threatened by the location of new light rail facilities (V.E.P. Homeowners Association)
3. Group representing West County suburban residents who commute to other parts of the metropolitan area (Multi-Modal Task Force)
4. Industrial suburb servicing North County industries (city of Sunnyvale)
5. Private organization representing industries located in Santa Clara County (Santa Clara County Manufacturing Group)
6. Business interests (San Jose Chamber of Commerce)
7. Private auto interests (Council for a Balanced Community)
8. Mass transit supporters (Modern Transit Society)
9. Environmental interests (Sierra Club, American Lung Association)
10. Representatives of minorities and low income families (Mexican American Community Services Agency, Confederacion de la Raza)
11. Good government advocates (League of Women Voters).
12. Metropolitan planning agencies for the San Jose area (Santa Clara County Transportation Agency and Planning Department)

13. Bay Area regional planning agencies (Association of Bay Area Governments, Metropolitan Transportation Commission)
14. Federal government (U.S. Department of Transportation).

After interviewing these actors, it becomes clear that a clustering of views existed concerning the surface transportation issue such that seven teams could represent the spectrum of actor's views.

Bay Area and Federal Planning Institutions (Association of Bay Area Governments, Metropolitan Transportation Commission, U.S. Department of Transportation)

Problem: The difficulties in the existing transportation system are not only interrelated with other aspects of the community, but they have largely been created by past land use decisions and continuing land use trends. Decisions having the most impact have been those related to the location of jobs and housing, with jobs locating in North County and housing in South County. If these policies are not modified, the transportation problems will most likely increase in severity by 1990 as the home-to-work commuting pattern extends beyond the county line and worsens within the county.[7]

The 1978 ABAG and MTC *Draft Report* of a comprehensive transportation study of the San Jose metropolitan area (see Figure 6.1) outlined two major areas of concern:

a. "Development patterns: Where will the jobs and homes be located in the county?"
b. "Transportation projects: What kind and how much transportation service can or should be provided?"[8]

As the study points out, in order to answer these two basic questions, numerous other important, underlying questions must also be asked and, it is hoped answered.

One basic question is what should be the most desirable land use or development pattern for the county. Since the extended distances between jobs and housing contribute not only to traffic congestion, but also to air pollution and unnecessary expansion of transportation facilities, an apparent answer seems to be to move the jobs and housing closer together. However, the question then becomes one of how to reconcile the existing development trends with the need to move these land uses closer together.

As shown in Table 6.1, more new jobs than housing units are

FIGURE 6.1. Surface Transportation System in Santa Clara County: 1978. *Source:* Association of Bay Area Governments and the Metropolitan Planning Commission, Joint Policy Committee. *Draft Report, Santa Clara Valley Corridor Evaluation* (November 1978).

Table 6.1 Population, Housing, and Jobs in Santa Clara County: 1975–90

	1975	1990 Projection	Estimated 1975–90 Change
Population	1,169,000	1,440,000	271,000
Housing units	411,000	570,000	159,000
Jobs	502,000	715,000	213,000

Sources: 1975 population and housing units from Santa Clara County Planning Department, Advanced Final Count of 1980 (April 1981): 1975 jobs from Santa Clara County Industry and Housing Task Force, Living Within Our Limits: A Framework for Action in the 1980's (November 1979); 1990 projections from Association of Bay Area Governments and Metropolitan Planning Commission, Joint Policy Committee, Draft Report, Santa Clara Valley Corridor Evaluation (November 1978).

expected to be generated during the 1975–90 period. The revelation that all currently available residential land in the county will be developed by 1990 forces consideration of additional problems, such as other housing solutions. These might involve higher density development or increased commuting from neighboring counties. How housing density can be moderately increased without disrupting the perceived quality of life in an area, and what effects increased commuting in will have on already overburdened county transportation facilities, are only two of the difficult questions arising from the basic proposal to modify the current growth patterns.[9]

The effects of the housing imbalance on commuting into the county were difficult to predict at the time of the study, but may be even more difficult to ascertain with the current gasoline situation. The possibility of stifled economic growth in Santa Clara County was briefly addressed by the ABAG/MTC Joint Policy Committee (JPC), but not heavily weighted. However, if the county continues to depend on long distance commuting and if energy resources continue to increase in price while becoming severely limited, the economic effects on the county may well be worth further examination. Such an occurrence may curtail the Bay Area residents' willingness to commute to work and, consequently, severely alter the current transportation and land use trends, as well as negate the question of commuters' overuse of county transportation facilities.

The transportation question also raises many other concerns. For example, the transportation section of the Draft Report is based on a consideration of whether dependence on highway improvements or conversion to alternative transportation modes is the answer. The latter option necessitates that the various choices be examined before a firm decision is made. And, of course, the entire situation must be placed within the context of the county's financial capabilities.

Appropriately, MTC, ABAG, and federal planning institutions, such as the Urban Mass Transportation Administration (UMTA) of the Department of Transportation, are concerned with the regional issues of intercounty travel and broad environmental impacts that could result from the recommendations of the corridor study.[10] The ABAG view of Santa Clara County as the new growth center of the Bay Area requires that future intercounty travel needs be considered and options included when formulating alternatives. However, although it was their responsibility to present the technical merits of these options for citizen consideration, it was not their intent to force these options on the county.[11] An example is the light rail proposal that attempts to maximize funding for Santa Clara County.[12]

The need to coordinate the transportation desires of the county can be seen when the various transportation plans of the cities and the county are added together. The cost of these plans far exceeds the maximum of $150 million that had been developed as a barely feasible figure. Even this amount will require the establishment of an additional 2 cent per gallon gasoline tax to provide matching funds for the Federal Aid Urban highway program. Even if that tax is not obtained and all the transportation features cannot be implemented, the priorities will already have been determined for the projects to be done, and the benefits of the land use recommendations can still be implemented.[13]

Solution: Clearly, the transportation problem in Santa Clara County is a very complex one, not only in terms of the physical problems, but also politically.The development of a solution involves numerous steps. As a preliminary aspect of the plan, ABAG and MTC, together with citizens and county and city policymakers, evaluated the various forms of development that could occur in the county. As indicated in the *Draft Report*, two development patterns were finally chosen for analysis as those most likely to occur and to be most acceptable:[14]

a. Alternative I—Policy trends. Development would occur in a manner consistent with recent trends, with jobs in the north and housing in the south. This alternative would allow for low density development and some loss of agricultural land.
b. Alternative II—Reduce commuting distance. More housing would be planned in the north and more jobs in the south. Density would be increased, especially along mass transportation routes and on already developed lands. Land around Gilroy would remain primarily in agricultural use.

These two development alternatives are based on the set of countywide job, housing, and population projections for 1990 shown in Table 6.1. The impacts of a faster rate of employment growth, such as those resulting from an additional 100,000 jobs, were also examined.

Each alternative was most heavily examined in terms of one of three transportation modes—bus, rail, or highway—with some analysis of the effects on other factors, such as the environment, the economy, waste-water disposal, social impacts, and energy. The exact impacts of the plan on these factors could not be readily determined because the evaluation was on a general level and the effects of the corridor study's recommendations were hard to separate from those of growth in general. More detailed analysis on a project basis, such as that which will occur in phase II of the UMTA Alternatives Analysis, should provide better data on these effects.[15]

The three transportation options were selected on the basis of currently known transportation technology, the transportation interests of the county, and the need to allow comparison with the status quo: the highways. The three options are the following:

a. Bus—"Emphasizing buses and reducing auto reliance"
b. Rail—". . . reducing auto reliance and providing transit on new rail facilities and bus transit"
c. Highway—". . . continuing reliance on the automobile."[16]

Each mode requires certain specific criteria in order to be successful. Thus, the best transportation choice cannot be determined without county and city development patterns being established. For example, a decision to increase residential densities may be conducive to rail, while low density housing will be better suited to buses.

In order to guide the course of the study and clearly define the overall objectives of the corridor evaluation, several generally agreed upon statements were provided in the *Draft Report*. The three basic guidelines established to direct the focus on the study were the following:[17]

a. The plan must be based on a realistic assessment of resources.
b. A better balance between jobs and housing.
c. Careful consideration of job locations, an adequate transit system, and investments in improving existing highways, not constructing new ones.

In accordance with the study's approach to the problem, specific recommendations made in the *Draft Report* were divided into two categories, development and transportation.[18] These preliminary recommendations are shown in Figure 6.2.

Recommendations for development were the following:

a. Encourage new job information and commercial development in central San Jose.
b. Encourage manufacturing jobs that depend on highway access to locate in the Northern San Jose/Milpitas area.
c. Encourage job development in the South San Jose neighborhood of Edenvale, served by existing highway and proposed transit improvements.
d. Encourage the development of higher density housing in North and Central County cities.
e. Support existing residential and industrial development policies of Gilroy, Morgan Hill, and the county in South County. Support maintenance of Coyote as an agricultural preserve.

Recommendations for transportation were the following:

a. Transportation projects should be used to reinforce the desired land use patterns.
b. Transportation projects should be selected that maximize the total system's effectiveness.
c. Where possible, options for the future should be preserved.
d. Strategies need to be defined that will support the county in its quest for state and federal discretionary funds.

☐ Specific highway recommendations and the funds required are shown in Table 6.2. These proposals do not include improvements to local arterials and expressways.
☐ The following recommendations for transit were also made:
   —The bus system should be expanded to approximately 750 vehicles to provide adequate local and express service within the urban limits.
   —Expansion beyond the basic 500 bus system should emphasize express service to downtown San Jose, express service from residential terminals to jobs in the industrial parks, and feeders to Southern Pacific railroad and regional bus connections with BART.
   —Southern Pacific rail service between San Jose and San Francisco should be upgraded as recommended in the MTC *Peninsula Transit Alternatives Project* (PENTAP).[19]
   —Development of a light rail line should proceed in the Edenvale cor-

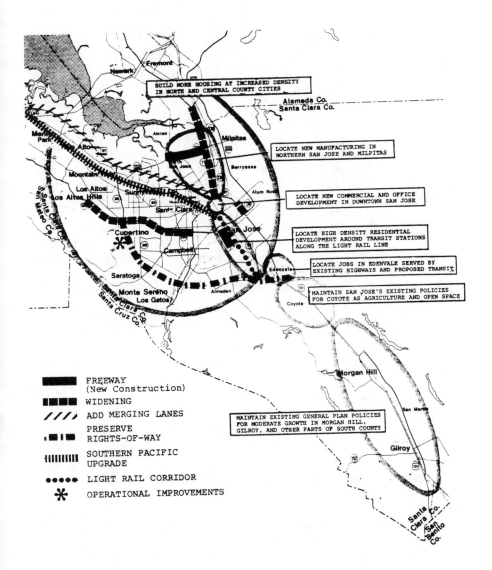

Legend:

■■■■ FREEWAY
(New Construction)

■■■■ WIDENING

//// ADD MERGING LANES

▪■▪■ PRESERVE
RIGHTS-OF-WAY

|||||||| SOUTHERN PACIFIC
UPGRADE

●●●●● LIGHT RAIL CORRIDOR

✳ OPERATIONAL IMPROVEMENTS

Map labels:

BUILD MORE HOUSING AT INCREASED DENSITY
IN NORTH AND CENTRAL COUNTY CITIES

LOCATE NEW MANUFACTURING IN
NORTHERN SAN JOSE AND MILPITAS

LOCATE NEW COMMERCIAL AND OFFICE
DEVELOPMENT IN DOWNTOWN SAN JOSE

LOCATE HIGH DENSITY RESIDENTIAL
DEVELOPMENT AROUND TRANSIT STATIONS
ALONG THE LIGHT RAIL LINE

LOCATE JOBS IN EDENVALE SERVED BY
EXISTING HIGHWAYS AND PROPOSED TRANSIT

MAINTAIN SAN JOSE'S EXISTING POLICIES
FOR COYOTE AS AGRICULTURE AND OPEN SPACE

MAINTAIN EXISTING GENERAL PLAN POLICIES
FOR MODERATE GROWTH IN MORGAN HILL,
GILROY, AND OTHER PARTS OF SOUTH COUNTY

FIGURE 6.2. Preliminary Land Use and Transportation Recommendations for Santa Clara County. *Source:* Association of Bay Area Governments and the Metropolitan Planning Commission, Joint Policy Committee, *Draft Report, Santa Clara Valley Corridor Evaluation* (November 1978).

175

Table 6.2   ABAG/MTC Highway Recommendations: November 1978

Route 85	Protect right-of-way and continue purchases as required. Develop and implement ramp metering and preferential treatment for buses where appropriate ($3-5 million)
Route 101	Widen from four to six lanes in vicinity of Alum Rock interchange ($5-10 million) Add auxiliary lanes (weaving lanes between interchanges) north of Route 17 ($4-6 million)
Route I-280	Add two inside lanes between Route 17 and Magdalena Road ($14-16 million)
Route 87	Construct four lane expressway with appropriate grade separations to connect with Almaden Expressway in the vicinity of Curtner Avenue ($18-20 million)
Route 237	Upgrade to a four lane freeway west of Route 17 ($20-25 million)
Route 17	Widen by adding one lane in each direction from Route 101 to Fremont ($8-12 million)
Route 85	Make operational improvements in Cupertino. The existing Caltrans project, which would cost approximately $7-10 million, to extend a freeway or expressway to Sunnyvale/Saratoga Road will be considered. The project is to be designed to avoid simply shifting traffic from Cupertino to San Jose and Saratoga streets.

Notes: In addition to the above projects, $4-6 million whould be committed to make safety improvements, particularly on Route 152 (Pacheco Pass).

All cost estimates in 1977 dollars.

Source: Association of Bay Area Governments and the Metropolitan Transportation Commission, Joint Policy Committee, *Draft Report, Santa Clara Valley Corridor Evaluation* (November 1978).

ridor, and the full existing right-of-way for the proposed Route 87 south of Almaden Expressway should be preserved for rail transit.

The corridor analysis identified two corridors, in addition to the Southern Pacific corridor, that had some potential for development of a rail system: Edenvale and Fremont. The results of the technical analysis alone, however, did not make an absolute case for rail in either corridor. The weakness in attempting to project a rail future based on 1978 conditions in Santa Clara County is that the justification of a rail system must assume changes in land use. Therefore, it was concluded that policy considerations and the ability to achieve consensus on the conditions that support a rail line are the most important factors in determining its feasibility.[20]

The report indicated that the potential for achieving a policy consensus is greatest in the Edenvale corridor.[21] Further, it pointed out that construction of light rail in this corridor would support three important objectives:

—The development of the central area of San Jose, particularly by connecting the different parts of this area
—The development of clusters of higher density housing and commercial areas on the rail corridor within the existing urban limits
—The interconnection with an existing regional rail service in the Southern Pacific corridor.[22]

The Edenvale corridor light rail recommendation was based on the condition that local government support for the transportation investment will result in adoption of the following policies:[23]

—Downtown San Jose should have the highest priority for jobs and commerical development with a strong parking management plan.
—Proposed station sites should be rezoned to permit higher density residential development and additional commerical development as appropriate.
—Transit system design should emphasize convenient interconnection between buses, Southern Pacific commuter rail service, and light rail service.
—The existing right-of-way for the proposed Route 87 south of the Almaden Expressway should be preserved for rail transit, and major new competing highway projects must be eliminated from the plan.
—The system design should discourage development that would leap-frog the existing urban limits.

Thus, the Bay Area and federal planning institutions were attempting to provide a comprehensive transportation plan for the San Jose metropolitan area—a plan that would balance land use patterns against a variety of transportation options, rather than relying solely on the automobile. In particular, they suggested a plan that provided options for reducing commuting distance by locating housing and employment centers closer together, and for increasing the use of mass transportation and high density housing.

The Metropolitan View (Santa Clara County Transportation Agency, and Planning Department)

Problem: The chief transportation problem in the San Jose metropolitan area is peak hour auto congestion.[24] Specifically, it is the home-to-work commutation, predominantly from the central and southern portions of Santa Clara County (along such highways as Route 101), and also from North San Jose, Milpitas, and Alameda County laterally to the peninsula (on such roads as Route 237).[25] Santa Clara County's development patterns are responsible for this difficult transportation pattern. The largest employers, electronics firms, are concentrated in the North County cities of Palo Alto, Mountain View, Sunnyvale, and Santa Clara, while the bulk of the county's housing is in or near San Jose.

The need for individual city General Plan revisions is recognized by the Santa Clara County Transportation Agency: "The trends and official policies contained in local plans are lengthening travel distance to work because new jobs are not being located close to new housing."[26] This contributes to congestion, pollution, and the need for new transportation facilities. Commuting from adjacent counties will increase as jobs are added faster than housing is built. For example, housing prices in Fremont and Newark have become competitive with those of South San Jose, and these Alameda County cities are closer to some jobs in Santa Clara County than is Morgan Hill. Thus the commute via Routes 17 and 237 is growing very rapidly.[27]

In contrast with the 1950s and the 1960s, less money is available today for transportation. The state gasoline tax of 7 cents per gallon has remained constant since 1963, and consequently, as the result of inflation, produces a much smaller proportion of total revenues than it once did. In 1978 highway maintenance costs were increasing at an annual rate of 15 percent and construction costs at 25 to 30 percent, while revenues were rising at only 8 to 10 percent per year.[28]

Furthermore, today's emphasis on reducing public expenditures has added to competition between localities for scarce funds, resulting in "...increased political pressure as a practical means of securing transportation projects that need Federal or State approval and money,"[29] in addition to competition by the county with projects elsewhere, in and outside of the Bay Area.

Solution: By influencing the current and future locations of jobs, we can more efficiently use existing roads and facilities. The Santa Clara County Transportation Agency argues as follows:

> ...development and transportation decisions must be mutually supportive. The location and growth of jobs are dependent on access to the labor market and, in turn, strongly affect congestion levels, trip lengths, and the effectiveness of transit.[30]

The Agency makes the following land use recommendations:[31]

a. Reverse current development trends by building more housing in the north county and creating more jobs near San Jose residential areas.
b. Target San Jose as a major center for new offices, commercial and housing [construction], especially high-rise developments.
c. Designate the "Golden Triangle" area—Milpitas, North San Jose, and Santa Clara—as a site for new industry and business dependent on rail and highway access, and generally low-density employment.
d. Bring new light manufacturing plants and research offices to Edenvale's industrial parks (high-density employment) in San Jose.
e. Where accepted by the cities, strive for high-density housing units in all of the urbanized areas of the county north of Coyote, a stretch of agricultural land between South San Jose and Morgan Hill.
f. Encourage self-contained economies for Morgan Hill and Gilroy. Supply the necessary stores, services, and jobs, so as to prevent them from becoming bedroom communities catering to jobs in the north.

The county believes that a collaborative approach, similar to that of the Industry and Housing Management Task Force established by the County Board of Supervisors, will be useful in implementing the above recommendations. This task force represents a coalition of contractors, industry, minority groups, environmental groups, and labor interests who are trying to improve development patterns in Santa Clara County.[32]

In addition, the County Transportation Agency's recommendations include the following transportation proposals:[33]

a. Given the prospect of limited funds for both highway and transit expansion, support a program of transportation systems management (TSM) measures. These include staggered work hours, car pooling and van pooling, and incentives to use transit.
b. Increase the state gasoline tax by 2 cents per gallon, or provide an equivalent means of revenue production.[34] This is needed to continue federal matching funds for highways and support the county's minimal highway construction program of $120 million (1977 dollars) through 1990.
c. Support as a top priority construction of high occupancy vehicle (HOV) lanes for the exclusive use of buses and car pools or van pools, where recommended, to widen county freeways and expressways.
d. Support detailed highway recommendations explained below.
e. Expand the bus system by approximately 250 vehicles (to 750 buses) as soon as possible, with the new vehicles being designated for a system of high speed, express routes primarily serving commuters.

f. Institute improvements to Southern Pacific's peninsula commuter line in order to provide greater service to county residents, including new stations and cars, and more trains and equipment.
g. Support a detailed, corridor-level alternatives analysis as defined by UMTA for a light rail transit line in the central San Jose to Almaden/Edenvale corridor(Guadalupe corridor). Encourage the implementation at the earliest possible date of construction of this line, assuming that the alternatives analysis demonstrates that light rail is the preferred mode.

The agency's detailed recommendations are presented below.[35]

Highways

Highway projects are categorized, by type and method of funding, into three groups: Federal Aid Urban (FAU), Federal Aid Primary (FAP), and Federal Aid Interstate (FAI).

FAU funds are allocated according to percentage of national population (of which Santa Clara County accounts for about 1 percent). They are used to improve local urban expressways such as Routes 85 and 87. The federal government matches 83 cents for every 17 cents of local money. FAP roads link two different urban areas, such as Routes 17, 101, and 152. The federal/local share is also 83/17. Interstate Route 280 benefits from the FAI program. The federal/local share is 90/10. Table 6.3 lists the county's recommended highway projects by program and priority order. Improvements to local arterials and expressways are not included.

HOV Lanes

County officials have indicated strong desires that any freeway or expressway widening should take the form of HOV lanes. As explained by John Perry, chairman of the County Transportation Commission, improving a freeway just to accommodate more automobiles—which, of course, perpetuates the problem—makes no sense.[36] James Lightbody, transit operations engineer, points out that HOVs are a necessary part of a successful express bus system.[37] All parties concerned with the corridor study have supported a bus fleet expansion, but the facilities to make such a system work have gone unmentioned. Santa Clara County encourages prompt consideration of HOV lanes, for the following reasons:

a. Many of the county's freeways and expressways are seriously congested, despite such devices as ramp metering and signal coordination. There will be no incentive to use an express bus or car pool or van pool if they, too, are detained in traffic jams.

Table 6.3   Santa Clara County Highway Recommendations: February 1979

	Cost (millions 1977 $)
Federal Aid Urban (FAU)	
1. Route 85 (West Valley Corridor) Protect right-of-way and continue purchases as required.	$5-10
2. Route 87 (Guadalupe Expressway) Construct four lane expressway with appropriate grade separations to connect with the Almaden Expressway in the vicinity of Curtner Avenue. Protect the remaining corridor ROW for future transportation purposes.	$18-20
3. Route 85 Make operational improvements in Cupertino, possibly including the existing Caltrans project to extend a freeway or expressway to Sunnyvale/ Saratoga Road. Widen between I-280 and 101 from 4 to 6 lanes, reserving the new lanes for exclusive use by buses and carpools (HOV lanes).	
Federal Aid Interstate (FAI)	
1. Interstate 280 Add 2 inside lanes between Route 17 and Magdalena Road (in Los Altos). The county recommends that these lanes be approved as high occupancy vehicle lanes, for exclusive bus and carpool use.	$14-16
Federal Aid Primary (FAP)	
1. Route 152 (Pacheco Pass, east of Gilroy) Widen to 4 lanes; add a median barrier and truck escape ramps between the Pacheco Creek Bridge and the existing 4 lane section in the vicinity of the summit. Numerous fatal accidents at this location prompted the county to name the project its overall first priority.	$6
2. Route 237 Add two HOV lanes between routes 85 and 17; construct interchanges at highest priority lacations. NOTE: Route 237 is now classified as an FAU project, but with only $9 million in FAU monies expected to be available over the next 12 years, the county recommends reclassification as an FAP project. Here, more money is expected to be available than would be required to take care of the recommended	$35-40

Table 6.3 *(Continued)*

	Cost *(millions 1977 $)*
improvements ($36 million) to current FAP freeways—101 and 17. Such a change (also sought for Route 87) will require approval from MTC, Caltrans, and the Federal Highway Administration.	
3. Route 101 (Bayshore Freeway) Widen from 4 to 6 lanes in the vicinity of Alum Rock interchange (from McKee to Tully).	$5-10
Add two HOV lanes between route 237 and Guadalupe Parkway.	$10
4. Route 17 (Nimitz Freeway) Widen from 4 to 6 lanes by adding 1 HOV lane in each direction from 101 to Alameda County.	$8-12
Also, though not numbered as a project:	
Develop and implement ramp metering and preferential treatment for buses where appropriate. Emphasize 101, 280, and routes 17 and 85.	$3-5
TOTAL COST	$154

Note: Total cost is considerably higher than the $120 million given in the county's *Recommendations*. The difference here is in the Route 85 widening (since proposed) at $15 million, and the additional $15 million that Caltrans estimates as the cost of widening Route 237.

Source: Santa Clara County Transportation Agency, *Recommendations Pertaining to the Santa Clara Valley Corridor Evaluation Study* (February 1979); and interviews with staff, Santa Clara County Transportation Agency, February and March 1979.

b. This may be the last opportunity to implement HOV lanes, since there will be no other rights-of-way available for additional lanes at a later date. Removing existing lanes from general traffic will prove to be extremely difficult.

c. Looking to 1990, it can be expected that additional travel demands will be made, essentially on the existing system.

To increase vehicle occupancies and the person-carrying capacity of the highway system, incentives to use car pools and buses must be provided.

HOVs have proved to be effective where lanes are added to highway; Marin County and Los Angeles have working examples. Santa Clara

County is at present working on a plot project with the City of Santa Clara to add HOV lanes to the San Tomas Expressway.

Transit

Further expansion beyond the currently planned system of 516 buses should emphasize express service between residential areas and industrial parks, with feeder lines to the Southern Pacific and BART. Measures such as bus preemption of traffic signals, bus bypass ramps on metered freeways, and reserved lanes for HOVs should also be considered as an integral part of this express bus system.

Recommendation		Operating Costs[38] (million 1978 $)
Continued arterial route service (450 buses)		$45
Express buses	(300 buses)	$21
	Total	$66

Given that the San Jose to San Francisco corridor is the most heavily traveled in the country, it is imperative that the existing Southern Pacific service be upgraded to attract and serve more patrons. Recommendations were detailed in an earlier study, called the *Peninsula Transit Alternatives Project.*[39] It suggested that new stations be established at San Antonio Road, Lawrence Expressway, and San Tomas Expressway. Approximately 24 daily trains should be added in three stages, so that by 1985–86, trains would run every eight minutes in the peak direction and every fifteen minutes in the nonpeak direction.[40]

Some residents and politicians have argued that the existing Southern Pacific tracks south of downtown San Jose should be opened to commuter service. In 1979, Assemblywoman Leona Egeland (D-Morgan Hill) introduced Assembly Bill 1196, which would establish a Southern Pacific station in South County.[41]

The county has not pursued such a plan. At the Transit District meeting of March 19, 1979, Supervisor Rod Diridon explained that the county's first choice for the Guadalupe corridor was the Southern Pacific. In turn, Southern Pacific threatened to bring a lawsuit against the county if it attempted to institute this service. (It is interesting that the Southern Pacific itself was then in court over whether it must continue to provide peninsula commuter service.) But even if the Southern Pacific were willing, a second track as well as new stations would be necessary. The system would still be generally limited to peak-hour commuter service rather than the regular, frequent all-day service that a rail system traditionally supplies. It is already heavily used by freight trains and Amtrak.

Recommendation	Operating Costs[42] (million 1978 $)
	County's share of improvements
Upgrade Southern Pacific service	$6.5–7.0

Light Rail

The most controversial element of the corridor study has been the proposed light rail line linking the Almaden/Edenvale residential areas in South San Jose to downtown San Jose, the Southern Pacific station, the Civic Center, San Jose Airport, and Marriott Park. This much-studied project was strongly debated among the county supervisors, who finally voted unanimously to approve a federally required alternatives analysis, which would select the best mode of transportation for the corridor. As the county's *Recommendations* state:

> Alternatives to be considered will include light rail, buses, Southern Pacific commuter rail and a full freeway . . . [After this,] final local and UMTA decisions would be reached on whether or not to fund a light rail line . . . .[43]

While waiting for the completion of the forthcoming study, the county recognizes two characteristics that make light rail a desirable alternative: land use effects and financing.

The rationale underlying the choice of the Edenvale corridor over the Fremont corridor for rail has been questioned, since the *Draft Report* data projected higher ridership on the Fremont line (to BART). Supervisor Diridon has said that the slightly higher ridership on Fremont was outweighed by the Edenvale corridor's effect of channeling more growth into downtown San Jose—a key land use recommendation of the study.[44]

Second, despite the high initial cost of light rail, its operating costs are lower than those of buses. It costs $3 million annually to run 25 light rail vehicles, which carry as many riders as 100 buses, compared with $10 million to operate 100 buses. Southern Pacific and light rail combined are expected to carry more than 28 percent of the daily transit ridership, yet would require only 14 percent of the total operating costs for transit.[45]

Overall, the county is in a good position to finance its proposed transit improvements. The local half-cent sales tax, plus state Proposition 5 monies (for fixed guideways construction) should cover the required 20 percent share of capital costs.

Recommendation	Operating Costs[46] (million 1978 $)
Arterial route service (450 buses)	$45
Express bus (300 buses)	$21
County's net share of Southern Pacific service	$ 7
Light rail (25 vehicles)	$ 3 to $4
18% for capital replacement and emergencies	$13.5
Total	$90

The county's *Recommendations* indicates that no new local or federal funding sources would be required to implement and operate the recommended transit system.[47]

The county is, in effect, pursuing a "transit first" direction in meeting the problems of peak hour congestion and limited funding, particularly for roads. TSM measures and HVO lanes can help to accommodate more riders at a given time on presently congested highways. An expanded bus system, with increased express runs, along with light rail and improved Southern Pacific facilities, will greatly improve service for commuters. Finally, land use decisions that bring housing and jobs closer together will reduce the need for people to commute long distances.

The Central City (San Jose)

Problem: San Jose, the largest city in Santa Clara County and the fourth largest city in California, had a population in 1975 of 610,500, or 52 percent of Santa Clara County's total population of 1,169,000.[48]

The City of San Jose has an imbalance with regard to jobs and housing. In 1975 employment within the city was 186,000, accounting for only 37 percent of Santa Clara County's employment of 502,000.[49] San Jose has a heavy population of workers who commute in an intricate network to places of employment, mainly to the electronics firms in cities in the northern part of the county. San Jose has a housing occupancy rate of 2.9 persons per housing unit, and between 1.1 and 1.4 workers per household.[50] With 174,500 households in San Jose in 1975,[51] a rate of 1.1 workers per household would result in 192,000 workers, and a rate of 1.4 workers per household would yield 244,000 workers. Yet, the 1975 data showed only 186,000 jobs within San Jose. Consequently, the jobs/housing imbalance creates the major transportation problem for San Jose residents: the long and inefficient journey to work.[52]

San Jose's jobs/housing rate can be contrasted with the situation in Sunnyvale, Santa Clara County's second largest city, with 102,100 residents (8.7 percent of the county's 1975 population) and 72,700 jobs (14.5 percent of the county's employment).[53] Sunnyvale is typical of the North County job rich communites that import workers from job poor San Jose.

Solution: The City of San Jose's position with regard to the Santa Clara Valley Corridor Evaluation is that all planned development by the City of San Jose, by private development, and by outside agencies must conform to the city's General Plan and to its Land Use and Transportation Elements.[54]

Most transit system priorities listed in the Corridor Evaluation conform to the action plan recommended by the Downtown San Jose Transit Mobility Improvement Project and adopted by the San Jose City Council in 1978.[55] This would bring together the Southern Pacific railroad line, Greyhound and Peerless Stage bus terminals, County Transit bus lines, airport limousines, and taxi stands in one facility.

San Jose and the regional institutions of ABAG and MTC agree that the industrial areas of the Edenvale Planning Area in South San Jose should be developed. These areas have been zoned for industry by the City of San Jose and have received ABAG/MTC approval to encourage reverse commutation on Route 101. During the rush hour, both northbound and southbound lanes would be fully utilized if workers living in North County drove south to work.

The city agrees with the ABAG/MTC stated objective that there should be a better balance of jobs and housing in the cities of Santa Clara County—that each city should more closely match available housing with employment opportunities. ABAG/MTC wants to ease transportation problems. San Jose wants to ease its fiscal problems. Housing and residents require services (schools, fire protection, police, parks, recreation) that industries do not, yet pay relatively little in taxes.

(However, the *Draft Report* does not address the impact of Proposition 13 on the tax structure and city income.)

Solving the economic problem of the jobs/housing imbalance is a major undertaking since functionally related activities and processes usually receive much economic advantage by locating near each other, and prefer to continue to do so. Housing is cost effective if it is built near other housing and can be served by common schools, libraries, parks. Similarly, commercial and industrial activities can benefit from agglomeration, being adjacent to a rail line, personnel offices, machinists, or other shared services.

San Jose's concerns regarding the *Draft Report* are in areas contrary to its General Plan. The proposal for a light rail line in the Route 87 (Guadalupe Expressway) corridor, with abandonment of the planned expressway south of Curtner Avenue, is contrary to the San Jose General Plan.

The construction and operation of a light rail line, even though less expensive than the heavy rail of the existing Southern Pacific line, requires a high density of population and transit users to be cost effective. The Edenvale Planning Area, designated to be the site of the proposed light rail line, has approximately 20 persons per acre. The evaluation calls for San Jose to increase its density on vacant land zoned residential in that area. The *Draft Report* gives no definition of "high density." The San Jose General Plan calls high density 12–35 dwelling units per acre (20 units per acre after allowing for streets). The General Plan defines very high density as 24–40 dwelling units per acre (30 units on the average). Other cities in the Bay Area, such as San Francisco and Oakland, might call such densities low.

Edenvale Planning Area had only 1,055 vacant acres of residentially zoned land in July 1978.[56] This land was zoned to accommodate from 1.2 to 40 units per acre.[57] Multiplying each vacant parcel by the density allowed shows that the Edenvale area, under current zoning, could accommodate 8,145 more housing units. At an occupancy rate of approximately 3.0 persons per unit, only an additional 24,400 more residents could be housed in Edenvale. Together with the present population of 101,000, the total population could be expected to be 125,000. Much of the vacant land is already under construction. Indeed, all the vacant land is expected to be occupied by 1990.

As mentioned earlier, the estimated number of workers per household ranges between 1.1 and 1.4. Applying these population figures to the expected number of 41,600 households[58] yields 46,000 to 58,000 workers for the Edenvale area.

These workers appear to be too few in number to generate enough commuters to make any rail system cost effective. Efforts are being made to develop a sizable industrial park in the Edenvale area. IBM, with approximately 8,000 employees, and Fairchild, with 3,000 workers, many of whom live in the Edenvale area, have already captured much of the expected ridership of the rail line.

The *Draft Report* is calling for the City of San Jose to increase its density in the Edenvale Planning Area to make the light rail feasible. In other words, the city is being asked to increase the number of residents in order to make the light rail successful, and to lose the Guadalupe Expressway possibilities in the Route 87 corridor. This recommendation is in direct opposition to San Jose's objective of reducing its jobs/housing imbalance by increasing jobs, not housing.

Also, the land south of Edenvale at the terminus of the rail line proposed in the Coyote Planning Area (reserved for agricultural and industrial use) is in the San Jose General Plan. This land will not be available for housing. Thus, San Jose is not likely to generate a high concentration of residential development in the vicinity of Edenvale.

Although a high hourly passenger volume would be necessary to develop a cost effective transit corridor, the *Draft Report* gives no data for projected ridership. A ridership of 10,000–15,000 per hour would be a minimum necessary for cost effectiveness.[59] Riders under the break-even point would be subsidized at the expense of the poor population, since the commuters on the rail line are expected to be workers living in Edenvale, a middle and upper-middle income area.

The *Draft Report* asks that the job rich cities take some of the needed housing in the future to alleviate the growing problem of a housing shortage. These cities do not seem anxious to comply with this request. For example, on May 1, 1979, the Sunnyvale City Council was presented with two proposed housing developments to be built on land currently owned by the City of Sunnyvale and offered for sale. Both developers offered the city the same price for the land, $500,000. One developer planned to build a 30 unit subdivision, with prices from $85,000 to $115,000, while the other builder wanted to develop a 21 unit subdivision of $140,000 houses. The Sunnyvale City Council accepted the bid of the developer proposing to build the 21 unit subdivision, saying it was the better plan.[60]

San Jose does not want to support a proposal of the *Draft Report* that could eliminate Route 87, which is shown on the Transportation Element of its General Plan, or to increase density in the Edenvale area to levels above those shown on the General Plan. The alternatives analysis for the light rail system will consider transferring the Southern Pacific line along Monterey Highway to public ownership. (A similar transfer was accomplished in San Diego, with the San Diego Transit District entering into a purchase and donation arrangement with the Southern Pacific.)[61]

Even though this proposal would be a great deal less expensive than the new light rail line proposed in the *Draft Report,* since the right-of-way and tracts are intact, a rail line still requires an intensity of ridership that the San Jose area may not be able to provide.

The Commuter View (Santa Clara Valley Manufacturing Group, City of Sunnyvale, V.E.P. Homeowners Association, Multi-Modal Task Force)

Problem: The major transportation problem of the San Jose metropolitan area is the daily peak commuting difficulties that residents of central, southern, and western Santa Clara County have in reaching their places of employment in North County industrial areas. Thus, groups representing the views of both employees and employers have a mutual concern over the transportation problem that threatens their collective well-being. They view this problem as the result of overreliance on single passenger automobile use and of government failure to provide an adequate highway system (incomplete highway routes 85, 87, 237); of insufficient public transportation (unreliable bus fleet); and of unbalanced land use patterns (the general plans of all 15 cities in the county will reinforce the concentration of new job growth in the northern part of the county, and residential growth in the south).[62]

Solution: Although there is some variation of views among the commuter groups, their transportation solutions generally involve the following:[63]

a. The present trend toward job growth in the central county should be encouraged. This action would enable a reverse commuting pattern whereby traffic would flow in both directions on existing roadways, rather than the current predominant pattern of south to north. Cities can facilitate this by doing the following:

Limiting the rate of new job growth in northern Santa Clara County
Increasing the housing supply to match planned job increases and, where fiscal or other pressures in a city cause a reduction in planned housing growth, corresponding limits on additional industrial construction
Increasing housing densities throughout the county, with particular emphasis on achieving maximum permissible densities in North County cities and utilizing suitable vacant land areas for housing
Maintaining present policies of Gilroy, Morgan Hill, and the county calling for moderate growth within already urbanized areas as appropriate elements of a balanced, rational countywide growth policy up to 1990.

b. Significant expansion of commuter-oriented bus service offers the most cost effective, near-term response to the county's travel needs.

The *Draft Report* of the Corridor Evaluation Study states that buses provide the kind of flexibility needed to serve a low density, dispersed area like Santa Clara County. Buses are also appropriate to meeting the near-term transportation demand because they do not require lengthy construction lead times. According to the planning staff of the Santa Clara County Transit District, the four long distance express bus routes linking residential and industrial areas have been quite successful.[64] Prior to the gas shortage in early 1979, ridership averaged 1,000 persons per day, or about 35 passengers per bus (35–45 passenger buses).[65] After petroleum shortages became acute during the spring of 1979, ridership doubled, with as many as 100 passengers per bus.[66] The Transit District plans to initiate two more express routes and, if the recommendations of MTC and ABAG are implemented, it may increase the express fleet by 300 buses, which would enable still more routes, and shorter headways on existing routes. With the recent dramatic increase in bus ridership, the Transit District has also received approval from the Board of Supervisors to take emergency measures as needed to meet the increasing demand. These measures include the possibility of leasing additional buses and contracting for service with private carriers.

Based on information from the Transit District, the commuter groups believe that commuter bus service can be more cost effective than other types of transportation, and claim that such bus arrangements would make possible an increase in service with a reduction in operating deficits.

c. Regardless of near term improvements in bus service, the county road network must be completed to meet projected long-term travel needs.

The *Draft Report* states that in 1990, 90 percent of the trips will still be made by automobile.[67] According to the commuter groups, some of the current traffic problems have been caused by residential development in the right-of-way of roads that were planned but never built. Roadways such as Routes 85 and 87 should be cleared and completed. According to Burton Epstein, chairman of the Santa Clara County Manufacturing Group's Transportation Task Force,[68] Route 85 should be developed in accordance with the Multi-Modal Task Force proposal that calls for the use of a combination of automobile, transit (bus or light rail) and bicycles modes.[69]

In addition, consideration should be given to reserving any new highway lanes for HOVs such as buses, van pools, and car pools. Such additional lanes would greatly enhance the potential for successful express bus service and ride sharing.

d. An upgrade Southern Pacific passenger service appears to be a reasonable, medium term transit objective only if there is a satisfactory arrangement for funding and operating the service.

Upgrading the Southern Pacific's passenger service, which was also recommended by PENTAP,[70] would include more intracounty service facilitated by additional stations, new equipment, and additional trains. This objective is considered reasonable by the commuter groups for several reasons:[71] The train has the greatest peak passenger carrying capacity of any transit alternative; the existing Southern Pacific right-of-way is close to most of the major work destinations in the North County; federal funds are available for upgrading existing rail service; upgraded intracounty service could demonstrate the cost effectiveness of rail transit; and fixed guideway reserve funds could be used to encourage federal funding and to supplement rail operations startup costs.

The feasibility and cost effectiveness of upgraded Southern Pacific service will depend on the following:[72] reaching a satisfactory agreement with Southern Pacific to operate an upgraded system, or to relinquish operations to a public agency; the frequency and reliability of service to all cities and stations; convenience of parking provided near the stations, as well as frequency and reliability of shuttle service to and from stations; and a reasonable cost for the service provided.

It is further recommended that the upgrading of the Southern Pacific be preceded by a pilot program linking feeder bus service to the existing Southern Pacific service.

e. The proposed light rail alternative requires significant additional evidence of transit ridership potential and cost effective bus operation before any final decision should be made.

The Santa Clara county Manufacturing Group and the City of Sunnyvale recognize that light rail could conceivably be a suitable long range alternative in the event of significant fuel cost increases and shortages, and higher density land uses.[73] However, these actors believe that at this time express buses and roads provide the flexibility in investment that will best meet the Santa Clara Valley's transportation needs. In addition, residential groups such as V.E.P. Homeowners Association[74] feel that light rail use of Route 87 would act to discourage the location of General Plan industrial uses that depend on the movement of goods, since industrial uses have traditionally relied on roads or heavy rail for the movement of freight. They also believe that the light rail line would induce growth in the Gilroy and Morgan Hill areas, and argue that the rail line in Edenvale would tend to reduce property values by encouraging unwanted high density residential development. Thus, both employer and employee groups are more supportive of bus transit than of rail transit: the employers, mostly on economic efficiency grounds, and the employees, for environmental-residential reasons.

The commuter groups are skeptical of the alternatives study proposed by MTC and ABAG to analyze the various modes, including light rail, for the selected Edenvale corridor.[75] In order to establish the feasibility of light rail, they believe the County Transit District should establish its ability to do the following:[76]

1. Increase bus ridership in the county, particularly in the Edenvale corridor (a minimum of 5 percent of all work trips for the 516 bus system)

2. Achieve better cost effectiveness in bus operation than is presently the case. Convenient commuter-oriented linkages between the proposed light rail line and an upgraded Southern Pacific line would also be essential for the success of the light rail line. Thus, these groups view a satisfactory agreement to fund and operate an upgraded Southern Pacific service as an additional condition of light rail's feasibility.

f. The commuter groups intend to cooperate with local government in developing and implementing near term transit improvements. For example, the Board of Directors of the Santa Clara County Manufacturing Group, the VEP Homeowners Association, and the Multi-Modal Task Force are quite willing to cooperate with public officials in developing ways to improve transportation in Santa Clara County.[77]

Environmental Groups (American Lung Association, League of Women Voters, Modern Transit Society, Sierra Club)

Problem: The Santa Clara Valley, which has grown from a small agricultural area to a large urban region, is faced with many problems related to this growth. One of these problems is the increasing inability of the regional transportation system to provide a convenient, cost effective, and environmentally acceptable means for people to commute to and from their jobs. Transportation is a problem in the San Jose area because of the dispersed settlement pattern with no single major, central employment focus.[78] This, in turn, led to the decline of transit service, the almost exclusive use of the automobile, and the construction of expensive and eventually congested and pollution-generating highways.[79]

The environmental groups argue that automobiles create more unhealthy, dirty air than other sources, more than half of all air polution in the county. In urban areas where the pollution is most serious, automobiles produce as much as 90 percent of the carbon monoxide, over 50 percent of the hydrocarbons, and up to 50 percent of the nitrogren oxides.[80] In addition, these groups believe that excessive use of the automobile utilizes far too much potentially taxable urban land for such facilities as highways, streets, and parking lots; causes many deaths and personal injuries, and much destruction of private property; consumes inordinate amounts of our petroleum energy resources; and has generally degraded the quality of our lives.[81]

Solution: The environmental groups favor fixed light rail transit (LRT) as an alternative to the automobile or the bus.[82] They agree that the auto should pay for itself in terms of the "hidden costs" of publicly supported parking, roadway improvements, and maintenance programs, and the overall costs of extending public services to dispersed urban growth. These measures would enable transit facilities to compete more equitably with the publicly supported, automobile-oriented transportation system.

LRT vehicles are usually electrically powered, and may run on any size rail or track; however, the cars are lighter and travel at slower speeds than heavier rail systems such as BART or Southern Pacific. MUNI streetcars in San Francisco are now being replaced with new, light rail vehicles.

Specifically, the environmental groups favor establishing a light rail starter segment on Route 87 for the following reasons.[83] During the next 10 to 20 years an important issue in preserving the standard of living in the Santa Clara Valley will be the transportation of people, especially commuters, along with the attending impacts on land use associated with all transportation systems. They believe that light rail is the best, next step investment in transportation for the county because it is proven world wide to be the most reliable and effective means for people to commute between home and work. Installation of a starter segment of a light rail network on this corridor should be the top priority because it is the only option that ensures the ability of many working people, living in the southern portion of the county and adjacent to the corridor, to commute to the majority of jobs in the northern part of the county and along the corridor for the rest of the century.

They believe the transportation goal of the San Jose metropolitan area should be to work for the expansion of the system, within five years of the construction of this first segment, in at least two stages.[84] The first expansion would be a second route, beginning in central San Jose at or near the Southern Pacific station and extending on the Vasona corridor to the vicinity of Los Gatos after crossing the West Valley corridor. The second expansion would be a line connecting the two north-south lines by an east-west route running parallel to Blossom Hill Road, possibly using the West Valley corridor. The third, southern portion of a triangular network would serve to collect commuter ridership onto the two north-south routes converging on the Southern Pacific station and the spur running into the industrial area north of 101, near the Marriott Hotel in the Great America facility.

Other issues relating to effective, long term transportation in the valley are raised by this proposal. The transportation of commuters and others between Santa Clara County residence and jobs along the peninsula will continue to require the existing Southern Pacific passenger service, and this proposal provides the most effective means to utilize that service.

Also, such a system would enhance and positvely interact with the growing county bus system that has been planned to expand to a fleet of 750 buses in the early 1980s. In addition, a light rail network in this valley would not replace cars; it would dramatically reduce the exclusive reliance on individual transportation mechanisms at the time of the day when most people need the use of their cars the least.[85] A light rail system would, in fact, allow for a more effective use of cars by reducing the competition for fuel and highway capacity.

In addition to serving the commuter, LRT would have a positive impact on accelerating the growth and development of downtown San Jose[86] The discussed relocation of the Southern Pacific station to First and Bassett Streets in conjunction with the recently funded downtown Transit Mall would result in a significant number of people entering the downtown area.

The Great America Marriott Park has attendance in the summer months in excess of 30,000 people per day; the northern San Jose industrial park employs more than 5,000 people; and the airport had a passenger use of more than 3 million people in 1979. Other sources of ridership include the Civic Center, the Center for the Performing Arts, several station sites along the edge of the Willow Glen area, Oakridge Mall, and IBM and Santa Teresa Hospital. Thus, by starting a light rail system at this time, the San Jose metropolitan area will be making a profitable investment in maintaining leadership as the center for commercial, industrial, and tourism activity.

A light rail system is the most promising alternative for mitigating the inflationary impact of government spending in the long run. An established light rail system can be expanded for as little as $3 million per mile.[87] And LRT, as proposed here, does not have the questionable, local tax draining liabilities associated with the proposed funding of express-ways on the corridor. It can be expected that the federal government would fund 80 percent of the costs of constructing the system.

In sum, a light rail system is the best alternative for dealing effectively with the needs of transit dependents, air and noise pollution, and the preservation of the tax base. In addition to benefiting commuters and the downtown, a double track, light rail line spans a width of only 50 feet, yet has the same passenger load capacity as a four lane freeway.[88] In many areas of the corridor, the existing right-of-way is more than 250 feet across.[89] The difference between the two alternative modes, then, is thousands of acres of land being lost or made available for housing or other tax-generating uses.

The Social View (Mexican American Community Services Agency, Confederacion de la Raza)

Problem: The little public transit that exists in Santa Clara County, especially in highly urbanized areas, has been the predominant mode of transportation for those who cannot afford or for some other reason do not own a car. But now transit systems are being thought of as options that will compete with the car in order to reduce traffic, air pollution, and the need for more highways. Transportation producers have taken the approach of trying to give some service to all interest groups, but with the primary concern of offering an alternative to the car for middle class households. From the social perspective of the poor, the handicapped, the elderly, and the minorities, they have received less consideration because they are, in many cases, already transit dependent and have been relatively less involved in transportation planning activities than other groups.[90] Public transit, which is provided along the most heavily traveled traffic corridors, may not reach these people because they do not generate much traffic. Also, these people have greater need for a personalized service that can get them to medical and nutrition centers, to educational facilities, or out to look for employment. And, though these groups and their needs are recognized by transit plans, their transportation needs usually are not well served.[91]

Although social concern has been a theme within modern urban planning, it has seldom been the dominant theme. The *Draft Report Corridor Study* partially reflects our need to increase the social sensitivity of physical planning, and to extend the scope of planning beyond the physical environment.[92] Most of the study dealt with social policy issues: Who is to live where? Where are public services to be located? However, these issues were dealt with superficially. That is, transportation planning was neutral with respect to the distribution of resources to different groups. It was more concerned with the global consevation of resources and with economic efficiency than with the desires of the pluralistic society that exists within Santa Clara County.

Against this presumed public interest position of the study, two Mexican American activist groups argue that there is a need for planning to advocate views on behalf of special social groups.[93] Their argument holds that there are special interests affected by urban development, and that certain groups—primarily the poor—have been neglected in plans prepared by official agencies acting in the presumed public interest.[94]

For the most part the main concern of these activist groups is that the value systems and behavior of their constituents differ greatly from those of the middle class professionals who design the programs that affect them.[95] They see planning as a process of redistributing resources through public action and as a way of redressing inequities that have arisen within our society.

Solution: A transportation philosophy should be developed that serves and protects the human environment. Accordingly, the transportation system that is to be devised should have an environmentally sensitive light rail emphasis. As a long-term objective, priority should be given to an extensive rail network once the densities of population and employment reach levels that can support such a system.[96]

In addition, feeder systems should be designed and implemented that would interconnect with rapid transit. Light rail instead of buses is more desirable for the following reasons:[97]

Light rail is less polluting than buses.
It could create more jobs in the region than buses.
Lower maintenance costs are associated with light rail, compared with nonrail alternatives.
Light rail has a greater capacity for carrying passengers per hour than buses.

A short term transportation objective should be the utilization and thorough upgrading of Southern Pacific facilities in Santa Clara County, including improved rail transportation to Gilroy, Monterey, and San Mateo County (through to San Francisco), as well as the rail segment across the bay and parallel to the Dumbarton Bridge from Fremont to Palo Alto.[98] Utilization of the Southern Pacific from Fremont to Palo Alto would relieve the congestion along the Dumbarton Bridge and could be put into operation soon. The Fremont station should be connected with BART so that there would be a continuity north to BART and across the bay to Palo Alto.

Another segment of rail should be upgraded in the short run to extend rail service south beyond Vasona lake to Los Gatos and Santa Cruz. In addition, the Confederacion de la Raza proposes that in time these rail lines could be electrified so as to be more economical and less harmful to the environment.

The social groups advocate that there be no further expansion of freeways or major arterials other than maintenance or conversion to bicycle lanes or public transit uses.[99] Part of a transportation study should include a well-defined maintenance program that sets forth the objectives clearly. Also, express buses should be utilized on main corridors on a 24-hour basis, with special lanes and safe, well-designed stations.

Bikeways should also be provided. The social groups believe that if continuous separate bikeways are not linked to major corridors and regional systems, they will not be developed at all. There is a need for a barrier to separate the bikeway system from automobile traffic, as well as for bike storage at origin and destination points. In sum, there is a need for a transportation plan that takes the bicycle into account as a significant means of short distance transportation (one to five miles).[100] This would relieve a great deal of the congestion caused by short commuting trips.

Another important transportation recommendation is that dial-a-ride be provided for senior citizens and the physically handicapped in the metropolitan area.[101] With regard to land use, county development should occur in accordance with historical and recent trends. There is a need to update and coordinate the General Plans of the local cities and county with regard to amounts of industrial development and housing available up to 1990 before any independent transportation studies are made. Reality dictates that employment will continue to develop in the Palo Alto-Santa Clara corridor. Therefore, in order to achieve a balance among jobs, housing, and commutation, each North County city should reduce its industrial development objectives and increase its residential growth policy objectives.

This concept suggests the importance of providing a viable plan for Santa Clara County based on an analysis of environmental, social, political, economic, and, above all, human needs.[102] Such a plan should take into account the maximum desirable population density in the county with respect to open space, water supply, agriculture, recreation, and social psychological, political, and economic needs of the population. The agricultural character of South County should be preserved, and housing and jobs located in such a manner throughout the county that would not only shorten the trip from home to work, but also create a more compact, less land-consuming urban development pattern.

In addition to the previously described transportation and land use recommendations, the following social concerns should be given careful attention:[103]

a. Housing. All future residential development, particularly high density housing, should be located close to key transportation corridors. A program should also be established that would provide funding, land banking, and housing for low income people in areas that are readily accessible to rapid transit and feeder systems, as well as in those areas designated to stay semirural. As the demand increases for housing in areas accessible to rapid transit, the price of housing in these neighborhoods will also increase. If left entirely to the market, this process would lead to the displacement of low income people from areas near the rapid transit system.

Similarly, in areas designated to remain semirural, demand for housing will increase because of the amenities associated with them. Again, this process would result in low income people being displaced into other, less desirable housing environments. The net effect of this process would be that low income people would be forced to live outside of the county or to live in those portions of it that are not adequately serviced by public transportation and have very few of the amenities of a semirural environment.

As an example, land banking could be used to guarantee that some low income people would have the opportunity to live in areas readily accessible to rapid transit by putting aside land for future low income housing in those areas where rapid transit and feeder systems are projected.

b. Employment. Present and future industrial sites should be easily accessible to public transportation. All employment centers must be made accessible to people living in predominantly low income and high unemployment areas. It is also recommended that new and expanded commercial and industrial activities develop training programs for new jobs, for the benefit of current residents of Santa Clara County.[104]

c. Hospitals. Hospitals and medical facilities should be easily accessible to the population they serve. Regional transportation policy ought to ensure that major hospitals, like Stanford University Medical Center, become accessible to the entire regional population.

d. Recreational facilities. Recreational facilities should be accessible to public transportation, especially for the low income groups and high density areas, such as central and southeast San Jose.

e. Neighborhood indentity. Transportation plans must reinforce, and above all must not violate, neighborhood identity or community patterns. Thus, proposed transportation facilities should be designed to minimize the destruction of low cost housing for minorities, elderly, and handicapped.

f. Affirmative action. All public projects, during both the planning and the implementation stages, should have an affirmative action program that guarantees the hiring of minorities and women. In addition, training programs for the unemployed should be set up in conjunction with existing schools or training centers and junior colleges. Labor and community organizations should be involved in the formulation and implementation of an affirmative action program and field training programs for any project related to public transportation.

g. Financing. Once adequate planning has taken place and an appropriate transportation system is selected and designed, it must be adequately funded and provide an equitable distribution of benefits and costs among the metropolitan population. A negative example is the half-cent sales tax approved for transit by the voters of Santa Clara County in 1976. This tax is inadequate because it doesn't provide sufficient funds for a bus fleet large enough to fully serve the county population, and is an inequitable burden on the low income taxpayer. Sales taxes are regressive because the poor end up paying a much higher percentage of their income than do the affluent. As is the case with BART, everybody pays the additional tax, yet it is the more affluent who seem to benefit most from the facility. The commuters to San Francisco are white collar workers, and there are enough feeder systems in San Francisco for them to go to all points from the BART stations. However, the reverse is not true. For example, it is difficult for a blue collar worker who lives in San Francisco to commute to Union City. There are no feeder systems in Union City for this worker to get to his or her job. In view of this drawback (the regressive half-cent sales tax), the social groups propose, in addition to funds that the county hopes to get from the federal government, the following means of financing and supporting the future transportation system of Santa Clara County:[105]

1. A substantial daily parking fee at all public transportation facilities
2. Imposing corporate taxes on industries and commercial enterprises that have been in the county for five or more years
3. An additional tax on gasoline.

Even though there has been minority group participation in the Metropolitan Transportation Commission's planning activities for the San Jose metropolitan area,[106] the Mexican American Community Services Agency and the Confederacion de la Raza perceive the ABAG/MTC *Draft Report* as an effort to plan services for the general population, not necessarily for the poor.[107] That is not to say that the needs of minorities and low income people and the needs of the majority do not coincide; it is quite evident that they often do. However, an analysis of ways of upgrading the physical environment is not enough. Proposals that reflect social needs, such as land banking, dial-a-ride for the elderly and handicapped, and affirmative action, are as important as physical planning, and should be brought into the framework of developing a transportation system.

The Private Sector (San Jose Chamber of Commerce, Council for a Balanced Community)

Problem: The combination of a dispersed settlement pattern, a spatial imbalance between jobs and housing centers, and a failure to complete necessary highway projects has led to a serious short range mobility problem in the San Jose metropolitan area.[108] While the bulk of employment opportunities remains in the North County, land available for residential use exists principally in the South County. The resulting imbalance creates the commuting pattern that represents the fundamental transportation problem of the metropolitan area.[109]

A continued reliance on the automobile as the sole mode of transportation will, in the long range, lead to increased congestion, deteriorating air quality, and a worsening fuel shortage.

Solution: One cannot expect an overnight abandonment of the automobile and the instant creation of a new supertransportation system.[110] The American economy has too much invested in automobile technology and highway infrastructure to implement such a policy without experiencing an economic collapse. If begun today, a rail or fixed guideway system capable of making a significant contribution to the solution of the mobility problems would take 10 years to complete.[111]

The transit proposals advocated in the *Draft Report* will still result in highways accommodating 90 percent of all daily trips by 1990.[112] Even the most optimistic view suggests that not more than 30 percent of all trips will be by public transit in 1990, which would still leave the auto as the primary transportation mode.[113] It is therefore folly to stop highway construction and maintenance until there is substantial evidence that a new system is capable of handling the bulk of future transportation demand.[114]

How will a new system be financed? At present, most funding for highway and transit development comes from state and federal gas taxes paid by automobile users. There is no public transit system that pays for itself out of the fare box. Bus fares recover 20 percent of costs, whereas light rail fares account for as much as 35 percent.[115] In order to lure commuters onto the bus, fares must be low. The deficit is then made up by the total population, most of whom continue to drive automobiles. One cannot expect automobile users to voluntarily assess themselves new taxes to finance a system they will not use.

Regardless of any policy choices, the inescapable fact remains that we are running out of petroleum. Although it may be 40 years before we run completely dry, it is likely that before this point is reached, the combination of high gas prices and shortages will seriously disrupt any petroleum-based transportation system. To ignore the problem entirely would be to ensure the ultimate collapse of the economy.

The Santa Clara County Transit Plan should make provisions for an "ultimate system," but it should be planned and designed so it can be implemented in phases utilizing a variety of modes.[116] The unique physical and social geography of Santa Clara County makes it unlikely that a single transportation approach will be able to satisfy the diverse transit needs. A multitiered system incorporating rural door-to-door taxi service, a bus feeder system to light rail, or possibly a fixed guideway system may be essential. More fuel-efficient personal vehicles will become utilized and bikeway facilities will be expanded.

Since it is unlikely that an ultimate system can be built immediately, a transitional plan designed to solve our short term problems and facilitate long range solutions would provide a practical approach. Such an approach would permit careful consideration of alternatives and minimize the time pressures that often result in poor planning.

The first phase would involve a bus-oriented system.[117] The newly expanded bus system is gaining acceptance as an efficient alternative to the auto. Freeways and expressways would continue to be built and maintained as multimodal systems providing express bus lanes, personal traffic lanes, and bike paths, and would ultimately serve as roadbeds for a light rail system. The Council for a Balanced Community endorses the West Valley Multi-Modal Transportation Corridor Task Force recommendation to develop Routes 85 and 87 as multimodal facilities.[118]

The second phase involves the utilization of light rail where rights-of-way and track already exist.[119] There are 100 miles of existing trackage in the county, owned by Western Pacific and Southern Pacific. The third phase would be the full implementation of a light rail system using existing freeways and expressways, based on the experience of successful bus routes. Buses would then be used as a local feeder system. The final phase, if it is still necessary and affordable, would be a fixed guideway system, predominantly used as an express line.

The Chamber of Commerce is reluctant to support any demonstration project, such as the Guadalupe light rail proposal, unless it is part of a coherent future transit plan, especially if it limits future alternative uses in that corridor.[120] If a short route is to be built, the chamber recommends a route extending from Marriott Park to the airport, the Civic Center, downtown, and San Jose State University to Highway 280, with large parking facilities at each end. This route would serve a greater portion of the county than the proposed Guadalupe line, and solve much of the critical downtown and university parking problem.

An estimate published in the Deleuw, Cather Report sets the capital costs for 45 miles of light rail serving five corridors at between $210 and $340 million—$4.5 to $7.5 million per mile.[121] The Santa Clara County Transportation Agency estimates the costs for a 35 mile system at $258 million, or $8 million per mile.[122] Although these estimates may seem high, they are still one-tenth the cost of a BART-type system.[123] Compared with BART, the lower cost of light rail reflects a less expensive right-of-way, a lack of total grade separation, and manual versus automotive control.

The criterion for evaluating transit alternatives should be based on cost and effectiveness. As stated in the county's *General Transit Plan*:

> The transportation system must be provided at the least cost, consistent with the provision of effective total transportation. The cost of the transit system must be less than any alternative means of providing effective transportation for the same number of people.[124]

The ideal system combines the convenience, comfort, flexibility, and privacy of the personal auto with the speed and efficiency of the fixed guideway. Unfortunately, the constraints of time, money, and energy may make the ideal system impossible until technological developments reduce capital and operating costs, or we decide to spend a greater part of our national income on transportation. A BART-type fixed guideway system requires at least 10 years from the design to the first ride. At current prices such a system would cost around $5 billion.[125] The carrying charges at 6 percent would total $300 million a year. This amount of money could provide the county with 1,250 buses at $120,000 each and allow $120,000 a year to operate each bus.[126]

In sum, the best, short range transportation solution for the San Jose metropolitan area remains the development of the bus system. At present the bus system accounts for only 1 percent of the county's 4 million daily trips. Before we invest in a light rail or a fixed guideway system, it seems reasonable first to develop ridership and efficient routes through experimentation with the bus system. Thus, highway construction and maintenance should be continued in the near future. For long term considerations, the regional transportation plan should provide for a fully integrated multimodal system. The diverse character of the county precludes solving the problem with a single mode of transportation.

With regard to development, future land use policies should be modified to encourage the blending of residential and industrial activity in order to shorten the journey to work.[127] Areas zoned as exclusively industrial should be redrawn to include residential use. The character of industrial development in Santa Clara County in no way precludes the juxtaposition of industrial and residential uses. In addition, multiple family and other types of attached residential construction should be encouraged, especially near mass transit facilities.

SUMMARY

While most of the actors had a similar definition of the transportation problem in the San Jose metropolitan area, their suggested solutions at first differed substantially. Proposals ranged from expanding the highway system and increasing dependency on the automobile to an almost exclusive use of a fixed, light rail transit system. Yet, most of the actors involved were also willing to suggest an area of maneuverability in resolving this metropolitan conflict. Thus, supporters of highway construction, such as private sector and commuter groups, recognized the long term importance of developing mass transit alternatives to the automobile. In fact, many of these groups actively support the expansion of the county's bus fleet.

Also expressing adaptability, the environmental interests indicated that their proposal for a light rail network would require a long term effort, which of necessity would have to rely upon the existing highway-oriented system in the short run. Even the most vigorous rail supporters, the Modern Transit Society, would condone the use of the automobile if it were not given hidden subsidies, such as publicly supported highway facilities, and competed equitably with transit facilities.

Accordingly, after an extensive multiple advocacy process of research and citizen participation involving over 200 public meetings and workshops during a three year period,[128] the ABAG/MTC regional planning activities attempted to reflect this diversity of views within the San Jose metropolitan area in the November 1978 *Draft Report, Santa Clara Valley Corridor Evaluation*,[129] which was circulated among the various communities, organizations, and special interests involved with this issue. ABAG and MTC assumed this arbitrating role even though they themselves represent Bay Area-wide interests that are more urban and transit-oriented than many local interests within Santa Clara County. Even when making light rail proposals, ABAG and MTC attempted to minimize local opposition by offering projects that would maximize Santa Clara County monies by keeping the dollars solely within the county and increasing the probability of obtaining UMTA funds. An example of this was the ABAG/MTC recommendation of linking downtown San Jose with an intracounty light rail line to Edenvale, the South San Jose neighborhood, rather than with an intercounty transit line to the Fremont BART station, although the two routes were found to be equal with regard to potential ridership.[130]

During the three month period between the issuance of the *Draft Report* and its consideration by the Santa Clara County Board of Supervisors, the report received great scrutiny.[131] Five public workshops were held throughout the county, and all city staffs were briefed. In addition, presentations were made to a number of other county agencies, such as the Inter-Governmental Council (IGC), the Transportation Commission, and the Board of Supervisors. All the City Councils discussed and took positions on the recommendations, as did civic organizations, business groups, and concerned individuals.

The final ABAG/MTC staff recommendations stated:

> In the past three months, participants in the review process have cooperated in developing a county-wide consensus on many of the land use and transportation recommendations. There is unanimous support for a better balance of jobs and housing. There is agreement on an improved and expanded bus system. There is widespread support for upgrading SP service. And there is recognition that land use and transportation decisions must be complementary.[132]

In March 1979 the *Draft Report* was approved, with relatively few revisions, by a unanimous vote of the Santa Clara County Board of Supervisors and by 14 of the 15 cities in the county.[133] All of the five development recommendations were essentially retained by the staff in its final recommendations to the JPC on March 14, 1979.[134] The only major change was in response to citizen concerns in the South County areas of Morgan Hill and Gilroy, where there are realistic fears of becoming bedroom communities. Wording in the final recommendations supported these cities' policies on industrial development, consistent economic and residential growth, and maintenance of Coyote as an agricultural preserve. In accord with these concepts, wording was also added concerning job development in the Edenvale area. This recommendation was modified to reflect the desire to balance those jobs with housing in San Jose, and to prevent establishment of a commuting pattern from Edenvale to Morgan Hill and Gilroy.[135]

In addition, a new recommendation was added by the staff, in order to encourage a balance between future increases in jobs and housing construction, and essentially to propose to "support construction of new housing at a rate commensurate with new job development."[136]

The final joint staff recommendations on transportation and land use were presented to the JPC on March 21, 1979. The prioritizing of these recommendations was essentially consistent with those adopted by the Board of Supervisors, showing the power of the county's input (see Table 6.4). Notable word changes were that improvements on Routes 280 and 17 would be for the use of car pools and buses, that rights-of-way on

Routes 85 and 87 should be protected, and that grade intersections on Route 237 should be changed to freeway interchanges.[137]

Route 152, which links Santa Clara County with I-5 in the Central Valley, had received increasing support during the review process and had been made the top priority for FAP highways by the Board of Supervisors. A recommendation was added by the staff that Route 152 be widened and truck escape ramps added. It is interesting to note that this is an interregional project that received strong county support.[138]

Virtually all of the staff recommendations shown in Figures 6.3 and 6.4 were adopted by the JPC in the form of a finalized study.[139] They did elect to leave Routes 101, 237, and 280 FAB projects of equal priority, although Route 152 had already received high priority status from MTC and the county. They also added widening of the Montague/San Tomas interchange at Route 101.

Recommendations for transit included comments emphasizing that the light rail proposal for the Edenvale corridor should be studied further in terms of alternatives. This is being done as part of the Phase II alternative analysis of the Guadalupe corridor required by UMTA.[140] In order to respond to pro-highway, low density housing interests in South San Jose, two supportive land use and transportation policies were softened. One change, while referring to light rail, specifically noted that Route 87 should also be studied for highway compatibility.[141] The second supportive statement was reworded to indicate that "The proposed land use plan for San Jose should be consistent with the development of the light rail corridor; . . . " and that any land use changes should be " . . . concurrent with federal commitment for construction," rather than the original phrasing "must be rezoned to permit higher density residential develoment."[142] The JPC adopted the recommendations of the staff, including the proposal for 750 buses and emphasis on express bus service, as well as upgrading of the Southern Pacific Railroad.[143]

By September 1979, ABAG and MTC had both approved the study as amended.[144] As such, it represented a major success of these Bay Area planning institutions.

While it may seem surprising that such a large and complex metropolitan area as Santa Clara County was chosen for only the second corridor study to be done by MTC,[145] the very size, importance, and character of its transportation problems virtually mandated that it be studied. Such a large scale evaluation was a difficult undertaking for the planners associated with the project, and consensus formation among the wide range of interests required extensive bargaining among the various actors, including the regional agencies, thus making it difficult to retain the plan's full technical integrity. It should be recognized, however, that the purpose of the study was to provide a locally accepted and viable plan,

Table 6.4 ABAG/MTC Highway Recommendations: March 1979

Federal Aid Urban (FAU)

1. Routes 85 and 87—Protect rights-of-way and continue purchases as required for these transportation corridors ($5-10 million).
2. Route 87—Construct four-lane expressway with appropriate grade separations to connect with the Almaden Expressway in the vicinity of Curtner Avenue ($18-20 million). The remaining corridor right-of-way should be protected for future transportation purposes.
3. Montague/San Tomas Interchange at Route 101—Widen the existing bridge over Route 101 from two to six lanes to match the roadway widths of the two adjoining expressways.
4. Route 85—Make operational improvements in Cupertino. The existing Caltrans project, which would cost approximately $7-10 million to extend a freeway or expressway to Sunnyvale Saratoga Road, will be considered. The project is to be designed to avoid simply shifting traffic from Cupertino to San Jose and Saratoga streets.

Federal Aid Interstate (FAI)

1. Route 280—Add two inside lanes between Route 17 and Magdalena Road. The possible use of these additional lanes exclusively by buses and carpools should be considered. Additional analysis should be undertaken to indicate how this type of preferential treatment would work in this location and how the development of the expanded bus fleet would be coordinated with this proposal ($14-16 million).

Federal Aid Primary (FAP)

1. Route 152—Widen to four lanes and add a median barrier and truck escape ramps between the Pacheco Creek Bridge and the existing four lane section in the vicinity of the summit. This widening is to be consistent with an ultimate four-lane facility on Route 152 ($6 million).
2. Route 237—Route 237 is currently in the Federal Aid Urban system. The County, the cities and Caltrans should determine the appropriate segment between Milpitas and Mountain View to recommend for conversion to the Federal Aid Primary system and should determine the priority for implementation of specific projects on this route ($20-25 million).
3. Route 101—Widen from four to six lanes in the vicinity of the Alum Rock interchange ($5-10 million).

The Joint Policy Committee voted to indicate that improvements to Route 152, Route 237 and Route 101 at the Alum Rock interchange would have equal priority at this time. Route 152, however, has already been supported as a high priority project by the County Board of Supervisors and MTC.

4. Route 101—Add auxiliary lanes (weaving lanes between interchanges) north of Route 17 ($4-6 million).
5. Route 17—Widen by adding one lane in each direction from Route 101 to Fremont. The exclusive use of these lanes by buses and carpools should be

considered in conjunction with the deployment of additional express bus routes that would utilize this facility ($8-12 million).

6. Develop and implement ramp metering and preferential treatment for buses where appropriate ($3-5 million). This particular recommendation does not have the project specific nature of the other recommendations included in this section. The position of this proposal is not meant to indicate that it has the lowest priority for the use of Federal Aid Primary funds. Rather, the intent of this recommendation is to insure that in the next ten years this magnitude of funding be allocated for ramp metering and transit and carpool preferential treatment on Federal Aid Primary highways. (Although no specific dollar amount has been developed, similar types of measures should be implemented, as appropriate, on Interstate and Federal Aid Urban freeways and expressways.)

Note: All estimates are in 1977 dollars.

Source: Association of the Bay Area Governments and the Metropolitan Transportation Commission, Joint Policy Committee, *Santa Clara Valley Corridor Evaluation: Summary* (March 1979).

not just the most technically correct one.[146] Community consensus and finalization of an approved plan increase the possibility that additional federal and state funds can be obtained to construct desired transportation facilities. ABAG and MTC recognized that a valid plan backed by the county as a whole would be more likely to withstand the jostling among other agencies' plans for priority rating at the state and federal levels and, consequently, to receive funding. This political reality may at times have appeared to overshadow the desire for public input even though over 200 public meetings and workshops were conducted. However, it should be remembered that funding is a political process, and the importance of concurrence cannot be underrated if the process is to be successful and monies are to be brought into the county.

Thus, MTC and ABAG did strive to have meaningful citizen input. Citizens and many groups, through their elected officials and numerous public meetings, were provided with the opportunity to make the plan responsive to their views. As a result the *Draft Report* already incorporated many of these views, and its acceptability was greatly enhanced. A second factor in the success of ABAG/MTC regional planning activities in Santa Clara County was the fact that these organizations, as well as their Joint Policy Committee, had substantial pro-transit representation from Santa Clara County itself. During the participatory process, especially while the *Draft Report* was being reviewed, the chairs of MTC (James Self, City Councilmember, San Jose) and ABAG (Rod Diridon, supervisor, Santa Clara County) and three of the seven members of the JPC were from the county.[147] These locally elected officials seemed

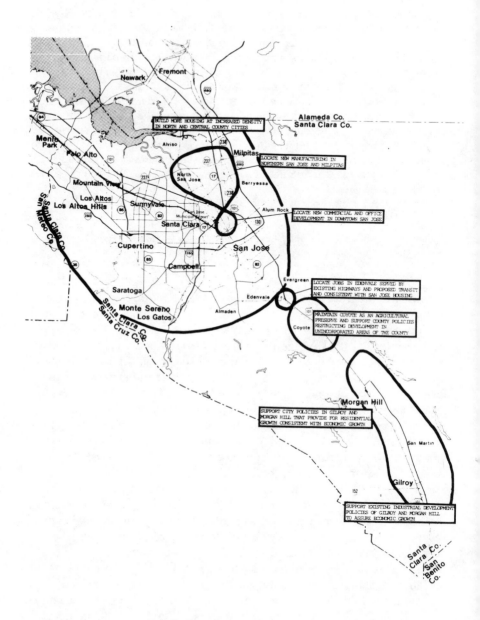

FIGURE 6.3. Land Use Recommendations for Santa Clara County.
Source: Association of Bay Area Governments and the Metropolitan Transportation Commission, Joint Policy Committee, *Santa Clara Valley Corridor Evaluation: Summary* (March 1979).

208

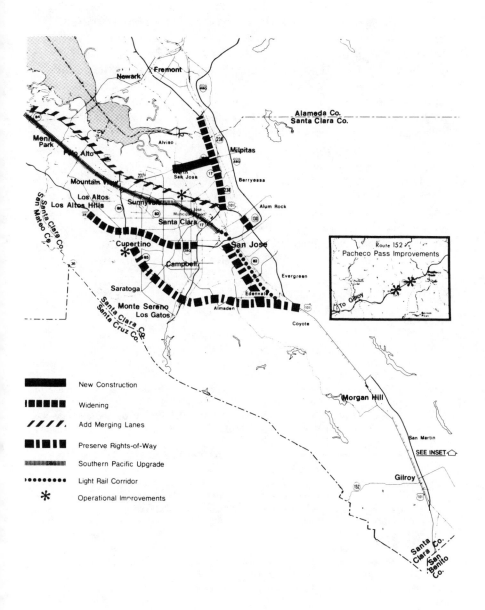

FIGURE 6.4. Transportation Recommendations for Santa Clara County. *Source:* Association of Bay Area Governments and the Metropolitan Transportation Commission, Joint Policy Committee, *Santa Clara Valley Corridor Evaluation: Summary* (March 1979).

to play a crucial role in convincing their constituents of the desirability of the ABAG/MTC plan, especially the mass transportation proposals.[148]

A third factor involved in this successful process was that most of the actors perceived the plan as either positive or neutral, because the plan generally promised to improve transportation throughout the county.[149] Only one group representing the South San Jose neighborhood, Edenvale, really perceived any direct negative aspects of the plan, since it was only their neighborhood that was specifically singled out for a possible light rail line and higher density housing.[150] Even their views were eclipsed by the residents in other San Jose neighborhoods, who generally supported the plan.[151]

Finally, the gradual increase in the cost and inconvenience of the highly automobile-oriented development pattern in the San Jose metropolitan area began to raise questions about transportation alternatives among the county residents themselves. Apparently, after more than 30 years of almost uncontrolled dispersed residential development, the citizens of Santa Clara County were ready to listen to the planners.

NOTES

1. This trend is well documented in Leo Grebler and Frank G. Mittlebach *The Inflation of House Prices* (Lexington, Mass.: Lexington Books, 1979); and in *Peninsula Times Tribune*, "Everything's Crowded," January 18, 1980, pp.1, 8.
2. In 1976 the voters in Santa Clara County voted a half-cent sales tax increase to support a County Transit District and a fleet of 516 buses.
3. For a report made during the early stages of the ABAG/MTC collaboration on the Santa Clara transportation issue, see *Corridor Evaluation, Summary Report, Phase III* (Berkeley: JPC, 1977).
4. See Frank Sweeney, "Supervisors Approve Most of Transit Plan," *San Jose Mercury*, March 6, 1979, pp. 1A, 18A.
5. A recent example of this problem was the local governmental rejection of the land use proposals in the ABAG-sponsored *Environmental Management Plan* (1978). See David E. Dowall, "Local-Regional Planning Conflicts: ABAG's Compact Growth Plan and Its Effects on the Metropolitan Housing Market," in David E. Dowall and Bruce D. McDowell, eds., *Making Regional Planning Work* (Urbana: Bureau of Urban and Regional Planning Research, University of Illinois, 1980), pp. 32–47.
6. See, for example, National Academy of Sciences, *Toward an Understanding of Metropolitan America* (San Francisco: Canfield Press, 1975).
7. Based on interview with Gordon Jacoby, senior planner, Association of Bay Area Governments, February 1979; interviews with Norman Steinman, Metropolitan Transportation Commission, February and May 1979; interviews with staff, Urban Mass Transportation Administration, U.S. Department of Transportation, December 1980; and Association of Bay Area Governments and the Metropolitan Transportation Commission, Joint Policy Committee (ABAG/MTC), *Draft Report, Santa Clara Valley Corridor Evaluation* (November 1978).
8. ABAG/MTC, *Draft Report*, p. 1.

9. Ibid., p. 5.
10. Interviews with Jacoby, Steinman, and staff, Urban Mass Transportation Administration.
11. Jack Ybarra, *Santa Clara Valley Corridor Evaluation: Public Participation Program* (Berkeley, Calif.: Association of Bay Area Governments and Metropolitan Transportation Commission, Joint Policy Committee, March 1979).
12. ABAG/MTC, *Draft Report*, p. 5.
13. Ibid., pp. 59–70.
14. Ibid., p. 3.
15. Such an alternatives analysis is currently under way for Route 87 (Guadalupe corridor). See James H. Graebner, "Santa Clara County in 1990: The Guadalupe Corridor," *Guadalupe Corridor Report*, January 1, 1980, pp.1–2.
16. ABAG/MTC *Draft Report*, p. 4.
17. Ibid., pp. 83–84.
18. Ibid., pp. 84–91.
19. Metropolitan Transportation Commission, *Peninsula Transit Alternatives Project* (1977).
20. ABAG/MTC, *Draft Report*, p. 90.
21. Ibid.
22. Ibid.
23. Ibid., p. 91.
24. Interview with David Minister, project director, Guadalupe Corridor Analysis, Santa Clara County Transportation Agency, March 1979.
25. Ibid.
26. Santa Clara County Transportation Agency, *Recommendations Pertaining to the Santa Clara Valley Corridor Evaluation Study* (February 1979).
27. Interview with Minister.
28. Bob Schmidt, "Gas Tax Increase Urged," *San Jose Mercury*, March 21, 1979, p. 1F.
29. Santa Clara County Transportation Agency, *Recommendations*, p. 3.
30. Ibid.
31. Ibid., pp. 3, 4.
32. Neil Peirce, "Valley's Suburban Sprawl Lends to Traffic Pollution," *San Jose Mercury*, April 17, 1979, p. 18.
33. Santa Clara County Transportation Agency, *Recommendations*, pp. 4–5.
34. The California Transportation Commission has recommended "a floating tax rate, pegged to inflation, which could be adjusted each year." See Schmidt, "Gas Tax Increase Urged."
35. Santa Clara County Transportation Agency, *Recommendations*, pp. 19–39.
36. Interview with John E. Perry, Jr., chairman, Santa Clara County Transportation Commission, March 1979.
37. Interview with James Lightbody, transit operations engineer, Santa Clara County Transit District, March 1979.
38. Santa Clara County Transportation Agency, *Recommendations*, pp. 32, 44, 49.
39. Metropolitan Transportation Commission, *Peninsula Transit Alternatives Project* (1977).
40. Santa Clara County Transportation Agency, *Recommendations*, p. 31.
41. *San Jose Mercury*, "Extend SP Commuter Service," April 2, 1979, p. 6B.
42. Santa Clara County Transportation Agency, *Recommendations*, p. 49.
43. Ibid., p. 54. Approved by Santa Clara County Board of Supervisors, March 19, 1979.
44. Santa Clara County Board of Supervisors meeting, March 19, 1979.
45. Santa Clara County Transportation Agency, *Recommendations*, p. 38.
46. Ibid., p. 50.

47. Ibid., pp. 44, 49.
48. Daniel Lopez, "Comparison of Balanced Estimate Development Plan and Local General Plans," in Association of Bay Area Governments, *Santa Clara Corridor Evaluation, Attachment No. 4* (August 1977). Other sources indicate a somewhat lower 1975 population for San Jose. See Table 2.1.
49. Ibid.
50. Interview with John Berg, planner, San Jose Planning Department, April 1979; ABAG/MTC *Draft Report*, p. 26; Interview with Joseph F. Bass, Transportation Division, Department of Public Works, City of San Jose, February 1979.
51. Santa Clara County Planning Department, *Info Highlights*, June 1978.
52. Interview with Bass.
53. Santa Clara County Planning Department, *Info Highlights*.
54. See correspondence of Janet Gray Hayes, mayor, City of San Jose, to Louise Giersch, chairman, ABAG/MTC Joint Policy Committee, February 22, 1979; and memorandum of John W. Hamilton, director of planning, City of San Jose, to mayor and City Council, City of San Jose, February 6, 1979.
55. San Jose City Council, *Downtown San Jose Transit Mobility Improvement* (December 1978).
56. San Jose Planning Department, General Plan work maps.
57. Ibid.
58. Calculated from ibid.
59. David M. Gordon, *Problems in Political Economy* (Lexington, Mass.: D. C. Heath, 1971), pp. 419–20.
60. Susan Yoachum, "More Costly Homes Win Sunnyvale Nod," *San Jose Mercury*, May 4, 1979, p. 4F.
61. Interview with Larry Daumbs, Metropolitan Transportation Commission, May 1979.
62. These views are based on interviews with Donald Stone, Santa Clara County Manufacturing Group, February 1979; Santa Clara County Manufacturing Group, "Views on the Land Use and Transportation Recommendations of the Santa Clara Valley Corridor Evaluation Study" (February 1979); interview with Robert Temmermand, Public Works Department, City of Sunnyvale, March 1979; interview with David R. Fadness, transportation chairman, V.E.P. Homeowners Association, March 1979; correspondence of David R. Fadness and James E. Cates, V.E.P. Homeowners Association, to the San Jose City Council, January 1979; interview with Mardi Gualtieri, chairman, West Valley Multi-Modal Transportation Corridor Task Force, February 1979: correspondence of Mardi Gualtieri to ABAG/MTC Joint Policy Committee, February 1979.
63. Ibid.
64. Interview with Lightbody.
65. Ibid.
66. Ibid.
67. ABAG/MTC, *Draft Report*, pp. 30–35.
68. Interview with Burton Epstein, chairman, Transportation Task Force, Santa Clara County Manufacturing Group, April 1979.
69. Interview with Gualtieri.
70. Metropolitan Transportation Commission, *Peninsula Transit Alternatives Projects* (1977).
71. Santa Clara County Manufacturing Group, "Views on the Land Use."
72. Ibid.
73. Ibid.; interview with Temmermand.
74. Interview with Fadness; correspondence of Fadness and Cates.

75. See for example, Santa Clara County Manufacturing Group, "Views on the Land Use"; Fadness and Cates correspondence.
76. Santa Clara County Manufacturing Group, "Views on the Land Use."
77. Interviews with Stone, Fadness, and Gualtieri.
78. These views are based on interview with Richard Baines, executive director, American Lung Association, April 1976; interview with Ralph Balmer, chairman, Transportation Committee, Loma Prieta Chapter, Sierra Club, February 1979; Correspondence of Ann Clifton, et al., League of Women Voters of Santa Clara County, to Board of Supervisors, Santa Clara County, January 30, 1979; Interview with Random Grabeel, Modern Transit Society, March 1979; and Alvin L. Spivak, "Transit Problems and Solutions" (Modern Transit Society, San Jose, Calif.: 1980).
79. Ibid.
80. Data from Federal Highway Administration, U.S. Department of Transportation (1979).
81. See for example, Spivak, "Transit Problems and Solutions."
82. Ibid.; interview with Balmer; correspondence of Lewis T. Ames, chairman, State and Federal Task Force, Modern Transit Society, to Donald Rothblatt, January 1980.
83. See Ames correspondence.
84. Ibid.
85. Interview with Grabeel.
86. Ames correspondence.
87. Ibid.
88. Interview with Grabeel.
89. Ibid.
90. These views are based on interviews with Jose Villa, executive director, Mexican American Community Services Agency, February and May 1979; interviews with staff, Confederacion de la Raza, April 1979; and Metropolitan Transportation Commission, Minority Citizens Advisory Committee, "MCAC Perspective: The Santa Clara Valley Corridor Evaluation" (November 1978).
91. Ibid.
92. ABAG/MTC, Draft Report.
93. Confederacion de la Raza and Mexican American Community Services Agency.
94. Interviews with Villa, and with staff, Confederacion de la Raza.
95. Ibid.
96. Ibid.
97. Ibid.
98. Ibid.
99. Ibid.
100. Ibid.
101. Interviews with Rosa Maria Hernandez, executive director, Mexican American Services Agency, February and April 1981.
102. Interviews with Villa and with staff, Confederacion de la Raza.
103. Ibid.
104. Metropolitan Transportation Commission, "MCAC Perspective."
105. Interview with staff, Confederacion de la Raza.
106. See Metropolitan Transportation Commission, "MCAC Perspective."
107. Interviews with Villa and with staff, Confederacion de la Raza.
108. These views are based on interview with Harry C. Kallshian, chairman, Transportation Task Force, San Jose Chamber of Commerce, February 1979; San Jose Chamber of Commerce, "Chamber of Commerce Position, Transit in Santa Clara County" (November 1975); San Jose Chamber of Commerce, "Chamber of Commerce

Position on Light Rail in Santa Clara County" (1977); San Jose Chamber of Commerce, "The Housing Price Crunch" (1978); interviews with Edward C. Steffani and Ralph Latine, Council for a Balanced Community, February 1979; *Council for Balanced Community Bulletin*, Spring 1979.

109. Ibid.

110. Interviews with Steffani and Latine.

111. Ibid.

112. ABAG/MTC, *Draft Report*, pp. 30–35.

113. Interview with Minister.

114. Interviews with Steffani and Latine.

115. Santa Clara County Transportation Agency, *Recommendations*, p. 51.

116. Interviews with Steffani and Latine.

117. Interview with Kallshian.

118. Interviews with Steffani and Latine.

119. Interview with Kallshian.

120. Ibid.

121. Deleuw, Cather and Company, *Rapid Transit Development Project: Phase I Summary Abstract* (San Francisco: January 1975).

122. Santa Clara County Transportation Agency, *Recommendations*, p. 47.

123. Interview with Kallshian.

124. Santa Clara County Transit District, *General Transit Plan* (September 1972).

125. Interview with Kallshian.

126. Ibid.

127. Ibid.

128. See for example, Ybarra, *Santa Clara Valley Corridor Evaluation*, pp. 1–29.

129. ABAG/MTC, *Draft Report*.

130. Ibid., pp. 90–91; interview with Steinman.

131. Ybarra, *Santa Clara Valley Corridor Evaluation*.

132. Chuck Forester, and William F. Hein, "Final Recommendations on the Santa Clara Valley Corridor Evaluation," memorandum to ABAG/MTC, Joint Policy Committee (March 14, 1979), p. 1.

133. See Sweeney, "Supervisors Approve Most of Transit Plan"; and Graebner, "Santa Clara County in 1990," pp. 1–2.

134. Forester and Hein, "Final Recommendations."

135. Ibid., pp. 3–4.

136. Ibid., p. 4.

137. Chuck Forester and William F. Hein, "Final Staff Recommendations on the Transportation Features of the Santa Clara Valley Corridor Evaluation," memorandum to ABAG/MTC, Joint Policy Committee (March 21, 1979), pp. 3–6.

138. Ibid., p. 4.

139. Association of Bay Area Governments and the Metropolitan Transportation Commission, Joint Policy Committee, *Santa Clara Valley Corridor Evaluation: Summary* (March 1979).

140. Interview with Graebner.

141. Forrester and Hein, "Final Staff Recommendations," pp. 6–8.

142. Ibid.; compare with ABAG/MTC *Draft Report*, pp. 14–15.

143. ABAG/MTC, *Santa Clara Valley Corridor Evaluation*, pp. 17–21.

144. Interview with Norma Mencacci, intergovernmental relations, Santa Clara County Transportation Agency, July 1980.

145. The first corridor study was conducted for San Mateo County.

146. See, for example, the statements on consensus formation in ABAG/MTC, *Draft Report*, pp. 1–4.

147. The three members of the ABAG/MTC Joint Policy Committee from Santa Clara County were Rod Diridon, supervisor, Santa Clara County; James Jackson, City Councilmember, Cupertino; and James Self, City Councilmember, San Jose.
148. Based on interviews with staff of ABAG, MTC, and Santa Clara County Transportation Agency, May 1980.
149. Ibid.; Ybarra, *Santa Clara Valley Corridor Evaluation*.
150. Ibid.
151. Interview with Bass; Hayes correspondence; Hamilton memorandum.

7

FINDINGS AND CONCLUSIONS

This chapter presents our findings and conclusions on the four case studies employing the multiple advocacy model in the San Jose metropolitan area. Our discussion examines the extent to which the model helped to facilitate conflict resolution and consensus formation with respect to regional planning problems.

FINDINGS

At first, the seemingly irreconcilable metropolitan battle lines appeared to be drawn for each issue. Not only were the suggested solutions different for most of the clusters of actors involved, but the definitions of the problems varied in half of the cases. It appeared that agreement about the character of each metropolitan problem was largely a function of the extent to which all the actors had knowledge about the issue, which in turn seemed to be based on how strongly all the actors were affected by the issue.[1] For example, the shortage and rapid increase in the cost of housing had become a problem not only for low income families, but also for a large part of the entire metropolitan community. Consequently, the level of actor knowledge of consensus on the character of the housing problem was relatively high. High consensus formation was also found with respect to the almost all-pervasive surface transportation problem in the area.

In contrast, there were great initial differences among the actors' problem perceptions about the relatively low visibility issues of expanding airport activities, which negatively affects a small minority of the regional population, and the open space and recreation issue, which involves

216

incremental space losses affecting only a few property owners at a time.[2] For these low visibility issues, problem perceptions initially varied from the extreme of too little collective action to that of too much government intervention in the marketplace. However, through the information it generated for the participants, the multiple advocacy process narrowed the differences in problem perceptions held by the actors involved with each metropolitan issue.

With regard to proposed solutions, across-the-board agreement was more difficult to establish than it was for problem difinition. A major reason for this difficulty in consensus building was the initial standing differences (sometimes called cleavages) that seemed to exist across issue lines between public and private actors, central city and suburbs, minority and majority populations, environmental groups and developers, and local communities and regional interests. Yet, as the multiple advocacy process unfolded and the actors involved became sensitized to one another's views and concerns, each was eventually able to suggest an area of maneuverability it might have in resolving a metropolitan conflict.

The degree of solution consensus seemed to depend on two sets of variables: issue attributes and situational characteristics.[3] The issue attributes involve such variables as the actors' perceptions of regional scale economies to resolve the issue, the degree of controversy of the issue, and the importance of resolving the issue. In part, results were similar to the typology shown in Table 7.1 and Figure 7.1, which suggests that solutions for Type I problems that have large economies of scale and are relatively noncontroversial, such as transportation and pollution control, would be the easiest about which to form a regional consensus for functional integration.[4] Conversely, metropolitan solutions for Type IV issues that seem to have low scale economies (or issues that residents want to control locally) and are relatively controversial, like housing and law enforcement, would be the most difficult to build a consensus about. Solutions for Type II and III issues with a mix of these characteristics, such as open space and recreation, were found to be moderately difficult for consensus formation. These findings were corroborated by studies in other metropolitan areas.[5]

The saliency or importance of resolving an issue can also induce consensus formation at the regional level.[6] While there was a metropolitan reluctance to build a strong consensus for dealing with the controversial housing problem with respect to economies of scale (see Figure 7.1), the growing importance of housing as an issue induced a relative increase in consensus formation about dealing with the housing problem (see Figure 7.2). This model[7] could help explain the recent public and private efforts to deal with the metropolis-wide housing problem in the San Jose area and the Bay Region.[8]

The situational variables could cover a number of influences exo-

Table 7.1 Regional Consensus-Forming Influences: Economies of Scale and Degree of Controversy

		Economies of Scale	
		High	Low
Degree of Controversy	Low	Pollution Control Transportation Solid Waste (I)	Open Space Recreation (II)
	High	Planning Economic Development Health (III)	Housing Law Enforcement Education Social Welfare (IV)

Source: Robert M. Stein, "Functional Integration at the Substate Level: A Political Approach," *Urban Affairs Quarterly* 16 (December 1980): 211–33.

geneous to the region, such as the state of the national economy and the availability of petroleum in world markets, that could affect such issues as housing and transportation. We will limit our discussion to those variables over which the regional actors have some influence: the extent of issue focus, the degree of citizen participation in developing a solution, the extent of trust formation, the distribution of benefits and costs, and the propensity of the metropolitan community to deal with the issue.

As both the airport and the surface transportation cases demonstrated, a well organized and extensive planning process with the potential (in terms of knowledge and financial resources) to actually deal with a regional problem can focus intense interest on an issue and increase the chance for forming a metropolis wide consensus.[9] In contrast, the open space and recreation issue, while less controversial than some of the other problems examined, received relatively little focused attention because of a lack of such a regional planning and potential action process.

It was also shown that extensive citizen participation, especially by the major actors, realistically modified proposed regional solutions and increased the acceptability of metropolitan plans. There may of course be diminishing returns to the consensus-building process when the social interaction costs of building high levels of agreement outweigh the regional benefits from project modifications[10] (see Figure 7.3). Yet, the transportation cases clearly demonstrated the importance of extensive participation in creating a trustful decision environment.[11] This was especially the case in the Corridor Evaluation Study, where a substantial

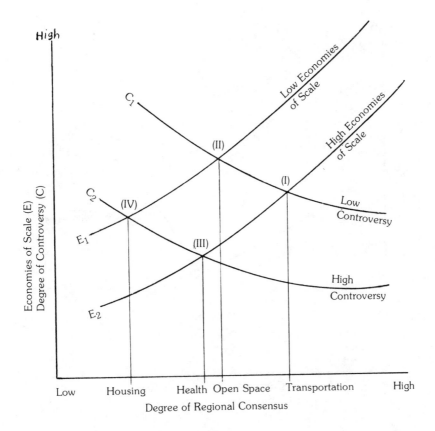

FIGURE 7.1. Regional Consensus-Forming Influences: Economies of Scale and Degree of Controversy. *Sources:* Robert M. Stein, "Functional Integration at the Substate Level: A Political Approach," *Urban Affairs Quarterly* 16 (December 1980):211–33; and Robert Mayer, Robert Moroney, and Robert Morris, eds., *Centrally Planned Change* (Urbana: University of Illinois Press, 1974), ch. 9.

number of decisionmakers (Joint Policy Committee of ABAG and MTC) were elected officials from the communities likely to be most affected by proposed plans for a regional transportation system. While functioning as a kind of co-optation process by the decisionmaking unit, this form of representation did create a trustful setting that helped facilitate trade-offs by local and regional actors that were needed for agreement.

Consensus formation also seemed more likely when the actors perceived that a solution would generate benefits for most of the metro-

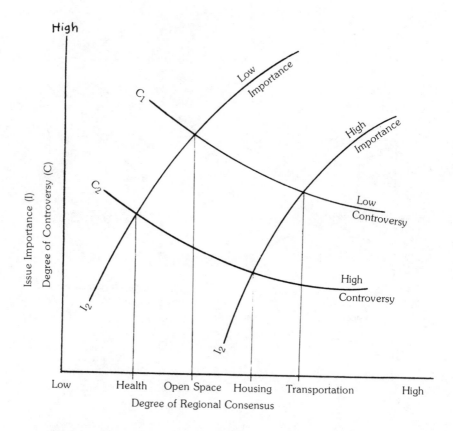

FIGURE 7.2. Regional Consensus-Forming Influences: Issue Importance and Degree of Controversy. *Source:* Robert Mayer, Robert Moroney, and Robert Morris, eds., *Centrally Planned Change* (Urbana: University of Illinois Press, 1974), ch. 9.

politan community and costs to a relatively small population.[12] This was especially true if side payments were made to compensate the groups incurring costs, as is the case with San Jose's plan to limit the environmental impact of its airport on surrounding areas. Conversely, when an existing problem generates low visibility costs for the metropolitan community and clear benefits for a few, such as the loss of open space, it was relatively difficult to form a consensus about a regional solution.

Finally, the degree to which the metropolitan area is prepared to deal with an issue (for instance, how ready a regional community is to cope with a particular problem) influenced consensus formation.[13] For ex-

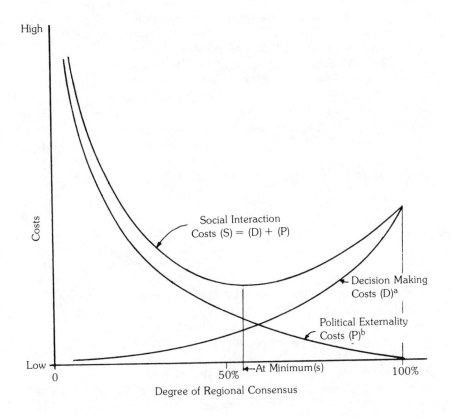

ᵃDecision Making Costs = time, effort, and direct outlays for consensus formation.

ᵇPolitical Externality Costs = costs borne by an individual forced to participate in collective action with which he or she does not agree.

FIGURE 7.3. Social Interaction Costs of Regional Consensus Formation. *Source:* Robert L. Bish, *The Public Economy of Metropolitan Areas* (Chicago: Markham, 1971), ch. 3.

ample, after three decades of low density, automobile oriented development, the San Jose metropolitan community began to raise questions about its environment and to consider alternative transportation and settlement patterns. By the late 1970s the metropolitan community was ready to carefully study the feasibility of a substantial increase in public transportation facilities, including a rail system—a study the San Jose region would not have seriously considered 10 years earlier.

Despite the varying degrees of consensus obtained for the solutions to different metropolitan problems, there appeared to be an across-the-board agreement on the approach or framework for developing a solution: regional guidance systems and cooperative efforts, especially public-private ventures. It seemed clear to most of the actors that some form of strengthened regional planning institution is needed to help guide the metropolitan community in dealing with its very serious areawide problems. There was also almost universal agreement that collaborative efforts among the various actors would be essential for problem resolution, not only because they become empathetic to one another's views, but also because they realized the importance of forming a consensus to generate the regional political and economic support needed to deal effectively with a regional problem.

CONCLUSIONS

Clearly, the multiple advocacy approach helped to facilitate the processes of consensus formation because it generated improved information, analysis, and communication among the actors involved in each metropolis-wide issue. As a result the region is probably a few steps closer to resolving some of the most important and difficult problems in the San Jose metropolitan area. To this end the multiple advocacy approach seemed to perform reasonably well the conflict resolution functions of openness, broad representation, fairness, hostility reduction, providing information, and responsiveness. While not entirely conclusive, it appears that the multiple advocacy approach helped to sensitize public decision-makers to the range of concerns and the proposals of the major actors involved.

In addition, the process enabled the participants to understand the interaction of the various issues and the trade-offs involved in proposed solutions. For example, programs designed to improve environmental quality through open space reservation in the suburbs could decrease housing opportunities for low income families in the central city;[14] policies to increase surface transportation facilities without modifying housing and industrial land use relationships could generate further traffic congestion;[15] and efforts to expand the metropolitan economy could place severe strains on the housing market, the public service system, and the quality of the regional environment.[16] Consequently, the actors came to view each problem with respect to a broad range of issues affecting the metropolitan community. As such, the multiple advocacy approach extended the comprehensiveness of collective decisionmaking and increased the rationality of the regional planning process.

NOTES

1. This finding is similar to the concept about the perceived need for collective action presented in Willis D. Hawley, "On Understanding Metropolitan Political Integration," in *Theoretical Perspectives on Urban Politics,* ed. Willis D. Hawley et al. (Englewood Cliffs, N.J.: Prentice-Hall, 1976), pp. 100–45.

2. For example, the low visibility and low importance of the parks issue was documented in Francis Tannian and John Stapleford, "Community Preference and Urban Policy", *Growth and Change* 12 (April 1981): 37–43.

3. This conceptualization is based in part on the model of community decisionmaking presented in Richard S. Bolan and Ronald L. Nuttal, *Urban Planning and Politics* (Lexington, Mass.: D. C. Heath, 1975), pp. 21–37.

4. Based on the typology developed in Robert M. Stein, "Functional Integration at the Substate Level: A Political Approach", *Urban Affairs Quarterly* 16 (December 1980): 211–33.

5. Ibid.

6. For a discussion on the significance of the relative importance of an issue in inducing regional consensus formation, see Hawley, "On Understanding Metropolitan Political Integration", pp. 113–18; and Tannian and Stapleford, "Community Preference and Urban Policy."

7. Based in part on the model presented in Robert Mayer, Robert Moroney, and Robert Morris, eds., *Centrally Planned Change* (Urbana: University of Illinois Press, 1974), ch. 9.

8. See, for example, Santa Clara County Industry and Housing Task Force, *Living Within Our Limits: A Framework for Action in the 1980's* (November 1979); and Bay Area Council, *Housing: The Bay Area's Challenge of the 1980's* (San Francisco: Bay Area Council, December 1980).

9. It has been argued that consensus formation is more likely when the actors associated with an issue believe that collective action might actually solve a problem about which people are concerned. See Hawley, "On Understanding Metropolitan Political Integration," pp. 105–13.

10. For a discussion of social interaction costs of consensus formation, see Robert L. Bish, *The Public Economy of Metropolitan Areas* (Chicago: Markham, 1971), ch. 3; and Mayer et al., *Centrally Planned Change,* ch. 9.

11. For a presentation on the importance of trust in resolving political conflicts, see Bernhardt Lieberman, "Coalitions and Conflict Resolutions," *American Behavioral Scientist* 19 (March/April 1975): 557–81.

12. This finding is also supported by Hawley, "On Understanding Metropolitan Political Integration," pp. 118–29.

13. See the discussion on developing a "sense of regional consciousness" as a necessary precondition for action to resolve a regional problem in Donald N. Rothblatt, *Regional Planning: The Applachian Experience* (Lexington, Mass.: C. C. Heath, 1971), ch. 5; and, in ibid, Hawley, "On Understanding Metropolitan Politcal Integration," pp. 134–38.

14. See David E. Dowall, "Reducing the Cost Effects of Local Land Use Controls," *Journal of the American Planning Association* 47 (April 1981): 145–53; Bernard J. Frieden, *The Environmental Protection Hustle* (Cambridge, Mass.: MIT Press, 1979); and Paul Davidoff and Mary E. Brooks, "Zoning out the Poor," in *Suburbia: the American Dream and Dilemma,* ed. Philip C. Dolce (New York: Anchor Press, 1976), pp. 135–66.

15. Association of Bay Area Governments and the Metropolitan Transportation Commission, Joint Policy Committee, *Santa Clara Valley Corridor Evaluation: Summary* (March 1979).

16. Santa Clara County Industry and Housing Task Force, *Living Within Our Limits.*

8

IMPLICATIONS FOR
METROPOLITAN AMERICA

This book argues for the growing need for a process to help resolve metropolitan area plannng problems. We presented and examined the potential ability of a multiple advocacy model for such a process. Using four case studies in the San Jose metropolitan area, the model was found to perform reasonably well the task required in conflict resolution, and seems to have the promise of broad application in metropolitan America.

Because of the communication it induced among the actors involved in regional issues, the multiple advocacy approach seemed to generate the information sharing process looked for by Stephen Skjei in his urban system advocacy concept for resolving complex planning problems:

> Cooperation between advocates and public agency planners, rather than an adversary relationship, might promote the integration of their different types of data. Advocates would provide a broad general basis for understanding social costs and benefits, and public agency planners would be responsible for improving the precision of definitions, analyzing alternatives, and providing advocates with the technical studies they need.[1]

For both theoretical and practical reasons,[2] it has been argued that citizen involvement is essential in the planning process in order to accommodate the movement for greater participatory democracy in our nation. In an age of governmental austerity, such participatory activity is likely to become increasingly important.[3] As Kelman, Clavel, Forester, and Goldsmith suggest:

> As budgets contract there will be less money for comprehensive studies and large-scale model building. . . . There will be less money for elabor-

ate plans. . . . And with less money around, planning staffs will have to pay more attention to mobilizing community resources, building coalitions, organizing support for particular proposals, and organizing resistance to others in the everyday scramble of a local planning agency's work.[4]

Equally recognized has been the growing importance of the large-scale management of our physical and social environments, such as regional planning activities.[5] What appears to be needed, particularly in metropolitan areas, is a democratic method to reconcile the dispersed and often locally autonomous interests with regionwide concerns.[6] The dilemma is described by Hudson, Wachs, and Schofer:

> We face an increased need to plan at the regional scale, and at the same time we are constrained by the effectiveness of localized planning mechanisms.[7]

Proposals have been made to encourage the creation of regional plans for metropolitan areas that, if certified to support national objectives by a federal agency such as HUD, would entitle participating metropolitan areas to additional federal assistance.[8] The multiple advocacy approach could provide an important decentralized, process oriented method for dealing with metropolitan problems that would complement the more centralized, product oriented, certified regional plan approach. While these two planning methods may appear to be conflicting,[9] they could in fact be mutually supportive and produce realistic plans capable of reconciling local, regional, and national interests. In the absence of regional government in metropolitan America, the multiple advocacy approach appears to be a promising method for resolving metropolitan conflicts and generating the agreement needed for adopting and implementing regional plans. As Rondinelli points out:

> Planning as it has been redefined, is a complex process of analyzing, intervening in, and resolving conflict that inevitably accompanies urban change . . . .[10]

The case studies of the San Jose area suggest that the multiple advocacy approach could help provide a relatively open and trustful[11] environment in which actors involved with a metropolitan problem can exchange information about their views and resolve differences whenever it is feasible. Such an environment seems most likely to occur if the advocacy is undertaken or facilitated by a respected and reasonably even handed institution, such as a local public communications medium, a professional planning organization, or a university. In this light, university planning programs[12] and chapters of the American Planning Association could be viewed as potentially important resources for helping to resolve urban and regional planning problems in metropolitan areas throughout the nation.

It may also be possible to have a regional planning institution, such as a Council of Governments, conduct the multiple advocacy process. As was shown in the surface transportation case in the San Jose area, the Bay Area regional planning agencies of ABAG and MTC performed this important metropolis-wide conflict-resolving task exceedingly well. In addition, almost all the actors in our case studies expressed a strong desire to increase the role of regional planning agencies in resolving areawide problems, despite economy drives on local government in the post-Proposition 13 era. Indeed, as studies in other parts of the nation suggest, these economy drives may actually encourage local governments to seek the economies of coordination and scale that regional institutions can provide.[13] Since regional planning agencies exist in almost every American metropolitan area, they could be used to quickly provide supportive institutional settings for establishing multiple advocacy processes.

It is even feasible to televise the actors' views and expose the entire metropolitan population to important regional problems, then ask for regional write-in or phone-in votes on alternative solutions.[14] In fact, the Urban and Regional Planning Department at San Jose State University, in collaboration with the public television station in the San Jose metropolitan area (KTEH) and the Corporation for Public Broadcasting, produced such a program on the San Jose Airport issue.[15] While the citizen feedback was not overwhelming (mostly because the project relied only on write-in votes rather than telephone polling), the results shown in Table 8.1 were considered carefully by local, regional, and state elected officials with the power to help resolve the airport issue.[16] With such interactive media techniques, the multiple advocacy approach can improve the visibility of metropolitan issues and give public dicision makers further guidance through increased citizen participation and democratization of the regional planning process.

As such, the multiple advocacy model has the potential to benefit the metropolitan community for issues that are regional in scope. However, as pointed out earlier, there are other issues that are best handled at smaller than regional scales of activity, and for which our model would not be appropriate. For example, politically sensitive services with important local impact, such as schools and police patrol, warrant decentralization in order to promote community control of neighborhood and suburban areas.[17] Thus, a dual centralization-decentralization approach, similar to the Committee for Economic Development's proposed two tiered system of shared powers, appears to be needed to deal with the full range of

Table 8.1 Voter Response to the Multiple Advocacy Approach for Expanding Air Transport Facilities in the San Jose Metropolitan Area: 1976

	Vote	
Alternative	Number	Percent
Limit the growth of the San Jose Airport to present traffic	34	33.5
Allow San Jose Airport to continue to grow	24	23.5
Move San Jose Airport to another site in the metropolitan area	32	31.0
Close the San Jose airport and use other airports in the Bay Area and ground transit	12	12.0
Total	102	100.0

Source: Donald N. Rothblatt, "Multiple Advocacy: An Approach to Metropolitan Planning," *Journal of the American Institute of Planners* 44 (April 1978): 193–99; and Channel 54 (KTEH), San Jose (June 1976).

problems in our metropolitan areas.[18] Indeed, such an approach may also bring much needed administrative and fiscal relief to our central cities, which are overwhelmed by most of our urban problems. Douglas Yates believes this dual solution would help our cities become more governable:

> . . . from the city hall perspective, this hybrid solution of centralization and decentralization would appear to go to the heart of the problem of administrative overload.[19]

To the extent that it relieves local governments of regionwide administrative burdens, the multiple advocacy approach has the ability to help the central city and other communities become more governable, while making the metropolis more plannable. These management improvements at different levels of governance are likely to be important preconditions for effective regional planning. In the end, our ability to plan the metropolis may depend on our capacity and willingness to resolve both local and regional problems for the benefit of the entire metropolitan community. For only with broad, metropolis-wide citizen participation and support will regional planning activities in a democratic society obtain the legitimacy needed for effective action.

NOTES

1. Stephen S. Skjei, "Urban System Advocacy," *Journal of the American Institute of Planners* 38 (January 1972): 22–23.
2. See theoretical arguments favoring the removal of social and economic inequities implicit in citizens' participation in Paul Davidoff,"Advocacy and Pluralism in Planning," *Journal of the American Institute of Planners* 31 (November 1965): 331–38, John Hamer. "Neighborhood Control." in *Neighborhood Preservation. Hearings Before the Committee on Banking, Housing, and Urban Affairs,* U.S. Senate, 94th Cong., 2nd Sess. (June 1976), pp. 139–57; Bryan D. Jones et al., "Bureaucratic Response to Citizen-Initiated Contacts: Environmental Enforcement in Detroit," *American Political Science Review* 71 (March 1977): 148–65; Kenneth R. Mladenka, "Citizen Demand and Bureaucratic Response: Direct Dialing Democracy in a Major American City," *Urban Affairs Quarterly* 12 (March 1977): 273–90: and Joseph W. McGuire. "The Role of Equity in Economics", *Review of Social Economy* 33 (April 1975): 74–84.

   For a discussion of the practical arguments supporting citizen participation for guidance in program design, implementation, evaluation, and acceptability, see Lloyd C. Irland. "Citizen Participation—Tool for Conflict Management on Public Lands." *Public Administration Review* 35 (May/June 1975): 263–69; Harvey R. Joyner, "Regional-Local Conflicts in Transportation Planning", *Transportation Engineering Journal of ASCE* 98 (August 1972): 53–57: Nicholas P. Lovrich, Jr., and G. Thomas Taylor, Jr., "Neighborhood Evaluation of Local Government Services: A Citizen Survey Approach," *Urban Affairs Quarterly* 12 (December 1976): 197–222; Robert S. Magill and Terry N. Clark, "Community Power and Decision Making: Recent Research and Its Policy Implications." *Social Service Review* 49 (March 1975): 33–45: Adepoju G. Onibokun and Martha Curry, "An Ideology of Citizen Participation: The Metropolitan Seattle Transit Case Study," *Public Administration Review* 36 (May/June 1976): 269–77; Steven F. Redburn, "On 'Human Services Integration,' " *Public Administration Review* 37 (May/June 1977): 264–69; Donald N. Rothblatt, "Multiple Advocacy: An Approach to Metopolitan Planning," *Journal of the American Institute of Planners* 44 (April 1978): 193–99; and Louise G. White, "Rational Theories of Participation: An Exercise in Definitions," *Journal of Conflict Resolution* 20 (June 1976): 255–78.
3. See Rothblatt, "Multiple Advocacy: An Approach to Metropolitan Planning."
4. Sander Kelman, Pierre Clavel, John Forester, and William W. Goldsmith, "New Opportunities for Planners," in *Urban and Regional Planning in an Age of Austerity,* ed. *Pierre Clavel, John Forester, and William W. Goldsmith (New York: Pergamon Press,* 1980), p. 5.
5. See David E. Dowall and Bruce McDowell, eds., *Making Regional Planning Work* (Urbana: Bureau of Urban and Regional Research, University of Illinois, 1980); Melvin B. Mogulof, "A Modest Proposal for the Governance of America's Metropolitan Areas," *Journal of the American Institute of Planners* 41 (July 1975): 250–57; and Donald N. Rothblatt, "National Development Policy." *Public Administration Review* 34 (July/August 1974): 369–76.
6. For example, it has been suggested that local political control may be a major end in itself for many metropolitan residents. See W. Bruce Shepard, "Metropolitan Political Decentralization", *Urban Affairs Quarterly* 10 (March 1975): 297–313. Also see Onibokun and Curry, "An Ideology of Citizen Participation"; and Rothblatt, "Multiple Advocacy: An Approach to Metropolitan Planning."
7. Barclay M. Hudson, Martin Wachs, and Joseph L. Schofer, "Local Impact Evaluation in the Design of Large-Scale Urban Systems," *Journal of the American Institute of Planners* 40 (July 1974): 256.

8. See Thomas L. Ashley, testimony on the Intergovernmental Coordination Act of 1977 (HR 95-4406), in *Congressional Record* 123 (March 3, 1977): E1202-03; and Robert C. Embry, "Embry Proposes Regional Solutions to Urban Problems," *Practicing Planner* 7 (September 1977): 4–6.

9. For a discussion of the perceptions of dualities in modern planning and the possibilities of balancing or synthesizing competing planning approaches, such as thinking versus acting, see Howall S. Baum, "Analysts and Planners Must Think Organizationally," *Policy Analysis* 6 (Fall 1980): 479–94; Richard S. Bolan and Ronald L. Nuttal, *Urban Planning and Politics* (Lexington, Mass.: D. C. Heath, 1975); John Friedmann, *Retracking America: A Theory of Transitive Planning* (Garden City, N.Y.: Doubleday, 1973); and Stephen Grabow and Allan Heskin, "The Foundations of a Radical Concept of Planning," *Journal of the American Institute of Planners* 39 (March 1973): 106, 108–14.

10. Dennis A. Rondinelli, *Urban and Regional Development Planning: Policy and Administration* (Ithaca, N.Y.: Cornell University Press, 1975), p. 260.

11. Studies of diplomatic settings (akin to the metropolitan political arena) suggest the importance of trust in resolving conflicts. See Bernhardt Lieberman, "Coalitions and Conflict Resolution," *American Behavioral Scientist* 19 (March/April 1975): 557–81.

12. Perhaps university planning programs could become appropriate public vehicles for planning research, experimentation, and evaluation, as has been suggested for government and professional organizations. See Melvin R. Levin, *Community and Planning* (New York: Praeger, 1977), ch. 10; and Seymour J. Mandelbaum, "On not Doing One's Best: The Uses and Problems of Experimentation in Planning," *Journal of the American Institutes of Planners* 41 (May 1975) 184–90.

13. For example, see Richard A. Aribes and John S. Hall, "Revolt of the Affluent: Fiscal Controls in Three States," *Public Administration Review* 41 (January, Special Issue, 1981): 107–21; and Robert M. Stein, "Functional Integration at the Substate Level: A Political Approach," *Urban Affairs Quarterly* 16 (December 1980):211–33.

14. For a discussion of the important consensus-building potential of public media, especially television, in contemporary American culture, see Amitai Etzioni, *Social Problems* (Englewood Cliffs, N.J.: Prentice-Hall, 1976).

15. This program, "Airport '76 . . . Destination '86," was broadcast by Channel 54 (KTEH) in San Jose on June 8 and 11, 1976.

16. Based on letters from representatives of the San Jose City Council, Santa Clara County Board of Supervisors, Association of Bay Area Governments, and the California State Assembly, 1977–80.

17. Robert L. Bish and Hugh O. Nourse, *Urban Economics and Policy Analysis* (New York: McGraw-Hill, 1975), ch. 5; James S. Heilbrun, *Urban Economics and Public Policy* (New York: St. Martin's Press, 1981), ch. 15; Kelman et al., "New Opportunities for Planners," pp. 1–9; and E. S. Savas, "Intracity Competition Between Public and Private Service Delivery," *Public Administration Review* 41 (January, Special Issue, 1981): 46–52.

18. Committee for Economic Development, *Reshaping Government in Metropolitan Areas* (New York: Committee for Economic Development, 1970), and Howard W. Hallman, *Small and Large Together: Governing the Metropolis* (Beverly Hills, Calif.: Sage Publications, 1977), ch. 18.

19. Douglas Yates, *The Ungovernable City* (Cambridge, Mass.: MIT Press, 1977, p. 192.

BIBLIOGRAPHY

BOOKS

Bay Area Council. *Housing: The Bay Area's Challenge of the 1980's.* San Francisco: Bay Area Council, December 1980.

Birmingham, Stephen. *The Golden Dream—Suburbia in the 1970's.* New York: Harper and Row, 1978.

Bish, Robert L. *The Public Economy of Metropolitan Areas.* Chicago: Markham, 1971.

Bish, Robert L., and Hugh O. Nourse. *Urban Economics and Policy Analysis.* New York: McGraw-Hill, 1975.

Bloomberg, William, Jr., and Henry J. Schmandt, eds. *The Quality of Urban Life.* Beverly Hills, Calif.: Sage, 1969.

Bogue, Donald J. *Population Growth in Standard Metropolitan Areas. 1900–1950.* Washington, D.C.: Housing and Home Finance Agency, 1953.

Bolan, Richard S., and Ronald L. Nuttal. *Urban Planning and Politics.* Lexington, Mass.: D. C. Heath, 1975.

Bollens, John C., and Henry J. Schmandt. *The Metropolis: Its People, Politics, and Economic Life.* New York: Harper and Row, 1975.

Bourne, Larry S., ed. *Interval Structure of the City.* New York: Oxford University Press, 1971.

Burchell, Robert W., and George Sternlieb, eds. *Planning Theory in the 1980's.* New Brunswick, N.J.: Center for Urban Policy Research, Rutgers University, 1978.

Carter, James E. *1980 President's National Urban Policy Report.* Washington, D. C.: U.S. Government Printing Office, 1981.

Chudacoff, Howard P. *The Evolution of American Urban Society.* Englewood Cliffs, N.J.: Prentice-Hall, 1975.

Clavel, Pierre, John Forester, and William W. Goldsmith, eds. *Urban and Regional Planning in an Age of Austerity.* New York: Pergamon Press, 1980.

Committee for Economic Development. *Reshaping Government in Metropolitan Areas*. New York: Committee for Economic Development, 1970.

Cowart, Richard, ed. *Land Use Planning, Politics and Policy*. Berkeley: Extension Publications, University of California, 1976.

Deleuw, Cather and Company. *Rapid Transit Development Project: Phase I Summary Abstract*. San Francisco: January 1975.

Dickey, John W., et al. *Metropolitan Transportation Planning*. New York: McGraw-Hill, 1975.

Dolce, Phillip C., ed. *Suburbia: The American Dream and Dilemma*. New York: Anchor Press, 1976.

Dowall, David E., and Bruce D. McDowell, eds. *Making Regional Planning Work*. Urbana: Bureau of Urban and Regional Planning Research, University of Illinois, 1980.

Downs, Anthony. *Opening up the Suburbs: An Urban Strategy for America*. New Haven: Yale University Press, 1973.

Dror, Yehezkel. *Ventures in Policy Science*. New York: American Elsevier, 1971.

Duhl, Leonard J., ed. *The Urban Condition*. New York: Basic Books, 1963.

Dyk, Robert G., and Bruce D. McDowell, eds. *Getting It Together in Regional Planning*. Urbana: Bureau of Urban and Regional Planning Research, University of Illinois, 1979.

Edel, Matthew, and Jerome Rothenberg, eds. *Readings in Urban Economics*. New York: Macmillan, 1972.

Eichler, Edward P., and Marshall Kaplan. *The Community Builders*. Berkeley: University of California Press, 1967.

Etzioni, Amitai. *Social Problems*. Englewood Cliffs, N.J.: Prentice-Hall, 1976.

Fishman, Richard P., ed. *Housing for All Under the Law*. Cambridge, Mass.: Ballinger, 1978.

Frieden, Bernard J. *The Environmental Protection Hustle*. Cambridge, Mass.: MIT Press, 1979.

Friedmann, John. *Retracking America: A Theory of Transactive Planning*. Garden City, N.Y.: Doubleday, 1973.

Gans, Herbert. *The Urban Villagers.* New York: Free Press of Glencoe, 1962.

Gilmour, Robert S., and Robert B. Lamb. *Political Alienation in Contemporary America.* New York: St. Martin's Press, 1975.

Glazer, Nathan, and Daniel P. Moynihan. *Beyond the Melting Pot.* Cambridge, Mass.: MIT Press, 1963.

Gold, Seymour M. *Recreation, Planning and Design.* New York: McGraw-Hill, 1980.

_____. *Urban Recreational Planning.* Philadelphia: Lea and Febiger, 1973.

Gordon, David M. *Problems in Political Economy.* Lexington, Mass.: D. C. Heath, 1971.

Gottmann, Jean. *Megalopolis.* New York: Twentieth Century Fund, 1961.

Grebler, Leo, and Frank G. Mittlebach. *The Inflation of House Prices.* Lexington, Mass.: Lexington Books, 1979.

Greer, Scott. *Governing the Metropolis.* New York: Wiley, 1962.

Haar, Charles, ed. *The President's Task Force on Suburban Problems.* Cambridge, Mass.: Ballinger, 1974.

Hahn, Harlan, and Charles Levine, eds. *Urban Politics: Past, Present and Future.* New York: Longman, 1980.

Hallman, Howard W. *Small and Large Together: Governing the Metropolis.* Beverly Hills, Calif.: Sage, 1977.

Hawley, Amos H., and Vincent P. Rock, eds. *Metropolitan America in Contemporary Perspective.* New York: Halsted Press, 1975.

Heilbrun, James. *Urban Economics and Public Policy.* New York: St. Martin's Press, 1981.

Heller, Alfred, ed. *The California Tomorrow Plan: The Future Is Now.* Los Altos, Calif.: William Kaufmann, 1972.

Horan, James F., and G. Thomas Taylor, Jr. *Experiments in Metropolitan Government.* New York: Praeger, 1977.

Jacobs, Allan B. *Making City Planning Work.* Chicago: American Society of Planning Officials, 1978.

Kouskoulas, Vasily, ed. *Urban Housing.* Detroit: National Science Foundation, 1973.

Lasswell, Harold D. *A Pre-View of Policy Sciences.* New York: American Elsevier, 1971.

Levin, Melvin R. *Community and Regional Planning.* New York: Praeger, 1977.

Lineberry, Robert L., and Ira Sharkansky. *Urban Politics and Public Policy.* New York: Harper and Row, 1978.

Marshall, Dale R., ed. *Urban Policy Making.* Beverly Hills, Calif.: Sage, 1979.

Masotti, Louis H., and Jeffrey K. Hadden, eds. *The Urbanization of the Suburbs.* Beverly Hills, Calif.: Sage, 1973.

Mayer, Robert, Robert Moroney, and Robert Morris, eds. *Centrally Planned Change.* Urbana: University of Illinois Press, 1974.

McHarg, Ian. Design with Nature. New York: Doubleday, 1971.

Meyer, John R., John F. Kain, and Martin Wohl. *The Urban Transportation Problem.* Cambridge, Mass.: Harvard University Press, 1965.

Michelson, William. *Environmental Choice, Human Behavior, and Residential Satisfaction.* New York: Oxford University Press, 1977.

Mogulof, Melvin. *Five Metropolitan Governments.* Washington, D.C.: Urban Institute, 1972.

_____. *Governing Metropolitan Areas.* Washington, D.C.: Urban Institute, 1971.

Mumford, Lewis. *The City in History.* New York: Harcourt, Brace and World, 1961.

National Academy of Sciences. *Toward an Understanding of Metropolitan America.* San Francisco: Canfield Press, 1975.

Owens, Bill. *Suburbia.* San Francisco: Straight Arrow Press, 1973.

Peat, Marwick, Mitchell, and Company. *An Economic and Planning Management Program for San Jose Municipal Airport: Airport Master Plan.* San Jose, Calif., January 1980.

_____. *An Economic and Planning Management Program for the San Jose Municipal Airport: Aviation Activity Forecasts.* San Jose, Calif., February 1977.

People for Open Space. *Endangered Harvest: The Future of the Bay Area Farmland.* San Francisco: November 1980.

———. *The Case for Open Space.* San Francisco: 1969.

———. *The Functions of Bay Area Farmland.* Background Report no. 2, Farmlands Conservation Project. October 1980.

Rodwin, Lloyd. *Nations and Cities: A Comparison of Strategies for Urban Growth.* Boston: Houghton Mifflin, 1970.

Rondinelli, Dennis A. *Urban and Regional Development Planning: Policy and Administration.* Ithaca, N.Y.: Cornell University Press, 1975.

Rothblatt, Donald N. *Regional-Local Development Policy Making: The Santa Clara Valley Corridor.* San Jose, Calif.: San Jose State University, 1981.

Rothblatt, Donald N., ed. *Regional Advocacy Planning: Expanding Air Transport Facilities for the San Jose Metropolitan Area.* San Jose, Calif.: San Jose State University, 1976.

———. *National Policy for Urban and Regional Development.* Lexington, Mass.: D. C. Heath, 1974.

———. *Regional Planning: The Appalachian Experience.* Lexington, Mass.: D. C. Heath, 1971.

Rothblatt, Donald N., Daniel J. Garr, and Jo Sprague. *The Suburban Environment and Women.* New York: Praeger, 1979.

Schnore, Leo F. *The New Urban History.* Princeton: Princeton University Press, 1975.

Stanford Environmental Law Society. *San Jose: Sprawling City.* Stanford, Calif.: Stanford Environmental Law Society, 1971.

Thurow, Lester C. *The Zero Sum Society.* New York: Basic Books, 1980.

Ural, Oktal, ed. *Proceedings of the Second International Symposium on Lower-Cost Housing Problems.* St. Louis: University of Missouri-Rolla, 1972.

Ward, David. *Cities and Immigrants: A Geography of Change in Nineteenth Century America.* New York: Oxford University Press, 1971.

Warner, Sam Bass. *Streetcar Suburbs: The Process of Growth in Boston, 1870–1900.* New York: Atheneum, 1969.

Webber, Melvin, et al., eds. *Explorations into Urban Structure.* Philadelphia: University of Pennsylvania Press, 1964.

Weiss, Rose. *Analysis of Affluence in Los Gatos.* San Jose, Calif.: Economic and Social Opportunity, April 1975.

Wikstom, Nelson. *Councils of Governments: A Study of Political Incrementation.* Chicago: Nelson-Hall, 1977.

Williams, Edward A. *Open Space: The Choices Before California.* San Francisco: Diable Press, 1969.

Williams and Mocine. *Saratoga Basic Data Report.* Saratoga, Calif.: May 1977.

Williams and Mocine. *Saratoga General Plan Report.* Saratoga, Calif.: May 1977.

Wood, Robert C. *1400 Governments. Cambridge, Mass.: Harvard University Press, 1961.*

————. *Suburbia: Its People and Their Politics.* Boston: Houghton Mifflin, 1958.

Yates, Douglas. *The Ungovernable City.* Cambridge, Mass.: MIT Press, 1977.

Zehner, Robert B. *Indicators of the Quality of Life in the New Communities.* Cambridge, Mass.: Ballinger, 1977.

ARTICLES

Alexander, James R. "Policy Design and the Impact of Federal Aid to Declining Communities." *Growth and Change* 12 (January 1981): 35–41.

Alonso, William. "Metropolis Without Growth." *Public Interest* 53 (Summer 1978): 68–86.

————. "A Theory of the Urban Land Market." In *Readings in Urban Economics,* edited by Matthew Edel and Jerome Rothenberg, pp. 104–11. New York: Macmillan, 1972.

Aribes, Richard A., and John S. Hall. "Revolt of the Affluent: Fiscal Controls in Three States." *Public Administration Review* 41 (January special issues 1981): 107–21.

Baldassare, Mark, and Claude S. Fischer. "Suburban Life: Powerlessness and Need for Affiliation." *Urban Affairs Quarterly* 10 (March 1975): 314–26.

Banfield, Edward C. "The Uses and Limitations of Metropolitan Planning in Massachusetts." In *Taming Megalopolis,* edited by H. Wentworth Eldredge, pp. 710–19. New York: Frederick A. Praeger, 1967.

Baum, Howell S. "Analysts and Planners Must Think Organizationally." *Policy Analysis* 6 (Fall 1980): 479–94.

Belser, Karl. "The Making of Slurban America." *Cry California* 5 (Fall 1970): 1–21.

Bylinsky, Gene. "California's Great Breeding Ground for Industry." *Fortune* 89 (June 1974): 129–35, 216–24.

Cason, Forrest M. "Land Use Concomitants of Urban Fiscal Squeeze." *Urban Affairs Quarterly* 16 (March 1981): 337–53.

Castillo, Elias. "Hunt for Low Income Housing Getting Worse and Worse." *San Jose Mercury News,* April 9, 1980. 1B.

Davidoff, Paul. "Advocacy and Pluralism in Planning." *Journal of the American Institute of Planners* 31 (November 1965): 331–38.

Davidoff, Paul, and Mary E. Brooks. "Zoning out the Poor." In *Suburbia: The American Dream and Dilemma,* edited by Philip C. Dolce, pp. 135–66. New York: Anchor Press, 1976.

Diamond, D. B. "Income and Residential Location: Muth Revisited." *Urban Studies* 17 (February 1980): 1–12.

Dorn, Michael. "The Position of an Outlying Community Threatened by the Location of a New Airport Site: City of Milpitas." *Regional Advocacy Planning: Expanding Air Transport Facilities for the San Jose Metropolitan Area,* edited by Donald N. Rothblatt, pp. 22–28. San Jose, Calif.: San Jose State University, 1976.

Dowall, David E. "Reducing the Cost Effects of Local Land Use Controls." *Journal of the American Planning Association* 47 (April 1981): 145–53.

_____. "Local-Regional Planning Conflicts: ABAG's Compact Growth Plan and Its Effects on the Metropolitan Housing Market." In *Making Regional Planning Work,* edited by David E. Dowall and Bruce D. McDowell, pp. 32–47. Urbana: Bureau of Urban and Regional Planning Research, University of Illinois, 1980.

Ekland, Kent E., and Oliver P. Williams. "The Changing Distribution of Social Classes in a Metropolitan Area." *Urban Affairs Quarterly* 13 (March 1978): 313–41.

Elder, Rob. "ABAG Suddenly Bay Area's No. 1 Political Topic." *San Jose Mercury* (February 19,1976): 1.

Ellson, Richard. "Another Perspective on Growth Management." *Urban Land* 38 (January 1979): 3–8.

Embry, Robert C. "Embry Proposes Regional Solutions to Urban Problems." *Practicing Planner* 7 (September 1977): 4–6.

Fischer, Claude S. "Toward a Subcultural Theory of Urbanism." *American Journal of Sociology* 80 (May 1975): 1319–41.

Fletcher, Thomas W. "Is Consolidation the Answer?" *Public Management* 62 (May 1980): 15–17.

Florestano, Patricia S., and Vincent L. Marando. "Urban Problems from State Commissions." *Urban Affairs Quarterly* 15 (March 1980): 335–44.

Frieden, Bernard J. "The New Regulation Comes to Suburbia." *Public Interest* 55 (Spring 1979): 15–27.

Frisken, Frances. "The Metropolis and the Central City: Can One Government Unite Them?" *Urban Affairs Quarterly* 8 (June 1973): 395–422.

Gilbert, Neil. "The Design of Community Planning." *Social Science Review* 53 (December 1979): 646–654.

Giliam, Harold. "The Bay Area Struggles for Space." *Planning* 46 (March 1980): 34–36.

Goldenberg, Edie N. "Evaluating Municipal Services." *Public Administration Review* 39 (January/February 1979): 94–98.

Grabow, Stephen, and Allan Heskin. "The Foundations of a Radical Concept of Planning." *Journal of the American Institute of Planners* 39 (March 1973): 106–14.

Graebner, James H. "Santa Clara County in 1990: The Guadalupe Corridor." *Guadalupe Corridor Report* (January 1, 1980): 1–2.

Greene, David L. "Recent Trends in Urban Spatial Structure." *Growth and Change* 11 (January 1980): 29–40.

Guest, Avery M. "The Changing Racial Composition of the Suburbs: 1950–1970." *Urban Affairs Quarterly* 14 (December 1978): 195–206.

Gulick, Luther, "Needed: A New Layer of Local Self-Government." In *Urban Government*, edited by Edward C. Banfield, pp. 150–60. New York: Free Press, 1969.

_____. "Metropolitan Organization." *Annals of the American Academy of Political and Social Science* 314 (November 1957): 57–65.

Hamer, John. "Neighborhood Control." In *Neighborhood Preservation, Hearings Before the Committee on Banking, Housing and Urban Affairs.* U.S. Senate, 94th Cong., 2nd Sess. (June 1976), pp. 139–57.

Harris, Charles W. "A Regional Response to Metro-Urban Problems." *Growth and Change* 6 (July 1975): 9–15.

Hawley, Willis D. "On Understanding Metropolitan Political Integration." In *Theoretical Perspectives on Urban Politics*, edited by Willis D. Hawley et al., pp. 100–45. Englewood Cliffs, N.J.: Prentice-Hall, 1976.

Heikoff, Joseph M. "Economic Analysis and Metropolitan Organization." *Journal of the American Institute of Planners* 39 (November 1973): 402, 404–07.

Hudson, Barclay M., Martin Wachs, and Joseph L. Schofer. "Local Impact Evaluation in the Design of Large-Scale Urban Systems." *Journal of the American Institute of Planners* 40 (July 1974): 255–65.

Hutcheson, John D., and James E. Prather. "Economy of Scale of Bureaucratic Entropy?" Implications for Metropolitan Governmental Reorganization." *Urban Affairs Quarterly* 15 (December 1979): 164–182.

Irland, Lloyd C. "Citizen Participation—Tool for Conflict Management on Public Lands." *Public Administration Review* 35 (May/June 1975): 263–69.

Jones, Bryan D., Saadia Greenberg, Clifford Kaufman, and Joseph Drew. "Bureaucratic Response to Citizen-Initiated Contacts: Environmental Enforcement in Detroit." *American Political Science Review* 71 (March 1977): 148–65.

Jones, Victor. "Bay Area Regionalism: Institutions, Processes, and Programs." In *Metropolitan Areas, Metropolitan Governments*, edited by Gary Helfand, pp. 98–165. Dubuque, Iowa: Kendall/Hunt, 1976.

Joyner, Harvey R. "Regional-Local Conflicts in Transportation Planning." *Transportation Engineering Journal of ASCE* 98 (August 1972): 53–57.

Kain, John F. "The Distribution and Movement of Jobs and Industry." In *The Metropolitan Enigma*, edited by James Q. Wilson, pp. 1–31. Washington, D.C.: U.S. Chamber of Commerce, 1967.

Kelman, Sander, Pierre Clavel, John Forester, and William W. Goldsmith. "New Opportunities for Planners." In *Urban and Regional Planning in an Age of Austerity,* edited by Pierre Clavel, John Forester, and William W. Goldsmith, pp. 1–9. New York: Pergamon Press, 1980.

Khadduri, Jill, and Raymond J. Struyk. "Improving Section 8 Rental Assistance: Translating Evaluation into Policy." *Evaluation Review* 5 (April 1981): 189–206.

Kilborn, Peter T. "Corporate Grants Invade the Residential Market." *New York Times,* February 15, 1979, pp. 1, 4.

LaTour, Stephen, Pauline Houlden, Laurens Walker, and John Thibaut. "Some Determinants of Preference for Modes of Conflict Resolution." *Journal of Conflict Resolution* 20 (June 1976): 319–56.

Lefaver, Scott. "Will Success Spoil Santa Clara Valley?" *Planning* 46 (April 1980): 22–25.

Lieberman, Bernhardt. "Coalitions and Conflict Resolutions." *American Behavioral Scientist* 19 (March/April 1975): 557–81.

Long, Norton E. "The Local Community as an Ecology of Games." In *Urban Politics: Past, Present, and Future,* edited by Harlan Hahn and Charles Levine, pp. 107–18. New York: Longman, 1980.

Lovrich, Nicholas P., Jr., and Thomas G. Taylor, Jr. "Neighborhood Evaluation of Local Government Services: A Citizen Survey Apprach." *Urban Affairs Quarterly* 12 (December 1976): 197–222.

Lucy, William H. "Metropolitan Dynamics: A Cross-National Framework for Analyzing Public Policy Effects in Metropolitan Areas." *Urban Affairs Quarterly* 11 (December 1975): 155–85.

Maass, Arthur. "Public Investment Planning in the United States: Analysis and Critique." *Public Policy* 18 (Winter 1970): 211–13.

Magill, Robert S., and Terry N. Clark. "Community Power and Decision Making: Recent Research and Its Policy Implications." *Social Service Review* 49 (March 1975): 33–45.

Maisel, Sherman, and Louis Winnick. "Family Housing Expenditures: Illusive Laws and Intrusive Variances." In *Urban Housing,* edited by William L. C. Wheaton et al., pp. 139–53. New York: Free Press, 1966.

Mandelbaum, Seymour J. "On not Doing One's Best: The Uses and Problems of

Experimentation in Planning." *Journal of the American Institute of Planners* 41 (May 1975): 184–90.

Marshall, Harvey. "Suburban Life Styles: A Contribution to the Debate." In *The Urbanization of the Suburbs,* edited by Louis H. Masotti and Jeffrey K. Hadden, pp. 123–48. Beverly Hills, Calif.: Sage, 1973.

Mazziotti, Donald F. "The Underlying Assumptions of Advocacy Planning: Pluralism and Reform." *Journal of the American Institute of Planners* 40 (January 1974): 38, 40–47.

McGuire, Joseph W. "The Role of Equity in Economics." *Review of Social Economy* 33 (April 1975): 74–84.

Miernyk, William H. "An Evaluation: The Tools of Regional Development Policy." *Growth and Change* 11 (April 1980): 2–6.

Mladenka, Kenneth R. "Citizen Demand and Bureaucratic Response: Direct Dialing Democracy in a Major American City." *Urban Affairs Quarterly* 12 (March 1977): 273–90.

Mogulof, Melvin B. "A Modest Proposal for the Governance of America's Metropolitan Areas." *Journal of the American Institute of Planners* 41 (July 1975): 250–57.

Morrall, John F. III, and Edgar O. Olsen, "The Cost Effectiveness of Leased Public Housing." *Policy Analysis* 2 (Spring 1980): 151–70.

Munson, Michael J. "Environmental Planning: Intraorganizational Aspects and Agency Effectiveness." *Growth and Change* 8 (January 1977): 3–10.

Nash, William W., Jr. "The Effectiveness of Metropolitan Planning." In *Taming Megalopolis,* vol. 2, pp. 698–710. 1967.

O'Gorman, Hubert J., and Stephen L. Garry. "Pluralistic Ignorance—Replication and Extension." *Public Opinion Quarterly* 40 (Winter 1977): 448–58.

Onibokun, Adepoju G., and Martha Curry. "An Ideology of Citizen Participation: The Metropolitan Seattle Transit Case Study." *Public Administration Review* 36 (May/June 1976): 269–77.

Pachon, Harry P., and Nicholas P. Lovrich, Jr. "The Consolidation of Public Services: A Focus on the Police." *Public Administration Review* 37 (January/February 1977): 38–47.

Peirce, Neil. "Valley's Suburban Sprawl Lends to Traffic Pollution." *San Jose Mercury,* April 17,1979: 18

Peninsula Times Tribune. "Everything's Crowded," January 18, 1980, pp. 1, 8.

Peterson, Paul E., and J. David Greenstone, "Two Competing Models of the Policy-Making Process: The Community Action Controversy as an Empirical Test." In *Theoretical Perspectives on Urban Politics,* edited by Willis D. Hawley et at. Englewood Cliffs, N.J.: Prentice Hall, 1976. pp. 67–99.

Piper, John. "The Position of a Community Group Representing People Suffering the Negative Environmental Effects of the Existing Airport Site". In *Regional Advocacy Planning: Expanding Air Transport Facilities for the San Jose Metropolitan Area,* edited by Donald N. Rothblatt, pp. 18–21. San Jose, Calif.: San Jose State University, 1976.

Redburn, F. Stevens, "On 'Human Services Integration.'" *Public Administration Review* 37 (May/June 1977): 264–69.

Reschovsky, Andrew. "An Evaluation of Metropolitan Area Tax Base Sharing." *National Tax Journal* 33 (March 1980): 55–66.

Rothblatt, Donald N. "Multiple Advocacy: An Approach to Metropolitan Planning." *Journal of the American Institute of Planners* 44 (April 1978): 193–99.

―――. "Issues Underlying a National Urban and Regional Development Policy." In *National Policy for Urban and Regional Development,* edited by Donald N. Rothblatt, pp. 325–37. Lexington, Mass.: D. C. Heath, 1974.

―――. "National Development Policy." *Public Administration Review* 34 (July/August 1974):369–76.

―――. "Improving the Design of Urban Housing." In *Urban Housing,* edited by Vasily Kouskoulas, pp. 149–54. Detroit: National Science Foundation, 1973.

―――. "Housing and Human Needs." *Town Planning Review* 42 (April 1971): 130–44.

―――. "Rational Planning Re-Examined." *Journal of the American Institute of Planners* 37 (January 1971): 26–37.

Rothenberg, Jerome. "Cost Benefit Analysis: A Methodological Exposition." In *Handbook of Evaluation Research,* vol. 2, edited by Marcia Guttentag and Elmer L. Struening, pp. 55–58. Beverly Hills, Calif.: Sage, 1975.

Rutman, Leonard. "Planning an Evaluation Study." In *Evaluation Research Methods: A Basic Guide,* edited by Leonard Rutman, pp. 15–38. Beverly Hills, Calif.: Sage, 1979.

San Jose Mercury. "Extend S.P. Commuter Service," April 2, 1979, 6B.

Savas, E.S. "Intracity Competition Between Public and Private Service Delivery." *Public Administration Review* 41 (January/February 1981): 46–52.

_____. "How Much Do Government Services Really Cost?" *Urban Affairs Quarterly* 15 (September 1979): 23-41.

Schmidt, Bob. "Gas Tax Increase Urged." *San Jose Mercury,* March 21, 1979: 1F.

Schoettle, Enid Curtis Bok. "The State of the Art of Policy Studies." In *National Policy for Urban and Regional Development,* edited by Donald N. Rothblatt, pp. 3–33. Lexington, Mass.: D. C. Heath, 1974.

Shepard, W. Bruce,. "Metropolitan Political Decentralization: A Test of the Life-Style Value Model." *Urban Affairs Quarterly* 10 (March 1975): 297–313.

Skjei, Stephen S. "Urban System Advocacy." *Journal of the American Institute of Planners* 38 (January 1972): 11–24.

Slovak, Jeffrey S. "Property Taxes and Community Political Structures." *Urban Affairs Quarterly* 16 (December 1980): 189–210.

Stein, Robert M. "Functional Integration at the Substate Level: A Policy Approach." *Urban Affairs Quarterly* 16 (December 1980): 211–33.

Stipak, Brian. "Citizen Satisfaction with Urban Services: Potential Misuse as a Performance Indicator." *Public Administration Review* 39 (January/February 1979): 46–52.

Stovall, Calvin. "What Price Home Ownership? " *San Jose Mercury News,* February 19, 1979, 1B.

Sweeney, Frank. "Massive San Jose Jetport Local Decision." *San Jose Mercury,* October 20, 1979, p. 1.

_____. "Supervisors Approve Most of Transit Plan." *San Jose Mercury,* March 6, 1979, pp. 1A, 18A.

_____. "San Jose Looking Anew at Airport Plan." *San Jose Mercury,* March 1974, p. 21.

Tannian, Francis, and John Stapleford. "Community Preference and Urban Policy." *Growth and Change* 12 (April 1981):37–43.

Tarr, Joel Arthur. "From City to Suburb: The 'Moral' Influence of Transportation

Technology." In *American Urban History*, edited by Alexander B. Callow, pp. 201–223. New York: Oxford University Press, 1973.

Taylor, Nigel. "Planning Theory and the Philosophy of Planning." *Urban Studies* 17 (June 1980):159–172.

Tiebout, C. M. "A Pure Theory of Local Expenditures." In *Readings in Urban Economics*, edited by Matthew Edel and Jerome Rothenberg, pp. 513–23. New York: Macmillan, 1972.

Trounstine, Philip J. "Study Shows 4 Council Districts Lagging Parks." *San Jose Mercury*, January 13, 1981, pp. 1B, 5B.

Usher, L. Charles, and Gary C. Corina. "Goal Setting and Performance Assessment in Municipal Budgeting." *Public Administration Review* 41 (March/April 1981):229–35.

U.S. News and World Report. "Profile of America: What '80 Census Will Show," April 7, 1980, pp. 64–67.

Warren, Charles R. "Developing Alternative Models for Servicing Metropolitan America." In *Organizing Public Services in Metropolitan America*, edited by Thomas P. Murphy and Charles R. Warren, pp. 3–14. Lexington, Mass.: Lexington Books, 1974.

Webber, Melvin M. "The Urban Place and the Nonplace Urban Realm." In *Explorations into Urban Structure*, edited by Melvin Webber, pp. 79–153. Philadelphia: University of Pennsylvania Press, 1964.

White, Louise G. "Rational Theories of Participation: An Exercise in Definitions." *Journal of Conflict Resolution* 20 (June 1976): 225–78.

Wikstrom, Nelson. "A Re-assessment: Metropolitan Consolidated." *Growth and Change* 9 (January 1978):2–7.

Yates, Douglas. "Political Innovation and Institution Building: The Experience of Decentralized Experiments." In *Theoretical Perspectives on Urban Politics*, edited by Willis D. Hawley, et al., pp. 146–75. Englewood Cliffs, N.J.: Prentice-Hall, 1976.

Yoachum, Susan. "More Costly Home Win Sunnyvale Nod." *San Jose Mercury*, May 4, 1979, 7F.

Zech, Charles E. "Final Effects of Urban Zoning." *Urban Affairs Quarterly* 16 (September 1980):49–58.

Zimmer, Basil. "The Urban Centrifugal Drift." In *Metropolitan America in Con-*

temporary Perspective, edited by Amos H. Hawley and Vincent P. Rock, pp. 23–92. New York: Halstead Press, 1975.

PUBLIC DOCUMENTS

Association of Bay Area Governments. *Regional Plan 1980*. Berkeley, Calif.: July 1980.

_____. *Bay Area Housing Opportunity Plan*. Berkeley, Calif., October 1979.

_____. *Projections 79*. Berkeley, Calif., 1979.

_____. *Ridgelands, Multijurisdictional Open Space Study*. Berkeley, Calif., May 1977.

_____. *Areas of Critical Environmental Concern*. Berkeley, Calif., May 1976.

_____. *Financing Open Space for the San Francisco Bay Region*. Berkeley, Calif., 1973.

_____. *Regional Airport Systems: Final Plan*. Berkeley, Calif., June 1972.

_____. *Regional Open Space Plan: Phase II*. Berkeley, Calif., 1972.

_____. *Phase I of the Regional Housing Element*. Berkeley, Calif., 1971.

_____. *Regional Plan 1970–1990*. Berkeley, Calif., 1970.

Association of Bay Area Governments, General Assembly. *Meeting Minutes*. Berkeley, Calif., March 27, 1981.

_____. *Economic Development Objectives and Policies*. Berkeley, Calif., December 1980.

Association of Bay Area Governments, Regional Planning Committee. *Meeting Minutes*. Berkeley, Calif., December 10, 1980, and March 11, 1981.

Association of Bay Area Governments and the Metropolitan Transportation Commission, Joint Policy Committee. *Summary of the Regional Airport Plan*. Berkeley, Calif., July 1980.

_____. *Regional Airport Plan: Draft Environmental Impact Report*. Berkeley, Calif., June 1980.

_____. *Santa Clara Valley Corridor Evaluation: Summary*. Berkeley, Calif., March 1979.

———. *Draft Report, Santa Clara Valley Corridor Evaluation*. Berkeley, Calif., November 1978.

———. *Corridor Evaluation, Summary Report, Phase III*. Berkeley, Calif., 1977.

California. *The Growth Revolt: Aftershock of Proposition 13?*. Sacramento, Calif.: Office of Planning and Research, 1980.

———. *State of California Planning and Zoning Laws and the Subdivision Map Act*. Sacramento, Calif.: Office of Planning and Research, 1979.

———. *Urban Development Strategy for California*. Sacramento, Calif.: Office of Planning and Research, 1977.

California Housing Finance Agency. *Annual Report 1978–79*. Sacramento, Calif., September 1979.

Gilroy. *General Plan*. November 1979.

———. *Residential Development Ordinance*. November 1979.

Lopez, Daniel. "Comparison of Balanced Estimate Development Plan and Local General Plans." In *Santa Clara Corridor Evaluation, Attachment No. 4*. Berkeley, Calif.: Association of Bay Area Governments, August 1977.

Los Gatos. *Housing Assistance Plans Guidelines: June 1980–83*. 1980.

———. *Below Market Rate Program Guidelines*. May 1979.

———. *General Plan*. "Housing Element." 1979.

Milpitas Planning Department. *Housing Survey*. April 1980.

Metropolitan Transportation Commission. *Peninsula Transit Alternatives Project*. Berkeley, Calif., 1977.

———. *Airport Accessibility in the San Francisco Bay Area*. Berkeley, Calif., January 1974.

Metropolitan Transportation Commission, Minority Citizens Advisory Committee. "MCAC Perspective: The Santa Clara Valley Corridor Evaluation." Berkeley, Calif., November 1978.

Metropolitan Transportation Commission, Regional Airport Planning Committee. *Airport Activity Statistics*. Berkeley, Calif., 1979.

Morgan Hill. *General Plan Policy Document*. 1980.

_____. *Background Data Report for the General Plan Update*. November 1979.

_____. *General Plan*. "Housing Element." July 1979.

_____. "Residential Development Control System." *Municipal Code*. 1978.

New Jersey Pinelands Commission. *New Jersey Pinelands Draft Comprehensive Management Plan*. June 1980.

President's Commission on National Goals. *Goals for Americans*. New York: Prentice-Hall, 1960.

San Jose. *Airport Master Plan and Airport Vicinity Area Actions*. July 1980.

_____. *Supplemental Report to Environmental Impact Report/Environmental Assessment for San Jose Airport Master Plan* June 1980.

_____. *Environmental Assessment and Environmental Impact Report on the Airport Master Plan and Airport Vicinity Area Actions*. April 1980.

_____. *General Plan*. 1980 as amended.

_____. *Community Development Plan and Program: July 1979–June 1982*. October 1979.

_____. *Housing Assistance Plan*. 1979.

San Jose City Council. *Downtown San Jose Transit Mobility Improvement*. December 1978.

San Jose Parks and Recreation Department. *Inventory of Parks and Special Facilities*. 1976.

_____. *Project '75*. 1975.

San Jose Planning Commission. *Report to the City Council on the 1981–86 Capital Improvement Program*. April 15, 1981.

San Jose Planning Department and the Parks and Recreation Department. *An Analysis of Parks and Recreational Needs for the City of San Jose*. November 1980.

San Jose Property and Code Enforcement Department. *Housing Condition Survey*. 1978.

Santa Clara County. *General Plan*. San Jose, Calif., November 1980.

———. *Postal Vacancy Survey*. San Jose, Calif., 1979.

———. *An Urban Development/Open Space Plan for Santa Clara County*. San Jose, Calif.: Santa Clara County Planning Department, 1973.

Santa Clara County Airport Land Use Commission. "Resolution of the Santa Clara County Airport Land Use Commission Relating to the San Jose Airport Master Plan and Vicinity Area Plan." San Jose, Calif., September 10, 1980.

———. *Minutes*. November 29, 1973.

———. *Land Use Plan for Area Surrounding Santa Clara County Airports*. San Jose, Calif.: Santa Clara County Planning Department, August 1973.

Santa Clara County Association of Planning Officers. *Meeting Minutes*. San Jose, Calif., December 3, 1980.

Santa Clara County Housing Task Force. *Housing: A Call for Action*. San Jose, Calif.: Santa Clara County Planning Department, 1977.

Santa Clara County Industry and Housing Task Force. *Living Within Our Limits: A Framework for Action in the 1980's*. San Jose, Calif., November 1979.

Santa Clara County Local Agency Formation Commission. *Guidelines and Policies*. San Jose, Calif., February 1978.

Santa Clara County Parks and Recreation Department. *Regional Parks and Recreation Area*. San Jose, Calif., 1978.

Santa Clara County Planning Department. *Advanced Final Count of 1980*. San Jose, Calif.: Santa Clara County, April 1981.

———. *The Fiscal Impacts of Proposition 13 on Local Governments in Santa Clara County*. San Jose, Calif., December 1980.

———. *Information*. San Jose, Calif., June 1980.

———. *Draft of the Housing Element Problem Statement: A Background Report for the General Plan Revision Project*. San Jose, Calif., April 1979; revised January 1980.

———. *Info Highlights*. San Jose, Calif., June 1978.

———. *1975 Countywide Census, Santa Clara County*. San Jose, Calif., 1976.

———. *1975 Special Census of Santa Clara County*. San Jose, Calif., 1976.

_____. *Housing.* San Jose, Calif., February 1980.

_____. *Housing Characteristics, Cities, Santa Clara County, 1970.* San Jose, Calif.: Santa Clara County Planning Department, 1971.

Santa Clara County Transit District. *General Transit Plan.* San Jose, Calif., September 1972.

Santa Clara County Transportation Agency. *Recommendations Pertaining to the Santa Clara Valley Corridor Evaluation Study.* San Jose, Calif., February 1979.

Saratoga Community Services Department. *Saratoga Parks 1st Ten Years.* Saratoga, Calif., January 1979.

Sunnyvale. *Housing and Community Revitalization Sub-Element.* March 1980.

_____. *1979 General Plan of the City of Sunnyvale.* February 26, 1980.

_____. *1972–1982 Application for Community Development Block Grant Funds.* 1979.

Sunnyvale City Council. *Moratorium on Addition of New Industry.* December 1979.

Sunnyvale Planning Department. *Housing Survey.* June 1979.

U.S. Air Force, Andrews Air Force Base. "An Installation Compatible Use Zone: A Report to the Citizens of Andrews Air Force Base Environs." December 1974.

U.S. Congress. *Congressional Record* 123 (March 3, 1977): E1202–03.

U.S. Department of Commerce, Bureau of the Census. *Preliminary 1980 Census.* March 1981.

_____. *1977 Census of Governments,* vol. 5, *Local Governments in Metropolitan Areas.* 1977.

_____. *Census of Population.* 1960, 1970.

U.S. Department of Housing and Urban Development. *Principal Program Areas.* May 1978.

U.S. Department of the Interior. *San Francisco Bay National Wildlife Refuge.* 1970.

U.S. Department of Transportation, Federal Aviation Administration. *Federal Aviation Regulations, Part 77—Objects Affecting Navigable Airspace.* January 1975 as amended.

_____. *Airport Development Aid Program: Authority, Program Policy, Eligibility and Allowability Criteria.* August 1971 as amended.

_____. *Airport Development Aid Program.* Advisory Circular no. 150/5100-7. January 1971 as amended.

_____. *Federal Aviation Regulations, Part 36—Noise Standards: Aircraft Type and Airworthiness Certification.* December 1969 as amended.

Ybarra, Jack. *Santa Clara Valley Corridor Evaluation: Public Participation Program.* Berkeley, Calif.: Association of Bay Area Governments and the Metropolitan Transportation Commission, Joint Policy Committee, March 1979.

UNPUBLISHED MATERIAL

Ames, Lewis T., chairman, State and Federal Task Force, the Modern Transit Society. Correspondence to Donald Rothblatt. January 1980.

Building Industry Association. "Affordable Housing Presentation." March 17, 1981.

_____. "Urban Service Programming." March 17, 1981.

Clifton, Ann, et al., League of Women Voters of Santa Clara County. Correspondence to Board of Supervisors, Santa Clara County. January 30, 1979.

Fadness, David R., and James E. Cates, V.E.P. Homeowners Association. Correspondence to San Jose City Council. January 1979.

Forester, Chuck, William F. Hein. "Final Recommendations on the Santa Clara Valley Corridor Evaluation." Memorandum to Joint Policy Committee, ABAG and MTC. March 14, 1979.

_____. "Final Staff Recommendations on the Transportation Features of the Santa Clara Valley Corridor Evaluation." Memorandum to Joint Policy Committee, ABAG and MTC. March 21, 1979.

Gissler, William A., mayor, City of Santa Clara. Letter to the San Jose Planning Commission concerning the Environmental Impact Report on plans to expand the San Jose Municipal Airport. June 11, 1980.

Graham, Gordon. Presentation on the British Columbia Provincial Agricultural Land Commission. Sonoma Farmlands Conference, April 1981.

Gualtieri, Mardi. Correspondence to ABAG-MTC Joint Policy Committee. February 1979.

Hamilton, John W., director of planning, City of San Jose. Memorandum to mayor and City Council, City of San Jose. February 6, 1979.

Hau, John C., staff coordinator, Santa Clara County Airport Land Use Commission. "Analysis of the Proposed Vicinity Area Plan for the San Jose Municipal Airport." Memorandum to Airport Land Use Commission Hearing Board. September 1980.

Hayes, Janet Gray, mayor, City of San Jose. Correspondence to Louise Giersch, chairman, Joint Policy Committee, Association of Bay Area Governments/ Metropolitan Transportation Commission. February 22, 1979.

Jacoby, Gordon, and Chris Brittle, Regional Airport Planning Committee, Association of Bay Area Governments and the Metropolitan Transportation Commission. "San Jose Municipal Airport Master Plan and Vicinity Area Plan Draft Environmental Impact Report." Letter to San Jose City Planning Department. June 4, 1980.

King, James R., assistant city manager, City of San Jose. Memorandum to Ted Tedesco, city manager, City of San Jose, on airport expansion and alternative sites. May 29, 1973.

Robinson, R., North Santa Clara City resident. Letter to the San Jose Planning Commission concerning the Environmental Impact Report on plans to expand the San Jose Municipal Airport. June 20, 1980.

Rothblatt, Donald N. "New Tools for Regional Planning." Paper presented at the American Planning Association National Conference. Boston, April 1981.

_____. "The Suburbs: Are They Alive and Well?" Paper presented at the American Planning Association National Conference. San Francisco, April 1980.

Tedesco, Ted, city manager, City of San Jose. "Airport Relocation Issue." Memorandum to mayor and City Council of San Jose. September 1975.

Records of Century 21 realtors. San Jose, Calif., April 1981.

Records of the San Jose Real Estate Board. San Jose, Calif., June 1981.

San Jose Chamber of Commerce. "Position Paper Criticizing Industry Management Task Force Report, Living Within Our Limits." January 1980.

———. *Airport Master Plan Recommendations.* September 1979.

———. "The Housing Price Crunch." 1978.

———. "Chamber of Commerce Position on Light Rail in Santa Clara County." 1977.

———. "Chamber of Commerce Position, Transit in Santa Clara County." November 1975.

Santa Clara County Manufacturing Group. "Views on the Land Use and Transportation Recommendations of the Santa Clara Valley Corridor Evaluation Study." San Jose, Calif., February 1979.

Spivak, Alvin L. "Transit Problems and Solutions." Modern Transit Society, San Jose, Calif.: 1980.

INTERVIEWS

American Lung Association
Baines, Richard, executive director. April 1976.

Association of Bay Area Governments
Hartzell, Chris, planner. February 1977.
Jacoby, Gordon D., senior planner. February 1979 and June 1980.
Lopez, Daniel, housing director. February 1980.
Morse, Linda, planner. February 1981.
Staff. May 1980.

Building Industry Association
Speno, Steven G., executive vice-president. February and April 1981.

California Fish and Game Department
Hall, Frank, biologist. February 1981.

California Office of Planning and Research
Staff. March 1981.

Committee for Green Foothills
Wordell, Cynthia. February and April 1981.

Community Housing Developers
Lofgren, Zoe, executive director. February 1980.
Smith, Linda, acting executive director. April 1980.

Confederacion de la Raza
Staff. April 1979 and April 1981.

Council for a Balanced Community
Latine, Ralph. February 1979.
Steffani, Edward C. February 1979.

Eureka Federal Savings and Loan Association
Kidwell, Kenneth, chairman. April 1980.

Federal Aviation Administration
Cartright, Donald, airport planning engineer. June 1980.

George S. Nolte and Associates
Abraham, Maurice, urban development director. March 1981.

Gilroy
Dorn, Michael, director, Planning Department. February 1981.

Housing Services Center
Sandoval, Manuel J., executive director, February 1980 and April 1981.

Los Gatos
Bowman, Lee, director of planning. February 1980.
Cannon, Ruth, City Councilmember. February 1980.
Cody, Jill, director of community programs. April 1980.

Metropolitan Transportation Commission
Brittle, Chris, airport planning engineer. June 1980.
Daumbs, Larry. May 1979.
Staff. May 1980.
Steinman, Norman. February and May 1979.

Mexican American Community Services Agency
Hernandez, Rosa Maria, executive director. February and April 1981.
Villa, Jose, executive director. February and May 1977, February and May
1979.

Midpeninsula Coalition Housing Fund
Moulton, Robert, executive director. March 1980.

Midpeninsula Regional Open Space District
Sessions, Steven, land manager. February 1981.

Milpitas
City staff. March 1981.

Connolly, James R., deputy city manager. March and June 1980, and February 1981.

Milpitas Planning Department
Burkey, Stephen M., assistant planner. March 1980.

Modern Transit Society
Grabeel, Random. March 1979.

Morgan Hill
Wyman, Beth, City Councilmember. March 1980.

New Jersey Pinelands Commission
Moore, Terrance, executive director. February 1981.

North Side Residents Association
Winton, Michael, president. June 1980 and February 1981.

Peninsula Open Space Trust
Huggins, Ellie. February 1981.

People for Open Space
Orman, Larry, executive director. February and April 1981.

San Jose
Bass, Joseph F., Transportation Division, Department of Public Works. February 1979.
Berg, John, Planning Department. April 1979.
Cohen, Margaret, planner, Housing Division. February 1980.
McEnery, Thomas, City Councilmember. February 1980.
Guisto, John, chief of parks planning, Parks and Recreation Department. February, April and May 1981.
Korabiak, Dennis, planner, Planning Department. February and April 1981.
Kramer, Carolyn, planner, Planning Department. April 1981.
Marin, Edward, airport planning engineer, San Jose Airport. June 1980.
Mettler, James, manager, San Jose Airport. June 1976.
Schoennauer, Gary, director, Planning Department. June 1981.

San Jose Chamber of Commerce
Kallshian, Harry C., chairman, Transportation Task Force. February 1979.
Tucker, James F., executive director, economic development and communications, June 1980 and March 1981.

San Jose Real Estate Board
Johnson, Robert. February 1980.
Mack, Daniel. February 1980.

O'Leary, Mary. February 1980.
Rogers, Gary. February 1980.

Santa Clara
    Downey, Michael, deputy city attorney. February 1981.
    Smith, Olney, director, Planning Department. June 1980.

Santa Clara County
    Errico, Felix, planner, Parks and Recreation Department. January and
        April 1981.
    Hau, John C., staff coordinator, Airport Land Use Commission and Planning
        Department. June 1980.
    Hunt, Dr. Lester, Office of Education. February 1980.
    Lightbody, James, transit operations engineer, Transit District. March 1979.
    McKinney, Steven, senior planner, Planning Department. February 1980 and
        February 1981.
    Mencacci, Norma, intergovernmental relations, Transportation Agency. July
        1980.
    Minister, David, project director, Guadalupe Corridor Analysis, Trans-
        portation Agency. March 1979.
    Perry, John E., Jr., chairman, Transportation Commission. March 1979.
    Vogl, Kim, planner. February, April and May 1981.
    Weden, Donald, associate planner, Planning Department. January, April and
        May 1981.
    Wilson, Susanne, supervisor. February 1980.
    Staff, Planning Department. February 1981.
    Staff, Transportation Agency. May 1980.

Santa Clara County Manufacturing Group
    Epstein, Burton, chairman, Transportation Task Force. April 1979.
    Staff. April 1980 and April 1981.
    Stone, Donald. February 1979.

Saratoga
    Rudin, Vicki, planner, planning department. May 1981.
    Sampson, Barbara, director of community services department. May 1981.

Save Our Valley Action Committee
    Hanson, Maureen, spokesperson. June 1980.

Sierra Club
    Balmer, Ralph, chairman, Transportaton Committee, Loma Prieta Chapter.
        February 1979.
    Carrell, Paula. April 1981.
    Lazarus, Clara Mae. February 1981.
    Staff. Apirl 1981.

South Santa Clara County Housing Development Corporation
    Sequin, Olivia, director. March 1980.

Sunnyvale
    Moore, Edward C., planning officer. April 1981.
    Staff, Planning Department. April 1980.
    Temmermand, Robert, Public Works Department. March 1979.

United New Conservationists
    Branon, Lilyan, president. June 1980.

U.S. Department of Housing and Urban Development
    Flo, Michael, family housing coordinator. April 1980.
    Sachs, Steven, community development coordinator. April 1980.
    Sperling, Mitchell, planner. May 1980.

U.S. Department of the Interior
    Staff. April 1981.

U.S. Department of Transportation
    Staff, Urban Mass Transportation Administration. December 1980.

V.E.P. Homeowners Associaton
    Fadness, David R., transportation chairman. March 1979.

West Valley Multi-Modal Transportation Corridor Task Force
    Gualtieri, Mardi, chairman. February 1979.

INDEX

ABOUT THE AUTHOR

DONALD N. ROTHBLATT chairs the Urban and Regional Planning Department at San Jose State University, and is past president of the Association of Collegiate Schools of Planning. His other works include *Human Needs and Public Housing, Thailand's Northeast, Regional Planning: The Appalachian Experience, Allocation of Resources for Regional Planning, National Policy for Urban and Regional Development*, and (as coauthor) *The Suburban Environment and Women*. He has studied planning in the United States and Europe, and holds the Ph.D. in city and regional planning from Harvard University, where he was on the planning faculty.

'ibra'